New Ways in
Content-Based Instruction

Donna M. Brinton and Peter Master, Editors

New Ways in TESOL Series II
Innovative Classroom Techniques
Jack C. Richards, Series Editor

Teachers of English to Speakers of Other Languages, Inc.

Typeset in Garamond Book and Tiffany Demi
by Capitol Communication Systems, Inc., Crofton, Maryland USA
and printed by
Pantagraph Printing, Bloomington, Illinois USA

Teachers of English to Speakers of Other Languages, Inc.
700 South Washington Street, Suite 200
Alexandria, Virginia 22314 USA
Tel 703-836-0744 ● Fax 703-836-7864 ● http://www.tesol.org/

Director of Communications and Marketing: Helen Kornblum
Managing Editor: Marilyn Kupetz
Copy Editor: Ellen Garshick
Cover Design: Ann Kammerer

Every effort has been made to contact the copyright holders for permission to reprint borrowed material. We regret any oversights that may have occurred and will rectify them in future printings of this work.

TESOL thanks Barbara Jacobson, the staff, and students of the ESL program at Northern Virginia Community College/Alexandria campus for their participation and assistance.

ISBN 0-939791-67-6
Library of Congress Catalogue No. 96-061208

Contents

Acknowledgments

Compiling innovative teaching ideas for the content-based ESL/EFL classroom is a challenging task, especially when the contributions arrive (as they did for this volume) in a wide variety of word processing formats via fax, e-mail, overnight mail, and snail mail from all corners of the globe. This project would not have seen completion without assistance and encouragement from a number of individuals. We would especially like to single out the following: Jack Richards, the New Ways in TESOL Series Editor, who conceived of the volume and convinced us to embark upon this task; Marilyn Kupetz, TESOL's Managing Editor, who gave much-needed expert guidance at every stage of the project; Ellen Garshick, who facilitated the completion of the manuscript; and, perhaps most important, our many colleagues around the world who so generously shared their ideas and expertise to co-construct this volume.

Sincere thanks are due to our home departments, the Department of TESL and Applied Linguistics at the University of California, Los Angeles (UCLA), and the Department of Linguistics and Language Development at San Jose State University, which provided financial support for outgoing mail, e-mail, fax, and telephone costs. Additional thanks go to the following UCLA students and colleagues: Gabriela Solomon and Joseph Plummer for their willingness to help with the translation of computer files; David Palmquist for technical assistance in creating a World Wide Web home page and getting our guidelines for submission out over the Internet; Diane Childs for tracking missing references; and finally Lyn Repath-Martos, who offered the services of her assistants in the UCLA ESL Media Center to scan and enter text.

Introduction

As an approach to second and foreign language teaching, content-based instruction (CBI) is a relative newcomer to the field. Growing out of its origins in immersion education, the language-across-the-curriculum movement, and English for specific purposes, it first appeared on the general language teaching scene in the mid- to late 1980s (see, e.g., the pioneering works by Benesch, 1988; Brinton, Snow, & Wesche, 1989; Cantoni-Harvey, 1987; Crandall, 1987; Mohan, 1986; Short, Crandall, & Christian, 1989). In spite of its short-lived presence in the pedagogical arena, CBI had assumed global dimensions by the mid-1990s—as attested to by its place of dominance at professional conferences such as TESOL's, by its strong impact on the ESL/EFL publishing field, and not least of all by the many contributions in this volume, which encompass a variety of settings across virtually all educational segments.

For the purpose of this volume, we define CBI quite widely to include theme-based L2 courses, sheltered content-area courses, and paired or adjunct arrangements in which language and content courses are taught in tandem, with mutually negotiated objectives. We also include contributions from language professionals working with younger learners in the elementary or middle school context, young adults in the high schools, and more mature learners in college preparatory or tertiary programs. As a result, the volume speaks to a broad potential audience of teachers in training, practicing teachers, materials developers, program administrators, and teacher educators.

In making the selections for this volume, we sought to include ideas that were generalizable in nature—ideas that, though sketched out by the contributor for a specific teaching purpose, setting, or audience, would allow readers to try them out in their own classrooms with a minimum of alteration in procedure—and that contributed to a more in-depth understanding of appropriate CBI methods and techniques. For ease of access, the contributions are divided into the following categories according to the type of activity the learner engages in:

- *Part I: Information Management:* sifting data into categories or finding examples given preestablished headings, arriving at names or headings for these categories, identifying similar characteristics within the category;
- *Part II: Critical Thinking:* going beyond simple classification to evaluate or analyze data (e.g., by determining a point of view or arguing from a given stance);
- *Part III: Hands-On Activities:* manipulating information via games, experiments, and other activities;
- *Part IV: Data Gathering:* (a) collecting and assembling facts, data, and references or (b) scanning for specific information; and
- *Part V: Text Analysis and Construction:* (a) breaking a text into its component parts, elucidating its rhetorical pattern, and examining text flow (cohesion and coherence) or (b) applying knowledge of oral and written discourse conventions to create a specifically patterned text with the goal of increasing fluency, accuracy, or both.

For an overview of the skill focus of each contribution, its topic, and the suggested learner level, see the Index to Activities at the back of this volume.

Each contribution follows a standard, easy-to-follow format. In the scholar's margin is information pertaining to the level of student for whom the activity is designed, its instructional goals or aims, the estimated preparation and class time needed, and the resources required. This information is followed by a summary of the activity and step-by-step procedures for the teacher to follow. Any additional suggestions or tips that the contributor wishes to pass on to users are contained in Caveats and Options, and References and Further Reading contains useful sources for follow-up. The Appendixes generally contain classroom handouts demonstrating how the suggested activity was applied in a specific classroom with a given set of learners. These materials are samples only and are not intended to be used without adaptation. Finally, the Contributors section provides brief biographical information on the author(s).

None of the activities included in this volume is a recipe to follow exactly. We encourage the readers of this volume, like good cooks, to experiment by adding their own ingredients to spice up an activity and adapt it to better suit the needs and interests of their learner population.

References

Benesch, S. (Ed.). (1988). *Ending remediation: Linking ESL and content in higher education.* Washington, DC: TESOL.

Brinton, D., Snow, M. A., & Wesche, M. (1989). *Content-based second language instruction.* Boston: Heinle & Heinle.

Cantoni-Harvey, G. (1987). *Content-area language instruction: Approaches and strategies.* Reading, MA: Addison-Wesley.

Crandall, J. (Ed.). (1987). *ESL through content-area instruction.* Englewood Cliffs, NJ: Prentice-Hall Regents.

Mohan, B. (1986). *Language and content.* Reading, MA: Addison-Wesley.

Short, D., Crandall, J., & Christian, D. (1989). *How to integrate language and content instruction: A training manual.* Washington, DC: Center for Applied Linguistics. (ERIC Document Reproduction Service No. ED 305 824)

Users' Guide to Activities

Part III: Hands-On Activities

Part IV: Data Gathering

Part V: Text Analysis and Construction

Part I: Information Management

Kimbunda Mwasa Jolie at Northern Virginia Community College, Alexandria, Virginia USA.

Vocabulary Classification

Levels
Intermediate +

Aims
Make connections in
order to remember
new vocabulary

Class Time
30 minutes

Resources
Vocabulary lists

A s students in adjunct classes study new vocabulary throughout the semester, their lists of words grow and can become unmanageable. This activity asks students to classify words, thereby helping them identify synonyms and words used in similar contexts. It also helps them review what they have been studying in their content class.

Procedure

1. Throughout the semester, keep a list of words the students have been learning in connection with their content class lectures and text.
2. Determine how the words on the list could be divided into categories. For example, in an ESL/humanities adjunct, the categories could be *baroque*, *rococo*, *neoclassic*, *romantic*, and *modern* or *sculpture*, *painting*, *architecture*, *literature, dance*, and *music*.
3. Select 20–30 words from the list to review. Either type them out for the students or write them on the chalkboard.
4. Divide the students into groups of three to five.
5. Ask the students to study the words and to group related words into separate lists. Then ask them to assign a title or heading to each list.
6. Have the students from each group share one of their categories and explain how and why they chose the words for that category.
7. As the discussion proceeds, review the definitions of the words and the way they have been used in the content class lectures and text.

Caveats and Options

1. These activities were used in an ESL/humanities adjunct class. The content class teacher used many adjectives and technical terms to describe paintings, sculptures, and other art and to describe the characteristics of art in various historical periods. Initially, the students were unfamiliar with most of these words, but this classification

activity helped them make associations and remember the works of art and historical periods.

2. In addition to giving the students the words to be classified, give them the categories and have them put the words in the correct category.

3. Do Step 1 as a contest in which the first group to categorize the words correctly wins. Keep in mind that some words may fit into more than one category.

4. Form a database composed of the words studied during the semester so that you can sort the words alphabetically and discard any repeated words, classify the words in various ways, and simplify test writing.

Contributor

Maureen Andrade is an Instructor at Brigham Young University, Hawaii, in the United States. Her interests include curriculum design, content-based instruction, and teaching writing.

Expanding Academic Vocabulary

Levels
Intermediate +

Aims
Become aware of the
difference between
general English
vocabulary and content-
specific terminology

Class Time
10–15 minutes

Preparation Time
None

Resources
Blackboard or butcher
paper

Tthis activity helps students deal with the large amount of vocabulary they confront in a semester-long content course. By learning to distinguish vocabulary associated with a particular content area from general academic vocabulary, they can focus on the terms that are most important to remember.

Procedure

1. Carefully discuss the difference between content-specific vocabulary (e.g., from U.S. history, *VJ Day*, *scalawags*, *New Left*) and unfamiliar words, terms, or phrases from reading assignments and lectures that do not specifically refer to the course content material but may impede understanding (*Alice in Wonderland*, *two-front war*, *Herculean task*).
2. Ask the students to assemble lists of examples from either the general or content-specific category from a given day's lecture.
3. Write the lists on the blackboard and disclose to the students that they can usually find content vocabulary from readings or lectures in the textbook's index or in a glossary; noncontent terms, however, frequently have colloquial, cultural, or anecdotal meanings.
4. Ask the students to determine priorities for addressing the more essential content vocabulary on the blackboard.
5. Urge the students to keep a running list of content and general academic terms (from the lectures and the textbook).

Caveats and Options

1. This activity was used in an ESL/U.S. history adjunct. In the Introduction to History class, students listened to the lecture and participated in class activities. In the ESL adjunct, the instructor opened the day's

activities by asking the students to identify "content" and "language" vocabulary that was critical to the understanding of the day's lecture.

2. If the list of content vocabulary made by your students appears too long, suggest that students split the list—an "A" tier for the terms they agree are obviously important and a "B" tier for less important terms to discuss if time allows.

References and Further Reading

Bernier, A. (1994). Diversity's challenge in the classroom: Language and history pedagogy from the student optic. *The History Teacher, 28,* 37–47.

Contributors

Anthony Bernier is a doctoral student at the University of California, Irvine, in the United States, where he was a study-group team leader with Project LEAP: Learning-English-for-Academic-Purposes. Marguerite Ann Snow is Associate Professor at California State University, Los Angeles, in the United States, where she conducts faculty training across the disciplines as Director of Project LEAP.

Divide and Classify

Levels
Intermediate +

Aims
Determine relevant
categories for a set of
details or main ideas
Sort information into
categories
Decide how to arrange
information in an
expository essay

Class Time
1 hour

Preparation Time
45 minutes

Resources
Handout with main
ideas or details
Blank paper
Scissors
Glue stick

This hands-on activity models a procedure academic writers can employ in the prewriting stage to classify information. Because this is a preliminary lesson in classification, the teacher identifies the key information for the students beforehand. This places the lesson's focus squarely on the skill of classification.

Procedure

1. Locate a source text that lends itself to the classification of information.
2. Ask the students to read over the text as homework before coming to class.
3. Type up the information to be classified (main ideas or details) in scrambled order in list form on a one-page handout (see the Appendix). Make one copy of the handout for each three to five students.
4. Seat the students in small groups of three to five, preferably at tables.
5. Distribute scissors, glue stick, blank paper, and one copy of the handout to each group.
6. Direct the students to study the listed information and discuss its relation to the assigned source reading.
7. Ask the students to cut the information into strips and classify the strips by placing them in separate piles by category.
8. Have the students create a name for each category and write the names at the top of each blank page of paper.
9. Have the students determine the order in which the information should be listed within each category and affix the sentence strips to the blank sheets of paper using the glue stick.

10. Ask the students to arrange the sheets of paper as they would organize the information in an essay of classification.

Caveats and Options

1. This activity lends itself particularly well to adjunct classes. In the psychology class of an ESL/psychology adjunct (Brinton, Snow, & Wesche, 1989), the students had been studying altered forms of consciousness such as visual distortions, delusions, and hallucinations. For the ESL assignment, they were given a text concerning the experiences of an individual who describes his physical and mental reactions to the drug LSD after ingesting it under experimental conditions (Asher, 1963). The details of this experience (see the Appendix) formed the basis of this prewriting activity, the purpose of which was to help prepare the students for the psychology assignment: to write a three- to five-page essay discussing the altered-consciousness experiences of the subject. Having the students cut the strips adds a kinesthetic dimension to the lesson and models an academic practice that they might want to emulate in their own prewriting activity.

2. In subsequent lessons, have the students themselves take the notes on the main ideas or details before engaging in the classification activity.

References and Further Reading

Asher, H. (1963, June 1). They split my personality. *Saturday Review*, *46*, 39–43.

Brinton, D. M., Snow, M. A., & Wesche, M. B. (1989). *Content-based second language instruction*. Boston: Heinle & Heinle.

Appendix: Sample Handout From Psychology Adjunct

Directions: Listed below are some of the effects of LSD that Harry Asher reports in "They Split My Personality." Using what you know about the effects commonly associated with altered states of consciousness, classify these effects, using the correct terminology. You may refer to chapter 8 of your psychology text or to your lecture notes.

feels nauseous
sees a spectrum at the edge of buildings
feels exhilarated and self-confident
has a tendency to laugh
notices the fluctuating quality of a patch of sunlight
notes "protruding" spectacles on the researcher's face
feels a "concertina" or "telescope" effect of his limbs
notices the corridor change in length
sees false teeth snapping in the air
[etc.]

Contributors

Donna M. Brinton is the Academic Coordinator of ESL Service Courses and a Lecturer in the Department of TESL & Applied Linguistics at the University of California, Los Angeles, in the United States. Marguerite Ann Snow is Associate Professor at California State University, Los Angeles, in the United States, where she conducts faculty training across the disciplines.

Advertising and the Audience

Levels
Intermediate +

Aims
Listen to and
comprehend U.S.
television commercials
Classify information
Make assumptions/
generalizations and put
them into categories

Class Time
20 minutes

Preparation Time
10 minutes

Resources
Chalkboard divided into
sections, or poster paper

Caveats and Options

In this activity students conduct a structured discussion of a product's consumers or its advertising audience. The focus is listening, speaking, classifying, and reasoning skills.

Procedure

1. For homework over a weekend or a few days, ask the students to watch television at different times of the day and night. Have them keep notes on what types of products are advertised at those times.
2. Ask the students to compare their notes in pairs.
3. Divide the chalkboard or paper into the sections *morning, afternoon,* and *night* (for other sample categories, see the Appendix).
4. Ask the students to write the names or types of products advertised in each time category in the appropriate section (see the Appendix).
5. Have pairs (or triads) of students discuss who will most likely buy such products.
6. Initiate a whole-group discussion regarding audience profile: Ask the students, "Who is buying the products based on the information you can gather from the time slot, programming, and type of product advertised?"

1. This activity serves as an awareness-raising and listening comprehension tool because students can pay close attention to the small doses of native speech in advertisements. It was used in American Society and Advertising, an intermediate ESL content course.
2. Put teams in charge of specific time categories and have them write profiles of the audience for that time slot.
3. Use magazine, newspaper, and radio advertisements to expose students to a variety of authentic materials.

4. Use the discussion of audience as a way of prompting or encouraging the awareness of audience in writing tasks. For example, this activity was used with diverse perfume advertisements in an intermediate ESL composition course.

References and Further Reading

Connell, E. L., Harrison, M. R., Hulse, M. L., Kling, J. M., Tickle, A., & Turner, J. (1995, March). *Building a content-based program: A dynamic dialogue*. Colloquium presented at the 29th Annual TESOL Convention, Long Beach, CA.

Hulse, M. L. (1994, March). *Developing a content course: A template*. Paper presented at the 28th Annual TESOL Convention, Baltimore, MD.

Simon, S., Howe, L., & Kirschenbaum, H. (1972). *Values clarification*. New York: Hart.

Stevens, P. (1972). *I can sell you anything*. New York: Peter H. Wyden.

Walker, J. A. (1994). *Art in the age of mass media*. Boulder, CO: Westview Press.

Appendix: Sample Categories

Time	6 a.m. to 12 p.m.
	12 p.m. to 5 p.m.
	5 p.m. to 11 p.m.
	11 p.m. to 6 a.m.
Products	Household items
	Cars
	Health and beauty aids
	Toys
Consumers	Mothers
	Fathers
	Children
	Teenagers
	Single women
	Single men

Economic level	Low
	Middle
	Upper middle
	High

Contributor

Eve L. Connell is an ESL Instructor and a Public Speaking and Business English Specialist for the MA programs at the Monterey Institute of International Studies as well as an ESL Instructor at Monterey Peninsula College, Monterey, California, in the United States.

Environmental Facts Around the World

Levels
Any

Aims
Read and listen to relevant factual information about world environmental crises
Memorize details
Sort information into categories for future study

Class Time
35–45 minutes

Preparation Time
20 minutes

Resources
Inflatable globe with world environmental statistical information
Index cards
Blank paper

This hands-on activity provides an enjoyable way to learn about world environmental issues and concerns. Students are assumed to have studied global environmental issues and to be familiar with the specialized vocabulary. The focus of this lesson is to practice speaking and listening, memorizing short factual data, and reviewing and classifying the data.

Procedure

1. Locate an inflatable globe printed with environmental facts.
2. Write on the index cards the names of the countries whose environmental facts appear on the globe. Write categories, such as *regions* or *problems,* on the blank paper to distribute in Step 11 (see the Appendix for sample categories).
3. Arrange the students in a circle, either seated or standing.
4. Hand out one or two country cards per student, depending on the group's size and level.
5. Have one student begin the game by holding the globe and reading aloud one or two times the environmental fact that is written over the country named on his or her index card.
6. Have the first student toss the globe to another student in the circle.
7. Have this second student read aloud the fact on the globe that is written over the country named on his or her card and toss the globe to a third student.
8. Allow the game to continue until all the students have caught the globe and read aloud their country's environmental fact.
9. Allow the students 5 minutes to write down all the facts they remember from the globe-tossing sequence.
10. Have the students compare their lists in pairs.

11. Pass out the category sheets and instruct the students to add their combined information to the sheets (e.g., *types of problems: air, water, soil pollution; regions: hemispheres, continents*).
12. Allow student pairs to present their findings to the class.

Caveats and Options

1. This activity works with any type of information that can be found on educational globes: environmental issues, animals, countries, continents, hemispheres, planets, stars, and constellations. In an intermediate ESL environmental issues course, this activity gave the students, who had been studying different environmental issues for a few weeks, the chance to practice familiar terminology, to challenge what they thought they knew about the issues, and to see and classify where in the world these problems were occurring.
2. In Step 9, divide the students into two teams and have them compete against the clock to write down as many facts as they collectively remember.
3. In subsequent lessons, call out a country and have the students write down the fact that they remember—or vice versa.
4. As a follow-up, create a handout that requires the students to match facts to the name of a country.

References and Further Reading

Connell, E. L., Harrison, M. R., Hulse, M. L., Kling, J. M., Tickle, A., & Turner, J. (1995, March). *Building a content-based program: A dynamic dialogue*. Colloquium presented at the 29th Annual TESOL Convention, Long Beach, CA.

Earth source: The environmental globe. [Available from Kaleidoscope, The Parent-Teacher Store, Capitola, CA, Telephone (408) 475-0210]

Ekins, P. (1992). *The Gaia atlas of green economics*. New York: Anchor Books/Doubleday.

Hammond, A. (Ed.). (1993). *Environmental almanac*. Boston: Houghton Mifflin.

Hulse, M. L. (1994, March). *Developing a content course: A template*. Paper presented at the 28th Annual TESOL Convention, Baltimore, MD.

Appendix: Sample Categories

Countries	*Regions*	*Environmental Problems*
Africa	Southeast Asia	Air Pollution
Indonesia	North America	Water Pollution
Brazil	South America	Deforestation
England	Western Europe	Landfill
China	Eastern Europe	Acid Rain
Taiwan		Nuclear Fallout
Germany		
Thailand		

Contributors

Eve L. Connell is an ESL Instructor and a Public Speaking and Business English Specialist for the MA programs at the Monterey Institute of International Studies as well as an ESL Instructor at Monterey Peninsula College, in the United States. Liz Bradbury is an ESL Instructor and Language Program Coordinator at the Monterey Institute of International Studies.

Observation or Interpretation, That Is the Question

Levels
Intermediate +

Aims
Differentiate
observations and
interpretations in social
science or science

Class Time
2 hours

Preparation Time
2–3 hours

Resources
Science or social
science magazines or
textbooks
Index cards
Magazine pictures or
photographs
Paper

This activity prepares students for further work in scientific reading and reporting on observations and interpretations. The focus of the activity is on developing the ability to recognize clues in written passages that aid the reader in identifying an example as an observation or an interpretation.

Procedure

1. Before class, collect a large number of photographs and magazine pictures that lend themselves to observation and interpretation. On the index cards, write examples of observations and interpretations from science or social science textbooks (see the Appendix).
2. Define the terms *observation* and *interpretation* for the students.
3. Divide the class into groups of three to five students.
4. Distribute the index cards to the groups.
5. Instruct the students to decide which cards are describing observations and which are describing interpretations.
6. Ask each group to report their decisions to the class.
7. Have the class discuss any disagreements in a noncritical fashion until everyone is in agreement on which category the cards belong to.
8. Display a large number of photographs or magazine pictures.
9. Distribute blank paper. Ask each student to choose one picture and write a corresponding observation and interpretation.
10. After the students have completed their assignment, again display the pictures.
11. Have the students read aloud their observations individually to the class. Ask the rest of the students to identify the picture that is being described.

12. Via written feedback from the students, evaluate how well they understand the difference between observations and interpretations.

Caveats and Options

1. This activity is designed to be used before activities in a social science or science course that require the students to understand the distinction between an observation and an interpretation.
2. Instead of supplying the pictures for this activity, have the students locate their own pictures to write about.
3. Ask the students in turn to read aloud either their observations or their interpretations and have the other students determine which it was.
4. Be sure to use authentic examples for this activity.

References and Further Reading

Richard-Amato, P., & Snow, M. A. (Eds.). (1992). *The multicultural classroom: Readings for content-area teachers.* White Plains, NY: Longman.

Appendix: Sample Cards

It appears that the patient is nervous.	The temperature of the liquid is 98 degrees Fahrenheit.
The liquid in the beaker is transparent.	This could be a result of the increased stress level due to finals.
The patient's palms were sweating.	The dinosaurs may have become extinct because of a change in the earth's temperature.

Contributor

Randi Freeman has taught ESL/EFL in Sweden and the United States. She has an MA in TESOL from the Monterey Institute of International Studies and teaches at Washington State University in the United States.

Feels, Tastes, Smells, Looks, Sounds Like . . . Emotions in English

Level
Low intermediate

Aims
Build vocabulary related to emotions
Scan texts
Classify emotion words
Describe emotions in terms of the five senses

Class Time
50–60 minutes

Preparation Time
30 minutes

Resources
Text containing references to emotion (e.g., journal article, novel)
Blackboard
Overhead projector
Blank transparencies and markers
Handout

This lesson serves as a prereading activity and a way for low-intermediate students working with advanced-level authentic texts to extract necessary information. The students work solely with the vocabulary related to emotions in order to apply it to the next step, discussing individuals' emotional responses to a given topic.

Procedure

1. Before class, divide the text into numbered sections (see Appendix A).
2. In class, ask the students how they are feeling. Elicit from the students as many emotions as they can identify and record them on a transparency displayed on an overhead projector.
3. Ask the students in pairs to scan the text and circle all the emotion words they can find.
4. Have each pair record the emotion words found in one numbered section of the text on the blackboard. Check to ensure that the pairs have found all of the vocabulary.
5. Ask the same pairs to group the emotion words recorded on the blackboard according to the categories on the handout (see Appendix B).
6. Assign the students to new groups of three or four. Ask the groups to choose one emotion from each category and to write a description of each emotion on a blank overhead transparency as follows:

   ● Feels like _____.

   ● Tastes like _____.

   ● Smells like _____.

- Looks like _____.
- Sounds like _____.

7. Have each group present its transparency to the class.

Caveats and Options

1. Expand the lesson by focusing on the formation of *-ed* and *-ing* adjectives.
2. The materials in the appendixes accompanied a lesson on responding to children's emotions that was designed for nonnative-speaking preschool teachers enrolled in a preservice training session.

References and Further Reading

Kostelnik, M. J., Stein, L. C., Whirren, A. P., & Soderman, A. K. (1993). *Guiding children's social development* (2nd ed.). Albany, NY: Delmar.

Appendix A: Sample Text

Skills for Responding to Children's Emotions:
How to Formulate Affective Reflections

1. *Observe children carefully before saying anything.* The context of a situation is important to its meaning. Pay close attention to children's facial expressions, voice tone, and posture as well as their actual words. If no words are spoken, you will have to rely on body cues alone. Because younger children tend to be more open about what they are feeling, the behaviors they display may be easier to interpret than those exhibited by older children. The emotions of grade schoolers, who have been socialized to respond in certain ways, or who have learned to hide their emotions, may be more difficult to decipher. With these children, you must pay particular attention to nonverbal cues. A child who is talking "happy" but looking "distressed" most likely is distressed.

2. *Be sensitive to the wide range of emotions children exhibit.* Children manifest numerous emotions. Some are extreme, some are more moderate; some are positive, some are negative. All of their emotions are important. If you only take the time to notice intense emotions, or focus solely on the negative ones, children soon learn that these are

the only emotions worth expressing. They get a broader perspective when all sorts of emotions are noticed and described.

3. *Make a nonjudgmental assessment of what the child is experiencing.* Form your impressions of the child's feelings using only evidence about which you are certain. Avoid jumping to conclusions about why children feel the way they do. For instance, you may observe Paul entering the room crying. It is obvious that he is either sad or angry, but why he is so distressed may not be evident. Although you may assume that he is missing his mother, he might really be upset about having to wear his orange sweater to school. Because you cannot be sure what is bothering him, an appropriate affective reflection would be "You look sad," rather than "You're sad because you miss your mom." Opening the interaction with the first statement is potentially more accurate than using the latter.

4. *Make a brief statement to the child describing the emotion you observed.* Keep your reflection simple. Do not try to cram everything you have noticed about the child's emotional state into one response. Young children understand short sentences best. This also is true for youngsters who do not speak English well, or those who are mentally impaired. Older children will appreciate longer sentences or combinations of phrases, but will resent being overwhelmed with a plethora of adult talk.

5. *Use a variety of feeling words over time.* Employ many different words to describe children's emotions. This emphasis on diversity expands children's vocabulary of feeling words and makes your responses more interesting to them. Begin by using words to describe the core emotions (happy, mad, sad, afraid). Gradually, branch out to include related words that make finer distinctions (variations of happy, such as delighted, pleased, contented, overjoyed). Once you have reached the latter point, think in advance of two or three words you have not used recently and plan to employ them on a given day. Each time a situation arises for which one of your words is suited, use it. Repeat this process with different words on different days. Finally, when you reflect using one of the more common feeling words in

your vocabulary, follow it with a second reflection using a slightly different word ("You seem sad. It sounds like you're disappointed the model didn't fly.").[1]

Appendix B: Handout

Directions: Write the vocabulary words from the blackboard in their appropriate place in the chart. An example is provided.

JOY	ANGER
happy	
SADNESS	FEAR

Contributors

Stephanie C. Perentesis, who has a master's in library science and an MA in TESOL, is the librarian for the College of Human Ecology; and Amy Tickle, who has an MA in TESOL, is a Lecturer in the English Language Center, both at Michigan State University in the United States.

[1]From *Guiding Children's Social Development* (pp. 128–129), by M. J. Kostelnik, L. C. Stein, A. P. Whirren, and A. K. Soderman. Copyright 1993 by Delmar Publishers, Albany, NY. Reprinted with permission.

Animal Classification

Levels
Beginning +; young
learners

Aims
Develop small-group
discussion skills
Utilize categorization
skills
Develop a concept of
scientific classification

Class Time
45 minutes +

Preparation Time
45 minutes +

Resources
Sets of black-and-white
illustrations of West
African animals
Blank paper (one sheet
per group)
Masking tape
Chalkboard or chart
paper

Part of an integrated seventh-grade English language development unit, this hands-on activity for early production and speech-emergent students crosses the curriculum boundaries between social studies (sub-Saharan medieval Africa), life science (classifications of living organisms), and language arts (West African folktale). As students sort illustrations into categories, they develop the social and language skills needed for small-group discussion as well as the scientific concepts required for academic success.

Procedure

1. Locate copyright-free illustrations of West African animals. Shrink or enlarge the illustrations on a photocopier to a standard size (e.g., 3.5 in. x 5 in.), mount them on card stock, and laminate them. Make one set for each group of four or five students.
2. Seat the students in groups of four or five.
3. Tape several illustrations to a wall or chalkboard.
4. Model for the students what they will do: Lay out the illustrations, study them carefully, and sort them into categories. Model the procedure for pictures of large and small animals and animals with two legs and four legs by moving illustrations appropriately, labeling categories, and listing the animal names. Be sure to demonstrate that an animal may appear in more than one category.
5. Elicit from the students suggestions for other possible categories. Check for comprehension and clarify as necessary.
6. Distribute one sheet of paper and one set of laminated illustrations of West African animals to each group.
7. Tell the students to lay out the illustrations so that everyone in the group can see them. Tell the students to look at the animals carefully,

sort them into as many categories as possible, and write down the categories and the names of the animals that belong in each.

8. When the students have completed the activity, ask them to name the categories they originated. Write them on the chalkboard or chart paper and ask groups to list the animals in the appropriate categories.

Caveats and Options

1. This activity presumes that the students have already been introduced to illustrations and common names of many West African animals.

2. If using this activity with intermediate students (speech emergent or intermediate fluency), ask them to think about how they determined the categories, which ones were obvious or subtle, and what information they used to put the animals into categories. Follow up by asking the students to write a description of the process they used to classify the animals.

3. Subsequent activities could move into an explanation of formal scientific classifications, comparison of student-originated with generally accepted scientific classifications, and analysis of features of both.

References and Further Reading

English language development curriculum, Grade 7. (1994). Alhambra, CA: Alhambra School District.

Dayrell, E. (1968). *Why the sun and the moon live in the sky*. Boston: Houghton Mifflin.

Harter, J. (Ed.). (1979). *Animals: 1419 copyright-free illustrations of mammals, birds, fish, insects, etc*. Mineola, NY: Dover.

Contributor

Linda Sasser is an ESL Program Specialist for the Alhambra (California) School District and an Adjunct Instructor in ESL at Pasadena City College, in the United States.

Identifying and Comparing Ancient Artifacts

Levels
Intermediate +

Aims
Identify, name, and compare two ethnic groups

Class Time
2 hours (advanced class)
2 hours + (intermediate class)

Preparation Time
1-2 hours

Resources
Museum with cultural artifacts, illustrations, slides, or teaching materials
Handout with archeological terms
Illustrated flash cards with descriptive text (if available from museum)
Paper or Styrofoam cups and colored pens (optional)

In this interactive activity, students visit a museum as part of a content-based unit on cultural anthropology or archeology. The activity focuses on vocabulary and comparative grammar forms. The students name simple characteristics of two distinct ethnic groups and their artifacts and then compare them.

Procedure

1. Arrange a museum visit (or acquire the materials for use in the classroom).
2. Ask the students to study the relevant terms before class (see Appendix A for a handout).

Introduction (20–30 minutes)

3. Review the topic-related vocabulary with the students.

Museum Visit (50–60 minutes)

4. Go to the museum (or group the students in class) and have them view at least five artifacts from two different ethnic groups or regions.
5. Ask the students to identify and name the following for each artifact viewed: color, number of colors, shape, and design.

Follow-Up (1 hour)

6. Review each illustration, name, and identification with the students.
7. Present the equative form (*like*) and simple comparative forms (*-er, more, less, fewer*). Model some examples of each form for the students.

8. Ask the students in groups to compare artifacts from the two ethnic groups using the equative and simple comparative forms.
9. Ask each group to write comparative sentences.
10. Have one student from each group orally present the group's sentences.

Caveats and Options

1. Many museums produce teaching packets that can easily be adapted for ESL teaching. Alternatively, produce your own materials. For example, Appendix B contains the flash cards produced to accompany an exhibit on ancient Peruvian ceramic artifacts. In groups, the students discussed the similarities and differences among the artifacts on the flash cards.
2. Pass out Styrofoam cups and colored pens. Have the students produce a replica of one artifact using the cups and pens. Then ask the students in pairs to orally compare their completed artwork and to use the flash cards to review and test each other's knowledge of the different artifacts.
3. Have the students act as archaeologists by putting together broken artifacts and making their own. This follow-up builds on the naming and comparison and encourages the students to talk about the art and the puzzles as they piece them together.

References and Further Reading

Kottack, C. P. (1993). *Researching American culture*. Ann Arbor: University of Michigan Press.

Fagan, B. M. (1985). *The adventure of archaeology*. Washington, DC: National Geographic Society.

Appendix A: Archaeological Terms

What is archaeology?
Archaeology is the recovery and study of physical remains from past human life and culture.

What is an archaeologist?
An archaeologist is a person who studies the lives and cultures of ancient peoples through the excavation and interpretation of material evidence of past human activity.

How does an archaeologist work?

Archaeologists work mainly by excavating places where people lived and worked and their burial places. Archaeologists also do research at universities and libraries and study modern people who have lifestyles similar to those of ancient people.

What is an archaeologist looking for?

Archaeologists look for artifacts and features that will give clues about the people who made them. An archaeologist also looks for relationships among the artifacts. For example, if the artifacts are found at the same depth in the ground, they probably are of the same age, and if two kinds of artifacts are usually found together, they may have been used together. Archaeologists are always looking for datable pieces of charcoal, bone, or other carbon-based materials that are found near the artifact to aid the dating process.

What is an artifact?

An artifact is an object made or modified by a human being.

What do archaeologists want to learn from these artifacts and features?

They want to learn how the people lived, when they lived, what was important to them, what their values were, and what their culture was like.

What is culture?

Culture can be defined as the attitudes, beliefs, customs, traditions, art, and achievements of a society that are transmitted from one generation to another.

What is looting?

Looting is the unsystematic removal of artifacts or any material culture resulting in a permanent loss of information.

Appendix B:
Illustrated
Flash Cards

North Coast

Shape: round with round bases or round with flat bases

Color: one or more

Spout: one or more

Description: North Coast vessels are round with flat bottoms, are decorated with one color, and have one stirrup spout.

North Coast

Shape: round with round bases or round with flat bases

Color: one or more

Spout: one or more

Description: North Coast vessels are round with flat bottoms, are decorated with one color, and have one stirrup spout.

South Coast

Shape: round with round bases or round with flat bases

Color: one or more

Spout: one or more

Description: South Coast vessels are round with rounded bottoms, are decorated with many colors, and have two spouts with a connecting bridge.

South Coast

Shape: round with round bases or round with flat bases

Color: one or more

Spout: one or more

Description: South Coast vessels are round with rounded bottoms, are decorated with many colors, and have two spouts with a connecting bridge.

Contributor

Michael Silverman is involved in applications of television and computer-based technologies and in academic, professional, and vocational content for ESL and EFL instruction.

Part II: Critical Thinking

Syed Imran Haider at Northern Virginia Community College, Alexandria, Virginia USA.

Support It!

Levels
Intermediate +

Aims
Distinguish between
generalizations and
supporting details
Decide whether a
generalization is correct
or incorrect
State reasons or
explanations to support
or refute a
generalization
Organize generalizations
and support in
expository writing

Class Time
30-50 minutes
(combined oral and
writing activities)
10-15 minutes (oral
activity alone)

Preparation Time
10 minutes

Resources
Lecture or text

This simple listening/speaking/writing activity is an effective way to review the concepts and vocabulary of any body of material that the students have learned from either lectures or readings. It can also improve the organization and content of the students' academic writing because it reinforces the "thesis + support" thinking that underlies much Western academic work.

Procedure

1. Have the students attend a lecture or read an article about any topic. If necessary, go over that material in class to ensure that the students understand the information.
2. Before the following class, write a series of four to six generalizations (some true, some false) on the lecture or reading material.
3. At the beginning of the next class, read each generalization aloud. After each generalization, call on a student to answer "true" or "false" and then to give at least one reason for that answer. Elicit additional reasons or explanations from other students.
4. Put on the blackboard a list of one or two key words for each of the generalizations you have just reviewed.
5. In pairs, have the students use the key words to reconstruct the generalizations they heard, correcting any that have been declared false. Circulate to help the students with their reconstructions.
6. Have each student choose the generalization from the list for which they have the greatest amount of support. This sentence will serve as the opening sentence of a paragraph.
7. Ask each student to compose a well-supported paragraph starting with the generalization selected.

Caveats and Options

1. This activity (or a variation of it) is used regularly in an adjunct class that is paired with a cultural anthropology course. The class generally discusses an anthropology lecture one day and reviews it the next day. This review is challenging, thought provoking, and focused, and it brings the whole class together.

2. Use the oral part of this activity, best done at the beginning of class, as a review. Start it just as a class is scheduled to begin with as many students as have come on time. You can even fire questions at late-arriving students as they straggle in, perhaps discouraging future tardiness!

3. Use this format for a quick-to-prepare pop quiz, with students writing their true-or-false answer and support/refutation, or as a review before the midterm or final examination. After the activity has become familiar and the students know what a generalization is, they can write their own statements and lead the activity.

4. In a subsequent lesson, use a student's paragraph as the basis for a lesson on transitions, as the students may initially string their support together without transition words.

Contributor

Melissa Allen is the Coordinator of the adjunct programs for the English Language Institute at George Mason University, Fairfax, Virginia, in the United States.

From Debate to Essay

Levels
Intermediate +

Aims
Think critically
Organize an argument
Analyze mistakes in
writing
Develop oral fluency
with target structures

Class Time
3 hours over two
sessions

Preparation Time
1 hour before the
second session

Resources
None

This two-stage activity encourages students to select their own topic independently of the tutor. The initial analytical work is followed by communicative work in which two subgroups prepare their arguments. By the time the debate proper comes, motivation should be very high. In the second part of the activity (mistake analysis and drill work), the two strands of analysis and communication are maintained. The activity comprises a complete study cycle that requires no initial input from the teacher and places complete responsibility on the students.

Procedure

Initial Lesson

1. Ask each student to write a motion on a topic (chosen before in a ranking exercise). Make it clear that the motion must be a controversial statement that is likely to provoke disagreement.
2. Write up to six motions on the blackboard. Check very carefully that all the students understand what the motions mean.
3. Ask the students to rank the motions according to interest.
4. Collate the marks, ranking the motions according to group interest.
5. Ask the students if they agree or disagree with the highest ranked motion. If there is a severe imbalance (of "agrees" and "disagrees"), continue down the interest list until you find a motion with a reasonable balance.
6. Divide the class into two subgroups. Tell each subgroup to prepare a logical argument to support their view. Ask each subgroup to choose a spokesperson. Visit the subgroups and offer your services as a language resource.

7. Reconvene the class for the debate proper. Ask each spokesperson to give an uninterrupted speech. Tell the opposing groups they may want to take notes during the speeches.

8. Encourage all the students to discuss their arguments in a less formal way. Make sure the reticent ones have a chance to speak. Note language errors that impede their communication and their correct equivalents on an error sheet.

9. Ask the two spokespersons to sum up the crux of their arguments in light of the debate.

10. Photocopy the error sheet and distribute it. Ask the students to write an essay that presents both sides of the motion.

Follow-Up Lesson

1. Correct the essays using only a code system, photocopy one of the essays (with the student's permission), and distribute the copies in class.

2. Ask individual students to correct the mistakes indicated by the codes. Then ask the students to check their work in pairs.

3. Ask individual students to read aloud the sentence that they have corrected. Confirm whether they are right or not; if not, say what is correct and elicit or say why.

4. Do some drill work based on the mistakes in the chosen essay. At the end, ask the students to write down one example sentence from each drill.

5. Ask all students to do a second version of their own essay (using the correction code guide for help).

6. Correct any remaining mistakes in the second version.

Caveats and Options

1. The activity works less well with a class that is highly dependent on the teacher. A degree of self-confidence is a prerequisite for success.

2. If you do not get a fair distribution of "agrees" and "disagrees" for any of the six motions, choose the most popular motion and ask some students to join a different subgroup (as an intellectual exercise).
3. This activity is adapted from "Milk it!" (Bress, 1994).

References and Further Reading

Bress, P. (1993, December). All correct. *Practical English Teacher*, 20–21.
Bress, P. (1994, October). Milk it! *Modern English Teacher*, 52–54.

Contributor

Paul Bress is a teacher and teacher trainer at Hilderstone College, Kent, England. His principal areas of interest are communicative strategies and learner independence.

Advocate Your Position

Levels
Experienced ESL/EFL
teachers and those in
training

Aims
Gain insight into the
need for negotiation
between content and
language faculty in
adjunct courses

Class Time
1 hour

Preparation Time
Minimal

Resources
Blackboard
Flexible table seating
(optional)
Name tags with role
identification
Meeting agenda
Role cards
Observation guide

This simulation provides those being introduced to adjunct instruction with a live model of the negotiation process, which is critical for the success of this cross-curricular model. By either assuming a role in the simulation or serving as outside observers, participants gain firsthand experience in the need to advocate their respective positions in an open-forum adjunct meeting. They also gain a deeper understanding of how idea exchanges and consensus reaching function within the adjunct model.

Procedure

Setup (15 minutes)

1. Explain to participants that they will be either actors in or observers of a simulated weekly meeting of adjunct faculty members. Divide them into these two groups.
2. Distribute the meeting agenda (Appendix A) to both groups and give a brief overview of the background, parties involved, and meeting agenda.
3. Distribute the name tags and simulation role cards (Appendix B) to all actors. Ask them to place these face down on the table or desk (see Caveats and Options, No. 2).
4. Distribute the observation guide (Appendix C) to all observers.
5. Set the ground rules for those serving as actors in the simulation:
   - All simulation participants must remain in character at all times and take an active part in the simulation.
   - Any statements made or actions engaged in must be in accordance with the role assumed.
   - Any agenda written into the role must be verbalized at an appropriate point during the simulation.

    ● It is the function of the program administrator to guide the meeting, keep the participants on topic, resolve any disputes or disagreements, and finish the business at hand within the 30 minutes allocated for the meeting.

6. Arrange the participants in the room, separating the actors and observers (see Caveats and Options, No. 3).
7. Allow time for clarification questions before the simulation begins.

Simulation (30 minutes)

8. Instruct the actors to put on their name tags and introduce themselves by role.
9. Ask the program administrator to begin the simulation.
10. After 30 minutes have elapsed (or sooner if the meeting comes to a natural end earlier), ask the participants to assume their original seats.

Feedback and Discussion (15 minutes)

11. Request feedback from the observers on the points listed in the Observation Guide.
12. Discuss with all participants how this experience relates to their previous understanding of the adjunct model and how it would influence them if they were to actually participate in such an instructional model.

Caveats and Options

1. This activity, designed to accompany chapter 6 of *Content-Based Second Language Instruction* (Brinton, Snow, & Wesche, 1989), assumes that the students are familiar with the concept of adjunct instruction. See References and Further Reading for other background readings.
2. If you wish, assign roles according to the personalities or abilities of the participants. We often have mixed native-speaking and non-native-speaking students of English in our MA in TESOL classes. Leave key roles such as the program administrator and psychology professor to those with strong linguistic skills.

3. If flexible seating is available, seat the observers in one corner of the room and arrange all the actors in the simulation around a large table or in a circle configuration.

4. The activity is written with 16–20 students in mind (13 simulation participants and 3–7 observers). If fewer students are available, collapse certain roles (e.g., the two English instructors, the two psychology teaching assistants, and the two English tutors). Alternatively, have all students participate in the simulation and, following the simulation, break the participants into smaller groups to complete the Observation Guide. Then have the groups each share their observations in a whole-class format.

References and Further Reading

Adamson, H. D. (1993). *Academic competence—Theory and classroom practice: Preparing ESL students for content courses*. New York: Longman.

Brinton, D. M., Snow, M. A., & Wesche, M. B. (1989). *Content-based second language instruction*. Boston: Heinle & Heinle.

Snow, M. A., & Brinton, D. M. (Eds.). (1992). [Theme issue on content-based instruction]. *The CATESOL Journal, 5*(1).

Appendix A: Meeting Agenda

Meeting Agenda: English/Psychology Adjunct

Background Information: It is Week 3 of the 6-week adjunct course in English and psychology. The occasion is the weekly coordination meeting, in which all members of the staff convene to discuss the progress of the linked courses. Attending this meeting are the following:

program administrator	psychology professor
English instructors (2)	psychology teaching assistants (2)
ESL instructor	psychology tutor
ESL tutor	academic counselor
English tutors (2)	dorm counselor

Agenda

Wednesday, July 23

1. Administrative update
   - payroll problems
   - final exam dates
     English—Aug. 3
     Psychology—Aug. 5
2. Cheating issue
3. Dorm update
4. Psychology paper assignment—Week 4
   - topic
   - degree of coordination
5. Other business

Appendix B: Simulation Role Cards

> You are the program administrator. It is your job to conduct the meeting and to ensure that decisions are made in accordance with the underlying philosophy of the adjunct course. You want to cover all items on the agenda and wrap the meeting up in approximately 30 minutes. You begin the meeting by telling the participants that, as a result of administrative problems beyond your control, their paychecks will be held up for 5 days.

> You are an English instructor. You took the job because it pays well. You are upset that you didn't receive your paycheck on the date it had been promised. Your rent was due 2 days ago. You have no money in your savings account and are really strapped financially.

You are an English instructor currently finishing up your doctoral dissertation (on Milton). You do not have much time to devote to class planning but have taught this level of English (in a nonadjunct setting) many times before. You would like to be able to teach your class as independently as possible, because any adjunct assignments require extra lesson planning.

You are the psychology teaching assistant in whose section all the ESL students are enrolled. Last week, there was an incident of cheating in your class. One of the male students, David, had his lecture notes open on his desk and was obviously copying information out of them. You confiscated his exam and gave him an *F* for it.

You are the ESL tutor. You are concerned about the dorm situation, which is not conducive to studying. This situation seems particularly bad for the ESL students, many of whom are so depressed by their performance on psychology quizzes that they have given up studying and spend much of their time in extracurricular activities such as playing Ping-Pong. Several students have broken tutoring appointments with you recently. One student, Rafael, was seen hanging out with nonstudent friends. They all seemed drunk.

You are the psychology tutor assigned to the ESL students. One of your students, David, came to you and said he had been caught cheating in the psychology section. He says lots of the other students did it too but did not get caught. He is very worried about his grade point average, because the exams are graded on the curve. David is a serious student, with lots of pressure from the home environment to succeed. He is a pre-med student.

You are the psychology professor. You have an idea for the next paper topic and want to discuss it. You also want to know what role the English instructors want to play in this paper assignment. Here is the topic:

Explain classical and operant conditioning. Then illustrate the two theories showing how the conditioning processes would differ. Target length: three to five pages.

You are the ESL instructor. Your students have been complaining about the weekly quizzes in psychology class. They are all multiple choice and depend on a lot of memorized detail. The students are very nervous and are not paying much attention to the English class because of their excess anxiety about psychology class. You would like to see them do more writing in psychology class because this would reinforce what you are teaching them.

You are a psychology teaching assistant for one of the sections with native speakers enrolled. Your students are having relatively few problems with the weekly quizzes, but you are concerned about the upcoming psychology paper assignment. You have worked as a teaching assistant for the psychology professor before, and his paper assignments tend to be straight out of the textbook. You feel this encourages plagiarism.

You are the head academic counselor for the Freshman Summer Program. You feel the students have hit a low point in their motivation due to the stress from the psychology class. Many students have simply given up. You and your counseling staff need more direct feedback from the instructors about individual students so you can arrange appointments with them to discuss their academic problems. You are upset that nobody consulted you about the cheating incident. This is the first you have heard of it.

You are an English tutor for one of the native-speaking sections. You are having problems motivating your students. They seem to view English tutoring sessions as extensions of the psychology tutoring sessions and most often come to you with questions about psychology. You are frustrated and want to discuss how to put the English class on an equal footing with the psychology class.

You are a psychology teaching assistant. You are not completely satisfied with the present format of the quizzes in the psychology discussion sections, which are all multiple choice. However, from what you have seen of the students' writing skills (your students are all native speakers of English), you are reluctant to have them write much. You're particularly concerned about the upcoming psychology paper assignment and want to get as much help from the English staff as possible. Ideally, you'd like to see this paper done as an adjuncted assignment (i.e., submitted to both classes, with each instructor assigning a grade for the paper).

You are the dormitory counselor. You feel that this summer's students are a relatively good group. However, the usual problems exist: students getting inadequate sleep, rowdy behavior in the recreation room, complaints about dormitory food, some racial tension. The ESL students seem to be anxiety ridden and do not mix with the other students.

Appendix C: Observation Guide

Observation Guide

Instructions: As you observe the various participants in the simulation, pay attention to the following issues. To what extent did they surface in the scenario? Jot down examples or points for discussion in the spaces below.

Staffing (e.g., instructor selection, pre-/in-service development):

Coordination (e.g., collaboration, assignments, personnel issues):

Resources (e.g., support services, facilities):

Course objectives (e.g., language goals, content goals, grading):

Student population (e.g., proficiency level, native language, ethnicity, motivation):

Contributors

Donna M. Brinton is Academic Coordinator of ESL Service Courses at the University of California, Los Angeles (UCLA), in the United States, and a Lecturer in the UCLA Department of TESL & Applied Linguistics. Marguerite Ann Snow is Associate Professor at California State University, Los Angeles, where she conducts faculty training across the disciplines.

"How Do You Feel About . . . ?"

Levels
Intermediate +

Aims
Explore differing
opinions on a theme or
topic
Express personal and
cultural values
Converse in an
authentic (discourse)
atmosphere

Class Time
1–2 hours

Preparation Time
10 minutes

Resources
Topic cards
Blank index cards

Students need opportunities to express their opinions, personal and cultural, in authentic settings. This discussion activity enables students to consider and explore their values and others' opinions on relevant, interesting, controversial topics through their communication skills.

Procedure

1. Prepare the topic cards (see the Appendix for sample topics).
2. Divide the class into small groups (three students per group is best).
3. Give each group a topic card.
4. Give the students 10 minutes to write their personal opinion about the topic on the card.
5. Allow the groups 15 minutes to discuss the issue and personal opinions.
6. Hand the groups five blank index cards. Ask the students to come up with five different opinion statements about their topic, ranging from liberal to moderate to conservative in point of view.
7. Have the groups exchange their five statement cards with those of another group.
8. Have the groups choose one card from the pack of five, discuss the new topic, and voice personal opinions.

Caveats and Options

1. This activity lends itself to discussing values and opinions of almost any type, although controversial, current, opinion-oriented topics are best. It is especially useful as a tool for aiding cross-cultural understanding, particularly in classes where students are having a difficult time seeing different sides of an issue.
2. Use the activity as preparation for a group presentation in which the students need to focus on cooperation and sharing. Have the groups

choose one card after Step 7 and prepare a 3- to 5-minute speech or opinion presentation. This activity encourages spontaneous, impromptu speaking, group work and organization, and perhaps the formal presentation of an opinion (not necessarily that of the speaker).

References and Further Reading

Connell, E. L., Harrison, M. R., Hulse, M. L., Kling, J. M., Tickle, A., & Turner, J. (1995, March). *Building a content-based program: A dynamic dialogue*. Colloquium presented at the 29th Annual TESOL Convention, Long Beach, CA.

Hulse, M. L. (1994, March). *Developing a content course: A template*. Paper presented at the 28th Annual TESOL Convention, Baltimore, MD.

Simon, S., Howe, L., & Kirschenbaum, H. (1972). *Values clarification*. New York: Hart.

Appendix: Sample Topics

U.S. aid to developing countries
Government funding of the National Endowment for the Arts
Health care reform
Welfare reform
The United States as world police

Contributors

Eve L. Connell is an ESL Instructor at the Monterey Institute of International Studies (MIIS) and Monterey Peninsula College as well as a Public Speaking and Business English Specialist for the MA Programs at MIIS, Monterey, California, in the United States. Douglas F. Werner served as ESL Instructor and Assistant ESL Coordinator at MIIS, where he specialized in Public Speaking and Communication Strategies. He is currently on a Fulbright Scholarship in Berlin, Germany.

Town Meeting

In this simulation activity, students evaluate the issues pertaining to a specific "problematized" situation, sift through information to locate the evidence that will support their assigned point of view, and bring this evidence to bear in arguing effectively for this point of view. The activity ideally follows the phase in a content-based unit in which the students have been exposed to a variety of source materials; it is an effective way to prepare the students for the unit's final writing activity.

Procedure

Day 1

1. Briefly review the source materials covered in the unit (e.g., by listing them on the blackboard and asking the students to provide a brief synopsis of the contents of each).
2. Explain to the students that they will be participating in a simulation activity in which they will be asked to assume a given role and argue persuasively in a town meeting format from their point of view. Further explain that they should draw the arguments from the materials studied for the unit and select evidence that supports their chosen point of view.
3. Group the students (four to five students per group is ideal) and distribute a role card to each group (see Appendixes A and B).
4. Distribute copies of the discussion guide to all students (see Appendix A). Explain that they should review the unit's source materials, "strategize" the arguments that will most effectively support their point of view, and fill in the discussion guide to prepare for the simulation.
5. As homework, ask the students to review the source materials for further ways to support their point of view.

Day 2

6. Set the stage for the simulation, selecting one member from each group to perform the roles. Explain the ground rules for the simulation (see Advocate Your Position, this volume, for suggested rules).
7. Have the selected students perform the simulation, limiting the time for the various group advocates to argue their point of view to a total of 20–25 minutes.
8. Follow up with discussion of the relative advantages and disadvantages of the ideas presented. If you wish, allow the student observers to vote for the most effectively presented argument.
9. Time permitting, allow additional student groups to perform the simulation.

Caveats and Options

1. Appendixes A and B contain the simulation handouts created to accompany units on the social causes and consequences of homelessness in U.S. society and on the psychological phenomenon of obedience to authority, respectively. Before participating in the simulation, university-level ESL students enrolled in a content-based academic writing class did extensive reading on the topic in a range of genres and viewed a video documentary. The simulation required the students to synthesize information from the various sources and served as preparation for the unit's final composition assignment.
2. Instead of having selected students perform the simulation in front of the class, divide the class into smaller groups and have them perform the simulation as a small-group activity.
3. Carefully tailor the simulation to the unit the students are studying. It works best when the source materials contain a variety of conflicting points of view. Take care to incorporate these points of view into the various roles created for the simulation.
4. Providing the students with pictures or photographs of the individuals whose roles they are assuming lends psychological reality to the task and serves to motivate the students. For example, in preparing the Obedience to Authority simulation (Appendix B), the students received a picture of Stanley Milgram from an introductory psychology textbook. Fictionalized "pictures" from magazines can also be used.

5. As with any controversial topic, the students may feel distressed if they are asked to represent a point of view that they disagree vehemently with or have negative personal experience with. Therefore, ask them if they are uncomfortable representing a particular point of view and redesignate the groups accordingly.

6. Create an additional group of "discussants" or "evaluators" whose role it is to take copious notes during the simulation and then to discuss the performance of the individual role players.

7. Videotape the simulations and, as a follow-up, analyze individual students' oral communication strategies. Students also enjoy watching their performances and often perform their roles more seriously when they are being videotaped.

8. As a follow-up writing assignment, ask the students to write a letter to the editor or a proposal to the city government representing their point of view.

References and Further Reading

Milgram, S. (1994). The perils of obedience. In L. Behrens & L. J. Rosen (Eds.), *Writing and reading across the curriculum* (5th ed., pp. 322–335). New York: HarperCollins.

Appendix A: Discussion Guide and Role Cards for Simulation on the Homeless

Background: You are about to take part in a town meeting at which residents will discuss the causes and possible solutions for the local homeless problem.

Setting: City Hall

Participants: The homeless groups represented are:

- The mentally ill homeless
- Homeless families
- Homeless teenagers
- Homeless Vietnam veterans
- Homeless rural people

Also participating is a city government mediator.

Task: Your job is to discuss the advantages and disadvantages of the solutions proposed by your group. Your criticisms of the proposed solutions should be based on your understanding of the causes of your own homelessness and the ways in which the solutions would affect you. Study the role card. Assuming the point of view of the person your group has been assigned, work together to suggest possible solutions for homelessness based on your own perspective and personal experience with the issue. Using the discussion guide provided, identify possible advantages and disadvantages of your proposals. Be prepared to support your evaluation with clear reasoning, with ideas from some of the unit readings, or from personal experience. Then, assuming the role of the group you are representing (i.e., a specific homeless group or city government official), present your point of view at the town meeting.

Discussion Guide: In your group, propose three possible solutions that society, the government, and citizens could implement to help alleviate the problems caused by homelessness. As you discuss these solutions, record the advantages and disadvantages of each. Draw ideas from the course materials we have used (i.e., the readings and videos).

Proposed solutions	Advantages	Disadvantages
Solution 1		
Solution 2		
Solution 3		

Role Cards

Mr. Jones: Representative of the mentally ill homeless

You suffer from a severe mental condition that requires constant medication. Before 1973, you lived in a state mental institution, but this hospital was closed in that year, and you were released into the community and provided with medication. Unfortunately, the funding for the community center in which you were supposed to live was cut. Because your family asked you to leave, you have been living on the street in various cities.

Mrs. Brown: Single woman with three children; homeless

Your husband abandoned you and your three children about a year ago, leaving you nothing and paying no money for child support. You have a job as a secretary in a small insurance company, but you have no health benefits. About 6 months ago, your youngest son became extremely ill and had to be hospitalized for several months. The high costs of his health care have wiped out all your resources. A month ago, your money completely ran out, and you were unable to pay your rent. You were evicted and have been living in a hotel for the homeless for the past 3 weeks.

Bob: 19-year-old homeless man

You have lived on the streets for the past 2 years. You ran away from your parents because both your father and your mother are alcoholics. Your mother neglected you, and your father used to beat and insult both you and your mother regularly. You cannot remember a time when this kind of abuse did not take place. Since going on the streets, you have become a drug user and have been forced to steal and lie to support your habit. You do not like being on the streets and wish someone would help you.

Alex: 45-year-old Vietnam veteran

You are a Vietnam veteran who returned from the war in 1972 after doing heavy combat duty for 3 years. Because of the kind of combat you saw in Vietnam, you were unable to readjust to your surroundings when you returned. Your marriage of 5 years ended in divorce, and you have been unable to hold a steady job since your return. You also suffer from post-traumatic stress disorder and severe flashbacks, which makes it difficult for you to work or live normally.

John: 50-year-old farmer

You have been a farmer since you were a small boy. You helped your father on the farm that had been in your family for 100 years and four generations—until a year ago. At that time, you suffered crop loss due to the previous summer's severe drought. As a result, you were unable to repay low-interest loans given to you by the government, and you lost the farm. You have been living with relatives, but the prospects are bleak for finding an inexpensive place to live because there is no low-cost housing in your community, and you have no job skills except farming.

Mediator: Representative from the city
seeking a solution to the homeless problem

You have been sent by the city government to meet with several homeless people in order to discuss proposals with them to eliminate or alleviate the causes of their homelessness. In proposing solutions, you should draw from the source materials covered in this unit (i.e., the course readings and video documentaries). It is your responsibility during the discussion to make sure that all participants voice their reactions (both positive and negative) to your proposals.

Appendix B: Discussion Guide and Role Cards for Simulation on Obedience to Authority

Background: It is a few years after the completion of Stanley Milgram's well-known experiments on obedience, and the famous scientist is eager to conduct another experiment on obedience to authority. This time he wishes to set up an experiment that would be conducted over a longer period of time. The results of his earlier studies on obedience are familiar to everyone within the scientific community and the general public. There has, of course, been much debate over the study itself and its conclusions.

Setting: The National Endowment for the Sciences has set up a committee to review Milgram's request for money. The committee consists of psychologists and members of the public who have a particular interest in research on obedience. This group of people will decide whether or not to approve the funding for his research. Milgram, for his part, is trying to convince the committee that there are valid reasons for him to receive grant money to further his research.

Participants: The members of the National Endowment for the Sciences Committee (NESC) are:

- Otto Schaeffer, a survivor of the Nazi death camps who now works for the Simon Wiesenthal Center in Los Angeles. He is an expert on the question of how Hitler convinced people to obey his commands and accept his ideology.
- Diana Baumrind, a psychologist who conducts research on human behavior but observes human behavior rather than setting up experiments in a laboratory. She has written books about why research on human behavior and psychology should not be conducted in a laboratory.
- Morris Braverman, a social worker and one of the subjects in Milgram's original experiments.
- Adolf Jones, a member of a special covert operations and torture unit for the U.S. Army. He has been with the military for 30 years, serving first in Vietnam and more recently in the Middle East during the Gulf War.

Task: Study the role card. Assuming the point of view of the person your group has been assigned, work together to evaluate Milgram's experiment. Using the discussion guide provided, identify which aspect of the study you are critiquing (e.g., the assumptions of the research, Milgram's conclusions, the relationship between the evidence and the conclusions). Support your evaluation with clear reasoning, with ideas from some of the unit readings, or from personal experience. Then, assuming the role of the person whose viewpoint you have been assigned to represent, present your point of view to the NESC.

Discussion Guide

Aspects of the study being critiqued	Support for your opinion

Role Cards

Otto Schaeffer

You are a survivor of the Nazi death camps and now work for the Simon Wiesenthal Center in Los Angeles. You are an expert on the question of how Hitler convinced people to obey his commands and accept his ideology. Because you lived in Germany during the time of Hitler, you know how people behaved. You had direct contact with the Nazi SS soldiers, with Hitler's policies to "free" Germany of Jews and other "undesirable" people, and you saw how ordinary citizens reacted to what was happening. You knew people who followed and said nothing when their Jewish neighbors were humiliated in the street or had all their property confiscated. You knew people who joined the Nazi party and participated. You also knew people who resisted Hitler's authority. But you knew how difficult it was to resist and the measures that the government and army took against someone who did not cooperate with Nazi policies and laws, and you knew the strong hierarchy that was in place to reinforce obedience.

Diana Baumrind

Like Milgram, you are a psychologist who conducts research on human behavior. However, you prefer to observe human behavior rather than set up experiments in a laboratory. You have written books about why research on human behavior and psychology should not be conducted in a laboratory.

Stanley Milgram

To "become" Stanley Milgram and support his research, reread Milgram's report of his research, "The Perils of Obedience."

Morris Braverman

You are a retired social worker and one of the subjects in Milgram's original experiments. You are the only member of the committee who has had actual experience with Milgram's research and how it was conducted. You had a very peculiar reaction during Milgram's experiment but nonetheless feel that it was a worthwhile experience for you. Reread the section in "The Perils of Obedience" entitled "Peculiar Reactions" (pp. 329–330) to familiarize yourself with your original reactions and your subsequent feelings about the experiment.

Adolf Jones

You are a member of a special covert operations and torture unit for the U.S. Army. You have been with the military for 30 years, serving first in Vietnam and more recently in the Middle East during the Gulf War. You are the only member of the committee who has had real-life experience inflicting pain on others as a direct result of your job and orders that you are given. You are proud of your work and feel that you take responsibility for your actions and know exactly why you agree to torture others when you are ordered to do so.

Contributors

Christine A. Holten is a Lecturer and ESL composition specialist in the Department of TESL & Applied Linguistics at the University of California, Los Angeles (UCLA), in the United States. Donna M. Brinton is the Academic Coordinator of ESL Service Courses at UCLA and a lecturer in the UCLA Department of TESL & Applied Linguistics.

The Cereal Connection

Levels
Intermediate +; young
learners

Aims
Develop an
understanding of
scientific concepts such
as identification of
criteria, analysis, and
evaluation
Engage in collaborative
discourse

Class Time
60–75 minutes

Preparation Time
20 minutes

Resources
Small boxes of different
types of cereal (three
per group)
Paper bowls
Large newsprint sheets
Overhead projector,
transparencies, and pens
(optional)

This interdisciplinary hands-on activity develops problem-solving and critical thinking skills. It also enhances group dynamics and collaborative discourse.

Procedure

1. Tell the students the problem: to determine which is the best cereal.
2. Outline the steps the students will take:
   - Select the set of criteria that will help you reach a consensus.
   - Analyze and evaluate the cereals based on these criteria.
   - Arrive at a conclusion.
   - Prepare a 2-minute presentation that explains the criteria selected and the process used to reach a consensus and arrive at a conclusion. The presentation should include graphics to illustrate feature analysis.
3. Post these steps on large newsprint sheets for all students to see.
4. Divide the students into small groups. Give each group three boxes of cereal, bowls, transparencies (or large newsprint sheets), and pens.
5. Have the students explore the problem and prepare their presentation. Facilitate and encourage exploration and creative ideas.
6. Have the groups deliver a brief presentation of their findings. Encourage class discussion of the presentations.

Caveats and Options

1. This activity is most successful with students 11 years old and above.
2. Encourage the students to explore criteria such as packaging design, price, and other marketing strategies.
3. Do the activity with other products.

4. Use the activity to develop library skills, to introduce students to consumer-oriented studies, and to expose students to interdisciplinary issues.
5. This activity evolved from one presented by Jacqueline Grennon Brooks at a joint session of TESOL and science teacher candidates at the State University of New York at Stony Brook.

References and Further Reading

Brooks, G. J., & Brooks, M. (1993). *The case for constructivist classrooms.* Alexandria, VA: Association for Supervision and Curriculum Development.

Davis, B. (1964). *Learning science through cooking.* New York: Sterling.

Nourse, A. E. (1977). *Vitamins.* New York: Franklin Watts.

Ontario Science Center. (1987). *Scienceworks: The Centennial Centre of Science and Technology.* Reading, MA: Addison-Wesley.

Patent, D. H. (1992). *Nutrition: What's in the food we eat?* New York: Holiday House.

Zubrowski, B. (1981). *Messing around with baking chemistry.* Boston: Little Brown.

Contributors

Dorit Kaufman directs the TESOL certification program in the Department of Linguistics at the State University of New York at Stony Brook, and Kathleen McConnell is a Counselor and Assistant Professor in the ESL Department at Suffolk Community College, Riverhead, New York, both in the United States.

Fruits for Thought

Levels
Advanced; young
learners

Aims
Develop analysis,
classification, and
evaluation skills
Observe the problem-
solving process
Solve problems
collaboratively
Cultivate multiple
perspectives in the
problem-solving process

Class Time
90 minutes

Preparation Time
20 minutes

Resources
Three different fruits
per group (e.g., kiwi,
peach, orange)
Paper plates
One knife per group
Napkins
Large newsprint sheets
or overhead projector,
transparencies, and pens
Handouts

This multisensory, hands-on activity is grounded in a learner-centered pedagogy that utilizes cooperative learning strategies and whole language approaches to help students acquire mathematical and scientific concepts and develop language.

Procedure

1. Divide the class into two equal groups: Group A (participants) and Group B (observers). Subdivide Groups A and B into smaller groups. Ask each Group B to observe a designated Group A.
2. Give Groups A three types of fruit, a knife, paper plates, napkins, and transparencies. They will engage in solving the problem while Groups B discover what that problem is and observe the ways Groups A arrive at a solution.
3. Give Groups A the handout entitled Solve This Problem (Appendix A). Give Groups B the handout entitled Observe Problem Solving (Appendix B).
4. Have Groups A negotiate and work through the problem-solving steps while Groups B record their observations of their designated Groups A. Facilitate and encourage discovery and collaboration.
5. Have Groups A reach a consensus and prepare a graphic presentation of their conclusions while Groups B continue to record observations.
6. Have Groups A give a brief presentation of their findings.
7. When the presentations of Groups A are over, distribute the handout entitled Reflections on the Problem-Solving Process (Appendix C) to Groups A for discussion. At the same time have Groups B discuss their observations and prepare their own brief presentation of the process they have observed.

Caveats and Options

This learner-centered activity can lead to numerous interdisciplinary thematic units. See References and Further Reading for sources of material.

References and Further Reading

Lovitt, C., & Lowe, I. (1993). *Chance and data investigations*. Carlton, Australia: Curriculum Corp.

Ontario Science Center. (1987). *Foodworks: Over 100 science activities and fascinating facts that explore the magic of food*. Reading, MA: Addison-Wesley.

Sakade, F. (Ed.). (1967). *Peach boy and other Japanese children's favorite stories*. Rutland, VT: Chas. E. Tuttle.

Appendix A: Solve This Problem

The problem: Determine the differences and similarities among these fruits.

1. Work as a group and follow these steps:
   - Select the criteria that will help you reach agreement.
   - Analyze and evaluate the data based on these criteria.
   - Draw your conclusions.
   - On the overhead transparency, create a graph or a table showing your conclusion.
2. Give a 2-minute presentation of your group's conclusions. Include an explanation of the criteria and the process you have used in order to reach a consensus.

Appendix B: Observe Problem Solving

1. What is the problem that Group A is trying to solve?
2. What criteria are being used?
3. How did Group A establish these criteria?
4. What is each learner's role in the problem-solving process?
5. Were there any learners who did not actively participate?
6. What problems did the group encounter in solving the problem?
7. What are some other ways the group might have solved the problem (e.g., selecting different criteria, using alternative approaches)?

Appendix C: Reflections on the Problem-Solving Process

1. What criteria did you use to solve the problem?
2. How did you establish these criteria?
3. What was each group member's contribution to the problem-solving process?
4. How would you have involved learners who were not active in the problem-solving process?
5. What difficulties did your group encounter in solving the problem?
6. What are some other ways your group might have solved the problem (e.g., selecting different criteria, using alternative approaches)?

Contributors

Dorit Kaufman directs the TESOL certification program at the Department of Linguistics at the State University of New York at Stony Brook, and Kathleen McConnell is a Counselor and Assistant Professor in the ESL Department at Suffolk Community College, Riverhead, New York, both in the United States.

Synthesizing Content on a Continuum

Levels
Any

Aims
Synthesize content from
multiple sources or
perspectives
Display relationships
graphically
Think critically by
looking beyond simple
dichotomies
Convert complex
relationships between
viewpoints and facts
into a visual
representation

Class Time
Variable

Preparation Time
Minimal

Resources
Content sources
Continuum handouts

This activity employs the continuum, a graphic representation with a deceptively simple appearance, as an aid to synthesizing information. Continua allow students to convert dense linguistic input, intricate concepts, and multiple perspectives into a simplified display of information. Like all graphic tools, continua are extremely versatile and can be used as endpoints in themselves or as springboards for related activities in content-based classrooms. The systematic use of continua and other graphic tools both within and across thematic units can lend an element of cohesion to a content-based classroom.

Procedure

1. Select and assign content sources that include a variety of opinions or perspectives, shades of meaning or factualness, degrees of similarity or difference, or chronologically ordered information.
2. Create a handout (see the Appendix):
   - Draw a straight line with endpoints.
   - Based on the content and the purposes of the lesson, label the endpoints appropriately (e.g., *agrees with X/disagrees with X, fact/opinion, similar to my culture/different from my culture, ancient/modern*).
   - Formulate a question that will require the students to place information along the continuum.
3. Contextualize the activity (e.g., say, "In the last few days, we have talked and read about . . ."), and then pose the question.
4. Distribute the handout.
5. Check that the students understand the prompt and the endpoints.
6. Have the students individually place information along the continuum.
7. Arrange the students in pairs or small groups. Have them compare their continua and discuss the reasons for discrepancies.

Caveats and Options

1. Content sources with complex information lend themselves to continua.
2. Use the filled-in continuum as a lead-in to another activity (e.g., a writing assignment that requires the synthesis of content or the analysis of different perspectives).
3. Modify the activity into an information-gap task. For example, during a thematic unit on animal communication in an ESL class, the students used three continua to synthesize opinions regarding whales (based on Cole, 1989; see the Appendix). One group of students completed the first continuum, and the other completed the second. Pairs of students composed of one student from each of the two groups completed the third continuum, which required the transfer of information from one student to the other. These activities led naturally into a writing assignment in which the students explained their own stance on whale communication.
4. Continua are just one among many types of graphic tools that can be used to synthesize content. Grids, flowcharts, network trees, and pie charts are among the most useful. Jones, Pierce, and Hunter (1988) and Tang (1992/1993) present a variety of graphic forms and suggest the types of content that fit each one. After using a number of graphic tools in class, relinquish control by allowing the students to decide which graphic tool would be most appropriate for the content under consideration.
5. Use graphic tools for skills feedback. For example, during oral presentations, provide feedback to the presenter (or have the students do so) by marking points between continua endpoints (e.g., *formal/informal* for vocabulary, *easy to understand/difficult to understand* for pronunciation, *too loud/too soft* for volume).

References and Further Reading

Cole, J. (1989). *Animal communication*. San Diego, CA: Greenhaven Press.

Jones, B. F., Pierce, J., & Hunter, B. (1988). Teaching students to construct graphic representations. *Educational Leadership, 46*(4), 20–25.

Tang, G. M. (1992/1993). Teaching content knowledge and ESOL in multicultural classrooms. *TESOL Journal, 2*(2), 8–12.

Appendix: Whale Communication

Part I: A continuum for half of the students

Directions: Where do three experts stand? Read pp. 32–39 and place the following experts on the continuum below. Be prepared to support your placement decisions in class discussion.

Experts: Victor Scheffer, Loren Eisely, Edwin Colbert

strongly believes that whales do not communicate   strongly believes that whales do communicate

Part II: A continuum for the other half of the students

Directions: Where do three experts stand? Read pp. 32–39 and place the following experts on the continuum below. Be prepared to support your placement decisions in class discussion.

Experts: Jacques Cousteau, Roy Gallant, John Lilly

strongly believes that whales do not communicate   strongly believes that whales do communicate

Part III: A final continuum for the information-gap activity

Directions: Where do all the experts stand? With your partner, consult the two continua to place all six experts on the new continuum below. As you negotiate, use the book to help you make your decisions.

strongly believes that whales do not communicate   strongly believes that whales do communicate

Contributors

Thomas Mach received his MA in TESL from Northern Arizona University, Flagstaff, in the United States, and teaches English at Technikon Northern Transvaal in Soshanguve, South Africa. Fredricka L. Stoller is Associate Professor in the TESL and Applied Linguistics programs and Director of the Program in Intensive English at Northern Arizona University.

A Gambit-Driven Debate

Levels
Intermediate +

Aims
Use conversational
gambits naturally
Analyze, synthesize, and
manipulate content for a
specific purpose
Prepare for formal
speaking situations
Gain confidence in
speaking
Work collaboratively

Class Time
Four class periods

Preparation Time
2 hours

Resources
Content that lends itself
to a debate
Handouts
Blank paper

This multistep activity enables students to debate an issue related to a thematic unit. Students prepare for the debate by analyzing, synthesizing, and manipulating course content. In addition, students engage in a variety of tasks (e.g., conversational gambit practice, prediction exercises) that help build their confidence for the upcoming debate.

Procedure

1. Design a debate format (for suggestions see Kayfetz & Stice, 1987; Ur, 1981), set a date for the debate, and invite a suitable audience (e.g., another class, parents, teachers, TESL graduate students).
2. Locate three articles from various sources with differing perspectives on an appropriate topic (e.g., controversial issues, opposing viewpoints) that lends itself to a debate.
3. Divide the class into two teams and each team into three groups. For homework, ask each group within each team to read one of the three articles.
4. In the next class, ask each group to summarize its own article for team members so that all members understand the content.
5. Have the class specify a pro/con issue raised in the readings, assign a side of the issue to each team, and introduce the debate format.
6. Introduce relevant gambits (see Appendix A) and give the students time to practice them.
7. Ask each group to reread its original article and extract information that could be used to support or refute its team's side.
8. Have each team fold a blank sheet of paper in half, label the halves *Pro* and *Con*, and list information from all three readings under the appropriate headings.

9. Have each team reorganize the content from the pro/con grid in order to define more succinctly its own major arguments and predict the major arguments of the opposing team.
10. Have each team use the grids on the Question Strategies handout (see Appendix B) to prepare for the question period of the debate.
11. Give the students a Debate Score Sheet (see Appendix C) to familiarize them with the criteria by which the audience will judge them.
12. Have the teams assign individual roles for the actual debate. Give the students time for individual and team preparation.
13. Hold the debate and have the audience evaluate each team using the Debate Score Sheet.

Caveats and Options

1. If you have a large class or an odd number of students, assign one or two students the role of debate moderator. The moderator will explain the format and score sheets to the audience, introduce and time the speakers, and facilitate the debate.
2. To make the activity especially effective, first have the students review and score a videotaped practice debate. This dry run will familiarize them with the debate format and help them anticipate difficulties they might encounter in the real debate.
3. Invite the audience to ask questions of each team at the end of the debate.
4. If you videotape the final debate, view the tape with the students in a subsequent class. Ask the students to score their performance using the Debate Score Sheet as if they were an audience. Compare the students' perceptions with those of the actual audience, analyzing each score sheet category. While watching the videotape, pause periodically to give the students feedback on aspects of their performance (e.g., gambit use, pronunciation, body language, communication breakdowns).

References and Further Reading

Kayfetz, J. L., & Stice, R. L. (1987). *Academically speaking*. Belmont, CA: Wadsworth.

Ur, P. (1981). *Discussions that work: Task-centred fluency practice*. Cambridge: Cambridge University Press.

Appendix A: Debate Gambits

Listed below are some useful gambits for different speaking purposes. On each blank line, add another gambit for the purpose stated on the left.

Purpose	Gambits
To begin a statement	*Basically, I believe ...* *I'd like to begin by saying ...* _____
To support a main idea	*For example, ...* *This is obvious in the case of ...* _____
To add another idea	*In addition, ...* *I'd also like to point out that ...* *Now, let's look at ...* _____
To signal that you are finishing	*In sum, ...* *I'd like to finish by saying ...* *Finally, ...* _____
To ask a question	*_____, would you please explain ...?* *_____, have you considered ...?* *This question is for _____ ....* _____
To solicit a response to a statement	*_____, I believe .... What do you think about this?* *_____, in my opinion, ... do you agree?* _____
To answer a question	*That's a good question. I believe ...* *I'm glad you asked that question because ...* _____

Appendix B: Question Strategies

In the grid below, list the questions that you think the opposing team will ask. Jot down possible responses to the questions as well as gambits that could be used.

Questions	Responses	Gambits

In the grid below, list the questions you might ask the opposing team. Also write down some gambits that may be useful in asking these questions.

Questions	Gambits

Appendix C: Debate Score Sheet

After the debate, complete this sheet for both teams. Remember that you are evaluating debating skill, not the position being argued. Rate each team on the categories listed below using a scale of 1 (poor) to 4 (excellent).

Poor			Excellent
1	2	3	4

Pro   Con

_____ _____ A. Analysis: The team presented the strongest possible arguments to support its position.

_____ _____ B. Evidence: The team supported its arguments with good examples.

_____ _____ C. Organization: The team's introductory and concluding statements were clear and well organized.

_____ _____ D. Questions: The team's questions (during the question period) were concise and exposed weaknesses in the opposing team's arguments.

_____ _____ E. Answers: The team's answers to questions were concise and to the point.

_____ _____ F. Presentation: The team members communicated their position effectively and persuasively by combining proper delivery, gestures, and eye contact.

_____ _____ G. Participation: All members of the team participated by making statements, asking questions of the other team, or answering the other team's questions.

_____ TOTAL   Winner: Pro _____ Con _____

Contributors

Thomas Mach received his MA in TESL from Northern Arizona University, Flagstaff, in the United States, and teaches English at Technikon Northern Transvaal in Soshanguve, South Africa. Fredricka L. Stoller is Associate Professor in the TESL and Applied Linguistics programs and Director of the Program in Intensive English at Northern Arizona University, in the United States. Christine Tardy received her MA in TESL from Northern Arizona University and is an Instructor of English for specific purposes at Sumikin-Intercom in Osaka, Japan.

Thanks for the Visuals

Level
Low intermediate; young learners

Aims
Gain access to social studies content via visual aids

Class Time
45–50 minutes

Preparation Time
30–60 minutes

Resources
Classroom text
Handout (optional)
Wall chart (optional)

A content-area class that contains both ESL students and native English speakers can pose a problem for instructors. Some ESL students may understand and be able to perform, others may have difficulty with some of the requirements, and still others may appear lost. Visual aids will help the teacher reach those students who are lacking in language proficiency, as the visual image makes an immediate impression and does not rely solely on written or oral language that may be beyond the learners' levels. Reading charts, graphs, and maps and studying diagrams and pictures allow students to do something useful without having to struggle with the language.

Procedure

1. Have higher level ESL students and native speakers do the regular civics lesson (e.g., "The English Settle America," Bernstein, pp. 23–29).
2. Have the lower level students read a teacher-made chart (see the Appendix) that gives them important information on the topic that would otherwise be inaccessible because of language difficulties.
3. Have the students answer oral and written questions about the material presented.

Caveats and Options

1. Limited English proficient students who are in a mainstream classroom may not learn everything in the lesson plan. The important thing is to expose them to as much language at their level as possible and to give them the opportunity to at least master some of the main points.
2. This exercise is useful for a multilevel class similar to the mixed-ability groups found in adult education programs or in a school setting where ESL learners are combined with native speakers.

3. Nonliterate learners will need more oral support and will rely on pictures rather than just on the printed information.
4. When presenting vocabulary, use words like *shoes* rather than lower frequency terms such as *footwear,* and allow long pauses between utterances.
5. Be aware that language learners go through a silent period of internal processing before they begin production. New students who seem uninterested or unable to participate are probably in this silent phase and will begin to communicate orally when they feel competent.

References and Further Reading

Bernstein, V. (1990). *America's story book one.* Austin, TX: Steck-Vaughn.
King, M., Fagan, B., Bratt, T., & Baer, R. (1987). ESL and social studies instruction. In J. Crandall (Ed.), *ESL through content-area instruction* (pp. 89–120). Englewood Cliffs, NJ: Prentice-Hall Regents.

Appendix

Where?	Who started the colony?	When?	Why?
Providence, Rhode Island	Roger Williams	1636	freedom of religion
Maryland	Catholics	1634	freedom of religion
Pennsylvania	William Penn	1681	freedom of religion
Georgia	James Oglethorpe	1733	to help the poor

Questions
1. Who started the colony in Maryland?_____
2. When did Roger Williams start his colony? _____
3. Which colony was started to help the poor?_____
4. Which colony was the first? _____
[Add other questions as necessary.]

(adapted from Bernstein, 1990, p. 28)

Contributor

Douglas Magrath teaches ESL at Seminole Community College and Embry-Riddle Aeronautical University and trains teachers in Volusia County and Lake County, Florida, in the United States.

Test Cram Session

Levels
Intermediate +

Aims
Understand how to
prepare for a test
Anticipate possible test
questions
Write clear and concise
test answers

Class Time
2 hours

Preparation Time
20 minutes

Resources
Blackboard
Content course
textbook
Student notes from
content class lectures
Paper

This activity gives students an opportunity to process the information they need to remember for a test in several ways: brainstorming questions, writing answers, and discussing answers.

Procedure

1. Divide the students into small groups.
2. Assign each group a chapter or section of the textbook.
3. Ask the students to look at the textbook and their notes from class and brainstorm one possible test question for each student in their group. For example, a question for a sociology class might be *Explain the difference between a more and a folkway and give an example of each*.
4. Have the students write each question on a separate piece of paper.
5. Collect the questions from each group, and distribute each group's questions to another group.
6. Have the students go to the blackboard one at a time and write their question and the answer on the blackboard.
7. Ask other students if they believe the answer is complete, and make changes or additions as suggested by the students.
8. If the answer is too wordy or contains irrelevant information, model how you would edit the answer for clarity.
9. Erase each answer when it is completed, and go on to the next question.

Caveats and Options

1. Because this activity can be very time consuming, divide it among several class periods.
2. Have students who are not at the blackboard copy down each answer as it is written on the blackboard; the result will be a study guide for the test.
3. As a follow-up activity, have the students form pairs and use their prepared study guides to quiz each other orally.

Contributor

Erin Morgan is an MA student in the Department of TESL & Applied Linguistics at the University of California, Los Angeles (UCLA), and a teaching assistant in the ESL Service Courses at UCLA, in the United States.

Speaking Out About the Issue

Levels
Intermediate +

Aims
Discuss a controversial
social issue
Represent a particular
point of view

Class Time
30–45 minutes

Preparation Time
About 5 minutes

Resources
Role-play cards

This activity allows students to examine the causes and consequences of a controversial social issue (e.g., homelessness, child abuse, date rape) by participating in an interesting and enjoyable role play. Role plays help draw the students into heated debates and encourage them all to participate.

Procedure

1. Have the students pick a partner that they are comfortable with to facilitate better communication.
2. Give the students one card each that describes their role in the game (see the Appendix).
3. Have the students read their role card silently and think about their role.
4. Tell them that they have 10 minutes to rehearse the role play with their partners in order to get comfortable with their roles, that they may take notes if it will help them remember, and that they will all have to perform their role plays in front of the class.
5. Have the partners interview each other in order to understand and act out their situations.
6. After 10–15 minutes of discussion, have each pair present their situation to the class.

Caveats and Options

1. This activity assumes that the students have previously discussed the issue, its causes, and its effects.
2. This activity lends itself particularly well to adjunct classes. It served as a follow-up exercise to the reading of several articles on child abuse in an ESL/psychology adjunct class. The purpose was to facilitate a discussion on the articles and the students' knowledge of

the topic. At the end of the role plays, the students wrote a paper on child abuse and the possible remedies for it.

3. In subsequent lessons, include role plays on a variety of subjects.

4. As a wrap-up exercise, ask the students how they were disciplined, how they will discipline their own children, and what they think the government should do about this terrible problem.

5. Students may feel some emotional discomfort when dealing with controversial issues. Because students may have firsthand experience with a given issue, exercise extreme sensitivity, and do not force students to participate in the role play if they appear distraught.

Appendix

Role Play 1

> You are a TEACHER. You have seen bruises on Scott, a 7-year-old boy in your class. You are worried that he may be an abused child, but you need more information in order to file a report with the school. Today is your first parent/teacher conference with Scott's mother, Sue Jones. Try to find out as much information as you can to help Scott.

> Your name is Mrs. Jones. You are Scott's MOTHER, and today you are in a parent/teacher conference discussion about your son's education. You are married to Mr. Jones, Scott's stepfather. You have to work every day to support the family because your husband is unemployed; he also drinks a lot of alcohol. You have noticed bruises on Scott, but you try to tell yourself that these occur at school. You do not want to believe that your husband is hurting your son.

Role Play 2

> You are a DOCTOR. Today Kathy, a 1-year-old baby girl, was brought to the hospital with a badly broken arm. When you x-rayed the arm, you saw that it had been broken twice before in different places. The mother said that Kathy fell down, but you do not believe her. You need to ask questions to find out if this baby is being abused so that you can contact the police and help her if she is in danger.

> You are Mrs. Connor, Kathy's MOTHER. You are divorced and on welfare. You have three other children and no family to help you raise them. You have no friends because you move around so much, and you cannot find employment. Lately you have begun to try to forget your troubles by drinking too much wine.

Role Play 3

> You are a SOCIAL WORKER. Mr. O'Neill has been suspected of abusing his children, Helen and Matt. The neighbors have called Child Abuse Prevention Services, and you are the social worker that has been assigned to this case. You want to see if Matt and Helen should be removed from their home.

> You are Mr. O'Neill. You are a SINGLE FATHER who loves his children with all of his heart. Your wife left you, and you have a hard time keeping a job because you need to look after the children. You are a good father, but you often lose your temper and shout. You punish your children when they deserve it, but you love them very much. You just want to keep the family together.

Role Play 4

> You are the PARENT of a child who attends day care while you are at work. Carrie (your 4-year-old daughter) returned home yesterday with her back and legs covered with bruises. The woman who runs the day care center said that your child had fallen off the swing, but the bruises are everywhere, and Carrie seems quiet and afraid. When you bring her back to the day care center today, Carrie begins to cry hysterically. You wonder if she has been abused.

> You are Mrs. White, a DAY CARE WORKER. You work with screaming children all day long and you do not even like them. Your marriage is falling apart, and you have begun drinking heavily.

Contributor

Lindsay O'Shea recently received her BA in English from the University of California, Los Angeles, in the United States. She is interested in a career as an ESL/EFL teacher and is hoping to teach in Italy.

Quiz Your Way to the Top With *Jeopardy!*

Levels
Any

Aims
Identify information to
review at the end of a
course
Organize and classify
information into
manageable groups
Review and retain
information through
interactive play

Class Time
Variable

Preparation Time
None

Resources
Index cards, one color
per category
Chalkboard
Prizes
Felt pens

This interactive activity gives students control over their own assess-ment. Because they design and write the questions, they control the level of difficulty and the material being tested and decide what is important information. Because of the competitive nature of the game, students routinely compose questions that are more difficult and more detailed than any the teacher might come up with. In addition, students who are competitive and love to win stay focused longer during this game than during a standard test.

Procedure

1. Establish the categories of information to be tested and the levels of difficulty (see the Appendix for examples). A good number is five categories and three levels.
2. Write a few questions with the students in class to establish a norm for levels of difficulty.
3. Pass out the colored index cards to the students. For homework, ask each student to write one question for each category and each level on a separate card.
4. Have the students submit the cards. Check them for grammar, content, and level of difficulty.
5. Collect prizes for the winning team, such as pencils, stickers, candy, and old textbooks.
6. On the day of the test, arrange the cards on a table in front of the chalkboard. Write the categories on the chalkboard, and mark the number of points for each category and each level to mirror the cards on the table. This helps the students see how the cards are arranged.
7. Divide the class into teams.

8. Play *Jeopardy*:
   ● Have the first team request an item to answer, saying, "I'd like [category] for [number] points, please."
   ● Read the requested card for that level.
   ● Give the team a fixed amount of time to discuss and answer the question (1 minute seems to be enough time).
   ● If the team answers correctly, erase the points for that category/level on the chalkboard and have the same team choose another question. If the answer is wrong, give the next team the choice of answering the same question or choosing another one.
9. Give the winning team the prizes.

Appendix

A sample student-generated *Jeopardy* game for the course Baby Boom: Four Decades follows on the next page.

Contributor

Penny Partch is a full-time ESL Professor at Monterey Peninsula College, California, in the United States, where she uses games to stimulate interaction and interest for students of all levels.

	History	Lifestyle	Music	Fashion	TV	Movies
The 1950s for 100	Who organized the bus boycott in Montgomery, Alabama?	What underground structure were people building in their yards?	Name a song by Elvis Presley.	What piece of women's clothing was named for a dog?	What popular TV show was named after a cartoon character?	Who starred in the movie *Giant*?
The 1960s for 200	Between which country and the U.S. did the missile crisis take place?	Name the slogan that symbolized the generation gap.	Name the location of a famous 30-day music festival.	Name the color dye process for clothing popular at this time.	What singing group had its own TV show?	Which actress starred in *Gentlemen Prefer Blondes*?
The 1970s for 300	Name the president involved in the Watergate scandal.	What percentage of marriages ended in divorce?	Name the music style made famous by the Bee Gees.	Name the "look" of the 1970s.	Name the TV show whose main character was Archie Bunker.	Name the movie(s) about a boxer.
The 1980s for 400	What country hosted the 1988 Summer Olympics?	Define yuppies.	Name the type of dancing done on street corners across America.	Name the "look" worn by teens to shock their parents.	Name the TV show that featured middle-aged women.	Name the famous nostalgia movie about the 1980s.

Social and Economic Awareness

Levels
Intermediate; secondary school

Aims
Study and discuss social and economic issues
Connect a role to real life
Determine the most relevant information in a text
Elaborate on the given information

Class Time
1½ hours over two classes

Preparation Time
30 minutes

Resources
Role-play cards
Newspaper or magazine article
Handout
Blank paper

This activity aims to encourage critical thinking, discussion, and writing about current economic problems and the government's role in generating and solving them.

Procedure

Before Class

1. Prepare role-play cards for pair work (see Appendix A). The cards should provide guidelines for the questions that Student A is supposed to ask and for the answers that Student B may provide. Cast Student A as a reporter interviewing Student B about an ongoing problem affecting B's social/economic segment.
2. Locate a newspaper or magazine article (published in English) that carries information about the social/economic issue in the learners' country. Adapt it to the learners' level of proficiency (see Appendix B for a sample article adapted for secondary school–aged, intermediate EFL learners).
3. Prepare a table like the one in Appendix C. Aim to elicit relevant information that outlines the sequence of events and the causes and consequences of such events.

In Class

4. Set the context, pair the students up, and allow them to choose their roles (i.e., interviewer or interviewee). Distribute the role-play cards and monitor the students' performance of the role play.
5. Change the context slightly (e.g., by saying, "A few days later a local newspaper publishes an article about the issue you've just talked about."). Supply each pair with a copy of the adapted article and the

table. Have the students read the article and fill in the table to help them prepare for the following task. Check the students' work.

6. Ask the students to write a letter to the editor of the newspaper using the information they have written in the table and the ideas and structures listed in the handout.

7. Have the students read their letters to the group. Encourage a group discussion about what advice or alternatives could be offered to the people affected by the issue in question.

Caveats and Options

1. This activity also works with students at a higher level of proficiency; adapt the article and the ideas and structures handout to the level aimed at.

2. The reading activity and table completion in Step 5 have to be well exploited to serve as a preparation for the writing activity in Step 6.

3. Assign the writing activity as homework to save class time. Start the following class with Step 7.

4. For the writing activity, write relevant language items on the blackboard.

5. At the end of the activity, discuss with the students how to develop an awareness of learning strategies. For instance, the students may discuss the importance of completing tables as a way of attending to and listing the most relevant information in a text, which will serve as input for a writing activity.

References and Further Reading

Oller, J. W., Jr., & Richard-Amato, P. A. (1983). *Methods that work*. Rowley, MA: Newbury House.

Regan, M. B. (1995, May 15). Big sugar may be about to take its lumps. *Business Week*, 31.

Appendix A: Sample Role-Play Cards

Student A
You are a newspaper reporter. You live in a rural town where the major economic activity is agricultural farming. You have been asked to write an article about the inhabitants' lifestyle and how the young people feel about this. You are going to interview high school students.
• Approach a student who is leaving school.
• Explain the purpose of the interview.
• Ask the student questions about his or her parents' occupation.
• Ask about his or her parents' free time activities.
• Ask about his or her feelings toward this lifestyle.

Student B
Your parents are fruit farmers. One day when you are leaving school, a newspaper reporter approaches you and asks you to answer some questions related to your parents' occupation.
• Ask why the reporter is asking these questions.
• Express willingness to answer the questions.
• Tell the reporter how hard your parents work on the farm.
• Express your feelings about your parents' lifestyle.
• Justify your feelings.

Appendix B: Sample Adapted Article

How Can We Harvest the Fruits of Our Work?

That is what 120,000 fruit growers spread around the Central and Southeastern regions are asking Congress after 72% of the voting Representatives voted YES to kill a federal subsidy program that provides $1.4 billion to fruit growers. Fruit farmers know they've had a great deal for years. Although the government doesn't give them direct cash subsidies, it provides them with low-cost loans from the Federal Bank and guarantees a price that is much higher than that on the world market, besides restricting imports. Fruit farmers say that now they'll try to export most of their harvest, and the little that is left for domestic consumption will be sold at higher prices.

(adapted from Regan, 1995, p. 31)

Appendix C: Handout

1. Fill in the table below with a summary of the information in the article you have read.

Problem:
People that caused the problem:
People affected:
Situation before the problem arose:

2. On a separate piece of paper, write a letter to the editor. Use the information in the table above. You may use the following ideas and structures:

Ideas

- How fruit farmers may get subsidies for the next season
- Changes in the supply of fruit to the domestic market
- The price of such produce in the domestic market

Structures

- I'm afraid _____ may (not)/will (not) _____.
- What I believe may/will unfortunately happen is that _____.

Contributor

Maria Alice Capocchi Ribeiro, an EFL teacher for 19 years, is also a materials writer at Centro de Linguistica Aplicada, Yázigi International, São Paulo, Brazil.

Feeling Empathy

Aims
Apply key concepts and
critical thinking
strategies
Express opinions and
emotions
Assume new roles
Relate classroom studies
to new situations and
problems
Become involved in
issues presented in class
lectures and readings

Class Time
45 minutes

Preparation Time
15 minutes

Resources
Handout that contains
situations

This activity takes learners beyond identifying and recalling the key concepts in the content class. L2 learners more readily understand abstract concepts if they can experience the concepts in some fashion. Using the handout, the students can apply important content principles and concepts presented in a course to situations and problems that people face in real life.

Procedure

1. Identify key concepts from the content course that are controversial and thought provoking, such as the principles of sustainable development (an environmental protection issue) or the morality of using the atomic bomb (a historical issue).
2. Create a set of situations that (a) illustrate a key content principle studied in the course and (b) place the student in the role of an imaginary character in the situation.
3. Prepare a handout that contains a number of these situations (see the Appendix).
4. Distribute a copy of the handout to each student.
5. Assign one situation to each student to read.
6. Clarify language problems (e.g., vocabulary, grammar) and any difficulties related to the understanding of the situation itself.
7. Have the students read the situation and prepare a personal reaction to the problem, a solution to the problem, or both.
8. Direct each student to assume the persona of the character in the situation, act the part of the character, and give a verbal response, preferably in the first person.
9. Take the opposing view (or assign other students to do so) and engage in a dialogue with each student, acting as a devil's advocate. In

this dialogue, encourage the student to use emotions and act the way the character probably feels. Set a time limit for each presentation and dialogue.

Caveats and Options

1. Have the students prepare and videotape a role play in pairs or small groups based on the description in each situation.
2. As a follow-up activity, hold a general class discussion on the issues raised in the activity.
3. If you devise problem situations for lower level students, provide more direction.
4. Take into account the native culture and beliefs of the L2 learners when creating the situations. It is better to avoid controversy in certain circumstances.

References and Further Reading

Chamot, A. U., & O'Malley, J. M. (1994). *The CALLA handbook: Implementing the Cognitive Academic Language Learning Approach*. Reading, MA: Addison-Wesley.

Short, D. (1991). *How to integrate language and content: A training manual* (2nd ed.). Washington, DC: Center for Applied Linguistics.

Appendix

A handout from a course on political science and environmental issues follows.

Personal Reaction Situations

1. Imagine that you are a parent who is living in a city in a developing country. You barely have enough money to support your family. The government in your country decides that it will double the monthly cost of water and electricity charges. It says that this big increase in charges is necessary because the extra money will be used to reduce water pollution. How do you feel? Are you for or against this increase? Explain your reasons.
2. You are the captain of a ship sailing in the Sea of Japan. You have been ordered to dump dangerous radioactive wastes in open waters. There is no waste disposal site within your own country. Suddenly people on a Greenpeace ship try to convince you not to dump the containers

into the Sea of Japan. What will you decide to do? Explain your reasons.

3. You are the new minister of the economy in your country. Your country's economy depends on the economic activity of its trading companies around the world. One trading company asks you for permission to cut down large areas of timber in your country. There is not much natural forest remaining. What do you tell the trading company? Give reasons for your decision.

Contributor

Michael Sagliano is an English Lecturer teaching adjunct courses at Miyazaki International College in Japan.

The 5W-1H Scan

Levels
Beginning +

Aims
Learn about the reading process
Use a prereading strategy

Class Time
Variable

Preparation Time
Variable

Resources
Nonfiction text
Scrap paper
Egg timer with bell
Blackboard
Overhead projector (optional)

This activity shows students how to use a prereading strategy to increase their reading comprehension. Through this strategy, students become aware of the questions they should be asking themselves as they read. The egg timer is an effective motivational device and sets limits on students' reading time, encouraging them to read more fluently.

Procedure

1. Locate a newspaper article, magazine article, or other nonfiction text with details that lend themselves to literal questions. Distribute the text to the students.
2. Ask the students to list the six English question words—*who, what, where, when, why,* and *how*. Introduce these words as the 5W-1H Scan.
3. Have the students skim the headline of the article, any subheadings, and photograph captions. Tell them to turn their papers over or put their texts aside. Distribute scrap paper.
4. Ask the students to form pairs and write on the scrap paper as many *who, what, where, when, why,* and *how* questions about the article as they can within 10 minutes. Each question must be expressed as a complete sentence (e.g., *Who won the lottery?*).
5. Collect the scrap paper and jot down the questions on the blackboard, asking the students which ones are the same as others and should be eliminated.
6. Distinguish between questions at the literal level, such as *When was the lottery?*, and those which are more comprehensive, for example, *How did the lottery operate?*
7. Set the timer for a fixed amount of time, usually 1 minute per question, and ask the students to scan the text to answer the literal questions.

8. When the bell rings, have the students check their answers with each other.
9. Show the answers on an overhead projector or quickly write them on the blackboard (while the students are checking with one another).
10. Ask the students to copy the comprehensive questions from the blackboard into their notebooks and to answer them as homework. Take up these questions for discussion in the next class.

Caveats and Options

1. As a prereading strategy, the 5W-1H Scan is best used with nonfiction, especially newspaper and magazine articles.
2. In subsequent classes, have the students use the 5W-1H Scan as a guide to writing summaries of books, films, and other events.
3. As with all learning strategy training, students need to use the 5W-1H Scan frequently to become both proficient at and accustomed to using it. In subsequent lessons, have students continue to practice using the technique.
4. Encourage the students to depend on each other for the right answers in this activity; this is more communicative and efficient than a long explanation by the teacher. Display your answers as quickly as possible because the point of the activity is to develop questions and to read the text selectively to find answers.

References and Further Reading

Carrell, P., Pharis, B., & Liberto, J. (1989). Metacognitive strategy training for ESL reading. *TESOL Quarterly, 23*, 647–648.

Shih, M. (1992). Beyond comprehension exercises in the ESL academic reading class. *TESOL Quarterly, 26*, 289–318.

Contributor

Gregory Strong is a full-time Lecturer in the English and American Literature Department at Aoyama University, Tokyo, Japan. He has also worked in Canada and China, where he was involved in testing for a Canadian foreign aid project and in teacher training.

Whom Should You Believe?

Levels
Intermediate +

Aims
Identify an expert's area
of expertise and point
of view
Determine the
credentials of experts
quoted
Evaluate sources on a
particular issue

Class Time
1–2 hours

Preparation Time
1 hour

Resources
Text
Content-based handout
as an anticipation guide
to the text

An important aspect of working with sources is being able to assess the biases and credentials of the "experts" quoted. This lesson is meant to foster an awareness of credible and noncredible sources and the biases and points of view that various experts have on a particular topic.

Procedure

1. Locate a text (e.g., from a newspaper, magazine, or video documentary) that includes quotations by experts and that relates to class content (e.g., homelessness, deforestation, energy sources). Prepare a handout similar to the ones in Appendixes A and B.
2. Distribute the handout in class. Identify the titles of quoted experts in an introductory statement to the topic under discussion.
3. Preview vocabulary. Ask the students to consider a list of titles or credentials of people who all feel competent to speak on a particular subject.
4. Based on a set of topics, ask the students to decide who they feel is best qualified to address a particular topic and who would be most likely to address the topic from a particular point of view (e.g., financial, religious, political, legal).
5. Based on a set of statements made by the people listed, ask the students to match as many quotations as possible to the person or title they think is the source.
6. Provide the students with the text and ask them to indicate which of the experts quoted are the most well informed, unbiased, and credible. Ask them to be ready to defend or explain their choices to others in a small group.

Caveats and Options

1. Ask the students to predict the point of view of a particular person before interacting with the text and then to see if their prediction is substantiated.
2. Ask the students to identify each expert's stance on a particular issue (e.g., *Would you give a homeless person money?*) and to identify the conditions expressed (e.g., *No, but I would buy him or her a sandwich.*).
3. When using a video or audio text, have the students listen for "quotable" quotes, possibly in the form of a modified listening dictation exercise for focused listening practice. Integrate the quotations into an expansion writing activity in which the students identify the issue and the points of view of each expert, introducing the expert by title and credentials and including quotations.

Appendix A: Timber Issue

A tribal head man, a forestry department official, a Japanese timber importer, a biologist, a logger, and a furniture manufacturer all feel competent to speak on any of the topics listed below. Who is really the best qualified?

1. Check to see if you know these words. Write a question mark next to any you cannot guess the meaning of. Ask the teacher to explain if you need help.

Any you can't guess?	Some clues . . .
___ exported	*ex-* out of, *exit*
___ repercussions	*-port-* carry, *transport*
___ depletion	*re-* again, *review*
___ projections	*pro-* toward, for, *proposal*
___ extent	*de-* away from, *depart*
___ recuperate	

2. In the blank in front of each topic, write the letter of the specialist (expert) qualified to speak on the issues below. The first one has been done for you. You may decide that more than one answer is possible.

A. tribal head man

B. forestry department official

C. timber exporter

D. biologist

E. logger

F. furniture manufacturer

G. stock consultant

_D_ endangered animals living in rain forest regions

____ amount of timber exported each year and to whom

____ number of trees cut per hectare in tribal areas in Sabah each year

____ the current price of timber used to make rosewood furniture

____ the impact of logging on waterways and food sources for jungle creatures

____ the quickest way to clear a forested area

____ projections for timber income in Malaysia throughout the next 20 years

____ the extent of illegal logging in Sarawak

____ the rights of indigenous people in Malaysia

____ how a forest can most quickly and effectively be reclaimed after slash-and-burn logging

3. Match each quotation in the left-hand column below with its likely source by writing a letter choice from the list of specialists above in the blank before the quotation. (You may decide that more than one answer is possible.)

Quotation	Correct?		Unbiased?
	✓ = yes	Which paragraph?	✓ = yes; Ø = no
___ "It was like our life itself was being burnt out when the forest clearing got out of control. Wild animals appeared, rushing from the jungle into our village. It was like seeing our brothers being burned."			
___ "We only cut selected trees and leave the jungle undisturbed."			
___ "There is no real control over the logging companies."			
___ "Loggers are not the problem. They practice reforestation. The problem is population pressure."			
___ "The issue of deforestation is not economic; it's political."			
___ "Trees grow like weeds in the rain forest. They'll never die out."			
___ "Natural resource management is not well-recognized by government sectors."			
___ "The key to forest management is to get local people involved."			

4. Whom should you believe? Look at the quotations in Step 3 and refer to the article to determine each person's position or title. Write a check mark next to the quotations you matched correctly and write down the number of the paragraph in which you found the information. Next, write a check mark next to those sources that you believe are the most reliable, well informed, unbiased, and credible and a Ø next to those you think are not. Be ready to defend or explain your choices to others in your group.

Appendix B: Homelessness Issue

The following people have been asked to discuss problems in U.S. society. Some are answering from a religious point of view; others, from a legal, medical, or other point of view.

1. Guess the basis for the following people's point of view (some are easy!). Use this key to write your answers:

R = religious person   S = scholarly person
P = political person   M = medical person
L = legal person   ? = impossible to judge

Point of view	Title/Identity
	New York Times columnist
	staff attorney, New York Civil Liberties Union
	theologian (study/teach religion)
	journalist
	U.S. surgeon general
	psychiatrist
	minister of a church
	president, Planned Parenthood
	chairperson, Committee for a Free World
	president, University of Utah
	U.S. Supreme Court Justice
	senior resident scholar, Georgetown University

2. Compare your answers with your neighbor's. Discuss them and feel free to change your mind or to ask questions.
3. Listen to the program *Ethics in America*. For each person listed below, answer the question, *Would that person help a homeless person?* (Circle *yes* or *no*.) Why or why not? What conditions or explanations are given? (Make a list, take notes, or both.)

Name and title	Would help homeless?	Why or why not? List conditions.
Quindlen *N.Y. Times* columnist notes/quotations:	yes no	because _____ _____ _____ only if _____ _____ _____
Shriver theologian notes/quotations:	yes no	because _____ _____ _____ only if _____ _____ _____
Koop U.S. surgeon general notes/quotations:	yes no	because _____ _____ _____ only if _____ _____ _____
Decter Committee for a Free World notes/quotations:	yes no	because _____ _____ _____ only if _____ _____ _____

4. Working with a partner, go back to Step 1 and see if your answers were correct, based on what you heard. Is each expert arguing from the point of view you expected?

Contributor

Kim Hughes Wilhelm is Curriculum Coordinator for the Center for English as a Second Language and Assistant Professor in the Department of Linguistics, Southern Illinois University, Carbondale, in the United States.

"Wh" the Issue—Where Is It? What Is It?

Levels
Any

Aims
Understand an issue
Identify the main issue
of an argument
Use power positions
and predictions from a
title to read efficiently

Class Time
20–45 minutes

Preparation Time
1 hour

Resources
Colored highlighting
markers
Index cards
Handout
Articles related to an
issue

Critical reading and persuasive writing typically require skill in speedy, accurate identification of issue statements. This lesson helps students recognize what issue statements are and where they are likely to be located and encourages them to think critically in finding and articulating them.

Procedure

1. The day before the activity, make sure each student has a highlighter. Present the definition of *issue* (e.g., an undecided question with at least two sides).
2. The next day, practice identifying issue statements from a set provided (see the Appendix).
3. Provide each student with an index card and a copy of a content-based (maximum two-page) article that expresses a point of view or describes an issue related to the content being studied in the class.
4. Solicit a few predictions from the title as to the main topic.
5. Remind the students that the *power positions*, the beginning and the end of most U.S. writing, are used to orient and "grab" the reader (beginning) and to reinforce the main message or purpose (end).
6. Ask the students to use the index card to move steadily through (speed read) the first paragraph and the last paragraph of the article. Model by reading the independent clauses aloud to locate key ideas.
7. Ask the students to highlight the *one* sentence that they think best describes the issue. Circulate and help the students as needed.
8. Debrief and discuss alternate answers. Decide on the best issue statement and explain why it is the best.
9. Practice again with at least one more article. Identify those students who are having trouble and those who have mastered the task.

10. Ask the students who have mastered the task to work in pairs with a new, shared article, to agree on and highlight the issue statement, and to compare their answer with that of other pairs. Next, have the students decide which issue of those in the three articles is the most interesting and label statements that identify the sides of the issue (use *1* and *2* or + and – to indicate arguments for and against). Ask the students to share their opinion on the issue with their partner and then report back to you whether they agree or disagree.

11. Meanwhile, with those needing extra work in issue identification, practice identifying issue statements as in Step 2 or in a third, easier article with a very clear issue statement. After the group successfully identifies the issue statement, lead the group through the identification of the sides and ask the students in turn to express their opinions. For homework, ask the students to highlight the issue statement and label the statements of each side in the article used in Step 10.

Caveats and Options

1. Include differentiation among issue, topic, and thesis statements in the handout and Step 2.

2. Do similar practice in issue identification with listening-based materials (see References and Further Reading for several sources). Prepare the students for the listening task by discussing the title and linking the content to that being covered in class. Ask the students only to listen the first time they hear the text. Have them listen again and nod at you or raise a finger when they hear the issue statement.

References and Further Reading

Light, R. L., & Lan-Ying, F. (1989). *Contemporary world issues: An interactive approach to reading and writing*. Boston: Heinle & Heinle.

Numrich, C. (1990). *Face the issues: Intermediate listening and critical thinking skills* [Audiotapes and text]. White Plains, NY: Longman.

Numrich, C. (1994). *Raise the issues: An integrated skills approach to critical thinking* [Audiotapes and text]. White Plains, NY: Longman.

Numrich, C. (1995). *Consider the issues: Advanced listening and critical thinking skills* [Audiotapes and text]. White Plains, NY: Longman.

Schinke-Llano, L. (1994). *Time: Reaching for tomorrow* [Audiotapes and text]. Lincolnwood, IL: National Textbook.

Appendix: Issue Identification Practice

Tiersky, E., & Chernoff, M. (1994). *In the news: Mastering reading and language skills with the newspaper* [Audiotapes and text]. Lincolnwood, IL: National Textbook.

Directions: Below are sentences written by Malaysian ESL students as issue statements for a persuasive paper. Read each sentence and decide whether it describes an issue. Label each issue statement with an *I*. Be ready to discuss what you think the "sides" would be for each issue identified. The first one has been done as an example.

<u> I </u> 1. Tax on foreign cars in Malaysia should be abolished.

_____ 2. Drunk drivers should be more severely punished than they are now.

_____ 3. There is a dark side to sports.

_____ 4. The Malaysian government shouldn't use the orangutan as a mascot for Visit Malaysia Year.

_____ 5. Which is better: working in the private sector or for the government?

_____ 6. Money is an incentive for athletes.

_____ 7. Should tourists have to get an AIDS test?

_____ 8. Parents are to blame for their runaway teenagers.

_____ 9. Students should be allowed to make their own rules in college.

_____ 10. Are schools and society biased in thinking that females have lower math ability than males?

_____ 11. Parenting skills are self-taught.

Optional: List the numbers of those statements that, in your opinion, are too broad or that need further definition.

Contributor

Kim Hughes Wilhelm is Curriculum Coordinator for the Center for English as a Second Language and Assistant Professor, Department of Linguistics, Southern Illinois University, Carbondale, in the United States.

Earth Summit: Think Globally, Act Locally

Levels
High intermediate +

Aims
Practice taking notes
Practice library research
skills
Scan reference sources
for specific information
Use oral/aural language
in an authentic
academic setting
Write in detail on
specific issues
Practice vocabulary
specific to social studies
and environmental
education

Class Time
Several class periods

Preparation Time
Variable

Resources
Reference materials on
environmental issues

This simulation allows students to combine the practice of an academic activity, research, with the real-life skills of debate, cooperation, and collaboration. Students who otherwise might find research projects boring are stimulated by the fact that they are investigating real issues within the context in which they exist, the school or university environment. The knowledge that they are debating feasible solutions that could actually be implemented is the motivating force behind this activity.

Procedure

1. Have the students think of a specific environmental issue that could be, but is not currently, addressed in their school or university. Examples are recycling, water conservation, and use of chemicals in the school environment.
2. Have the students in groups brainstorm what they already know about the issue. Have them determine what information they need to gather in order find a viable solution to the problem and write out specific questions to research.
3. Assign each student a role within the school or university setting, including, for example, administrator, teacher or professor, student, parent, janitor, secretary, school board member, and supplier.
4. Have the students use library resources to find the answers to the questions they have posed. Have them research their role by interviewing people in that role at their institution.
5. Have the students use the information they have obtained to write a resolution proposing a solution to the problem (see References and Further Reading and the Appendix). They must accurately represent the point of view of their "character" when preparing the resolution.
6. Allow the students to share their resolutions with each other in informal debate. Encourage them to collaborate on a resolution that

they agree with or to modify their own resolutions. Two or more students may decide to submit one resolution together if they agree with the solution it presents. Ask the students to make any revisions at this stage.

7. Collect the final drafts of the resolutions. Distribute copies of each resolution to each student.

8. Hold an earth summit simulation. Ask the students to form a semicircle and label their desks with their "characters." Act as chairperson, and sit facing the semicircle. Determine the amount of time that each resolution will be debated.

9. Have the students debate one resolution at a time, following formal debating guidelines as much as possible. Allow amendments to resolutions as a result of the debate as long as a majority agrees.

10. Close the summit by having the students vote on the resolutions. Present the resolution that receives the most votes to the school's student government or administration in a class letter.

Caveats and Options

1. Depending on their level and previous experience with research, students may need direct instruction on note-taking and using library resources.

2. Ask your local Model United Nations Club (if there is one) for samples of UN resolutions.

3. If necessary, remind the students that they must stay in character throughout all stages of the debate.

4. If possible, videotape the debate to use later for assessment. (It is difficult to assess the students accurately on their speaking or debating skills while acting as chairperson.)

5. If the class is large, have the students research and debate two or more issues.

References and Further Reading

Guide to delegate preparation. (1993). New York: United Nations Association of the United States of America. (updated every year)

Appendix: Format for a Local Earth Summit Resolution

1. Submission line: states which people or groups are submitting the resolution
2. Issue line: states the issue the resolution addresses
3. Preambulatory clauses: submitters state their opinion of the situation
4. Operative clauses: submitters state specific suggestions for dealing with the situation
5. Amendments: may be submitted by anybody debating the resolution during debate time; must be voted on before being added to the resolution

Sample resolution:

> *Submitted by:*
> Teachers' Union, Student Council, and Maintenance Personnel
>
> *Issue:*
> Recycling paper and waste
>
> *Convinced* that the unnecessary waste of paper and plastic on campus must stop immediately,
> *Considering* the limited room for waste disposal in our community,
> *Believing* that these problems can be solved without much additional cost or effort by the school community,
>
> 1. *Urges* all departments to develop a plan for collecting used paper and plastic.
> 2. *Recommends* that labeled recycling bins be placed around campus.
> 3. *Strongly recommends* that food services restrict themselves to purchasing items only in recyclable packaging.
> 4. *Suggests* that these actions be taken no later than 1 month from the date of the adoption of this resolution.

Contributor

Deborah Wilson-Allam is ESL Coordinator at the American International School in Egypt. She is working on an ESL textbook focusing on global issues.

Know Thyself!

Levels
Intermediate +

Aims
Build awareness of
issues in successful
language learning and
second language
acquisition
Develop language
learning strategy goals
Activate and build
schema for reading
comprehension

Class Time
Two 50-minute class
periods

Preparation Time
30 minutes

Resources
Language learning
questionnaire
10 Commandments for
Good Language Learning
handout
Prereading writing
handout
"Successful Language
Learners" reading
Reader response
composition handout

This reading-based composition activity provides a model for the first module in a thematic unit on L2 learning issues. The unit builds metacognitive awareness through a prereading questionnaire and discussion, a prereading writing activity, a reading activity, and a postreading activity that culminates in a composition assignment.

Procedure

1. Distribute the language learning questionnaire (see Appendix A) and ask the students to complete it in pairs by interviewing each other.
2. Discuss and explain each of the 10 Commandments for Good Language Learning (see Appendix B).
3. Divide the class into groups. Assign each group one of the commandments to discuss, and tell the groups to decide what they think the rationale is behind it.
4. Have one member from each group present the group's rationale to the class.
5. Have the class adopt the commandments as their class rules.
6. Distribute the prereading journal entry assignment (see Appendix C), giving the students approximately 10 minutes to complete it.
7. Distribute the reading "Successful Language Learners: What Do We Know About Them?" (Omaggio, 1978; see Appendix D).
8. Have the students look back over their language learning questionnaires with instructions to choose as their language learning goal one item that they had a poor response to.
9. Have the students discuss their choice with their groups before writing an entry in their journal stating which item they chose and why they chose it.
10. Distribute the reader response composition assignment (see Appendix E).

Caveats and Options

This activity could be used in a thematically arranged reading-based ESL composition course or in an ESL/psychology adjunct course.

References and Further Reading

Brown, H. D. (1994). *Principles of language learning and teaching*. Englewood Cliffs, NJ: Prentice-Hall Regents.

Omaggio, A. (1978). Successful language learners: What do we know about them? *ERIC/CLL News Bulletin, 4*(2).

Appendix A: Language Learning Questionnaire

Fill in one circle for each item that best describes you. Circles A and E indicate that the sentence is very much like you. Circles B and D indicate that the sentence is somewhat descriptive of you. Circle C indicates that you have no inclination one way or the other.

	A B C D E	
I don't mind if people laugh at me when I speak.	○ ○ ○ ○ ○	I get embarrassed if people laugh at me when I speak.
I like to try out new words and structures that I'm not completely sure of.	○ ○ ○ ○ ○	I like to use only language that I am certain is correct.
I feel very confident in my ability to succeed in this language.	○ ○ ○ ○ ○	I feel quite uncertain about my ability to succeed in learning this language.
I want to learn this language because of what I can personally gain from it.	○ ○ ○ ○ ○	I am learning this language only because someone else is requiring it.
I really enjoy working with other people in groups.	○ ○ ○ ○ ○	I would much rather work alone than with other people.

	A B C D E	
I like to "absorb" language and get the general gist of what is said or written.	○ ○ ○ ○ ○	I like to analyze the many details of language and understand exactly what is said or written.
If there is an abundance of language to master, I just try to take things one step at a time.	○ ○ ○ ○ ○	I am very annoyed by an abundance of language material presented all at once.
I am not overly conscious of myself when I speak.	○ ○ ○ ○ ○	I monitor myself very closely and consciously when I speak.
When I make mistakes, I try to use them to learn something about the language.	○ ○ ○ ○ ○	When I make mistakes, it annoys me because that's a symbol of how poor my performance is.
I find ways to continue learning the language outside of the classroom.	○ ○ ○ ○ ○	I look to the teacher and the classroom activities for everything I need to be successful.

(Adapted from Brown, 1994, p. 129)

Appendix B: 10 Commandments for Good Language Learning

1. Fear not!
   Don't be afraid to make mistakes. Share your fears and laugh with your classmates.
2. Dive in!
   Take risks. Make an effort. Try. Just do it!
3. Believe in yourself.
   Develop self-confidence. Focus on your progress and successes.
4. Seize the day!
   Motivate yourself. Remind yourself of the rewards of learning English.

5. Love thy neighbor.
    Cooperate with your classmates. Think of your class as a team working together toward a common goal.
6. Get the BIG picture.
    Don't worry about details. Read quickly—skim. Do rapid "free writes."
7. Cope with the chaos.
    Ask questions when you don't understand.
8. Go with your hunches.
    Guess! Make predictions! Use your intuition!
9. Make mistakes work FOR you.
    Make a list of your common errors and work on them on your own. Be aware of your own problems and needs.
10. Set your own goals.
    Go beyond the classroom goals. Set and work toward your own personal goals independently. Take responsibility for your own learning.

(Adapted from Brown, 1994)

Appendix C: Prereading Journal Entry

1. What strategies helped you learn English? Which were useful and which were not?
2. What personality characteristics helped you learn English? Which personality characteristics may have interfered with your language learning goals?

Appendix D: Reading Passage

Successful Language Learners: What Do We Know About Them?

Only a cynic would argue with the statement that most people learn their native language with a fair degree of success. Although some people seem to have more verbal skills than others, almost everyone can acquire his or her first language easily and well. Why is it, then, that the success record for acquiring skill in a second or foreign language in a formal classroom setting is so poor for so many students? What makes some foreign language learners succeed—often in spite of the teacher, the textbook, or the classroom situation—while others fail to acquire basic skills, even in the best learning situation?

Several researchers have been interested in these questions in recent years and have designed studies that attempt to discover what makes the "good" language learner good. They argue that if we know more about what successful learners did, we might be able to teach these strategies to poorer learners and thereby increase their chances of success. The studies have typically focused on three aspects of the problem:

1. What personality characteristics and learning styles are most frequently associated with good language learners?
2. What specific strategies and techniques do good language learners tend to use when approaching various language learning tasks?
3. Can these techniques be taught to students? If so, what kinds of language learning activities do they suggest for the classroom?

Personality Characteristics and Learning Style

Many researchers have attempted to determine which personality characteristics and learning styles are associated with successful language learners. Their findings, though limited and preliminary, provide some tentative conclusions, which are listed below:

1. *Selectivity:* Good language learners can select important linguistic points to attend to and ignore unimportant or inappropriate ones.
2. *Tolerance of Ambiguity:* Researchers characterize the successful language learner as one who can tolerate a certain amount of uncertainty while completing second language tasks. That is, they are able to cope with new, complex, and difficult to solve tasks. In contrast, more intolerant learners may react to ambiguity in the language learning situation with dislike, depression, or avoidance behaviors.
3. *Moderation:* Studies suggest that the good language learner does not overgeneralize or take a narrow-minded approach to language, but rather adopts a "middle-of-the-road" position in analyzing and categorizing linguistic data. When errors do occur, successful learners tend to overgeneralize from within the language rather than transferring rules or structures from their native language.
4. *Extroversion:* Several researchers have found a significant relationship between oral fluency and extroversion. Characteristics associated

with extroversion include assertiveness, emotional stability, and a willingness to take risks.

Strategies and Techniques

The following language learning strategies have been identified from interviews, observations, research, and insights from experienced language learners and teachers. These learning strategies are frequently associated with successful language learning.

1. *Successful language learners have insight into their own language learning styles and preferences.* They adopt a personal style or positive learning strategy that fits their needs and preferences. They can adapt to various teaching methods and materials and know how to analyze and understand the linguistic information they confront. Poor learners, by contrast, lack insight into their own learning difficulties and the nature of language learning tasks. They are often frustrated by methods that are not appropriate for them. They cannot organize linguistic information into a coherent system; instead, they regard the incoming data as an untidy assortment of separate items.

2. *Successful learners take an active approach to the learning task.* They make learning goals for themselves and make an effort to use the language. They will seek out opportunities to communicate in the second language with native speakers and to understand the communication. They are sensitive to the culture of the second language. Poor learners, on the other hand, often rely too much on the teacher and have a passive attitude toward learning.

3. *Good language learners are willing to take risks.* They are willing to appear foolish sometimes in order to communicate and try to communicate their message in any way they can. This may involve the creative use of gestures or linguistic invention.

4. *Good language learners are good guessers.* They use clues and make inferences. For example, successful reading comprehension strategies that involve guessing include using the context and grammatical information to determine the meaning of unknown words.

5. *Good language learners attend to form as well as meaning.* They use grammar, spelling, punctuation, and pronunciation patterns and

rules to understand meaning. They monitor their own language and seek correction from others.

6. *Successful learners actively attempt to develop the second language into a separate reference system.* That is, they try to think in the second language without translation as soon as possible. They correct mistakes and learn from them.

7. *Good language learners generally have a tolerant and outgoing approach to the second language, its speakers, and their culture.* They are able to understand the cultural point of view of native speakers and may accept some of their values.

(adapted from Omaggio, 1978)

Appendix E: Reader Response Composition Assignment

Write a letter in which you give advice to a newcomer on language learning strategies. Draw on your reading and your own experiences.

Contributor

Christine Wu is a graduate assistant and student in the MATESOL program at California State University, Sacramento, in the United States. She coordinates the reading and vocabulary development and oral skills tutorials and is an instructor in the ESL computer writing lab.

Write Your Congressman!

Levels
High intermediate +

Aims
Develop inferencing
skills
Build critical reading
and thinking skills
Become active and
involved in relevant
political issues
Learn formal letter
writing

Class Time
Two 50-minute classes

Preparation Time
45 minutes

Resources
Copies of articles from
several newspapers on a
relevant political issue
Copies of letters to the
editor from one or more
newspapers on that
issue
Copies of editorials
from one or more
newspapers on that
issue

This reading-based composition lesson is part of a thematic unit on political issues that concern ESL students, such as immigration and affirmative action. Each lesson in the thematic unit should be based on a different issue.

Procedure

1. Distribute copies of newspaper articles on a political issue that concerns ESL students from two or three different publications (e.g., *The New York Times, USA Today, The Christian Science Monitor,* a local newspaper, an alternative newspaper).

2. Have the students read the articles.

3. Seat the students in small groups of three to five students each and have them compare different perspectives on the issue by listing similarities and differences from the articles.

4. Have the groups discuss the issue and write a reader response journal entry on their opinion.

5. Distribute copies of letters to the editor dealing with the issue. Have the students read the letters and write a response letter in their journals.

6. Have the students compose a letter to a political leader involved in the issue, such as the president of the United States, a member of the U.S. Congress, the governor of the state, or a state senator or representative.

7. Mail the letters and wait for a response.

Caveats and Options

1. This activity lends itself well to thematically arranged reading-based composition instruction, as well as an ESL/ethnic studies or an ESL/government adjunct class.
2. Culturally heterogeneous classes may want to have a formal debate on the issue prior to writing the letters to get exposure to different perspectives and to clarify the issue.
3. In subsequent lessons, show the students a relevant segment of a television news magazine (e.g., *Nightline*), the local news, or CNN.
4. In classes that utilize a computer writing lab, have the students e-mail the letters to the president of the United States.

Contributor

Christine Wu is a graduate assistant and student in the MATESOL program at California State University, Sacramento, in the United States. She coordinates the reading and vocabulary development and oral skills tutorials and is an instructor in the ESL computer writing lab.

Part III: Hands-On Activities

Wilailuck (Lucky) Uthensut at Northern Virginia Community College, Alexandria, Virginia USA.

Poster Sessions by Experts

Levels
Any

Aims
Synthesize information
from content sources
Reinforce content
visually
Integrate skills
Interact with academic
community
Work independently

Class Time
3 hours

Preparation Time
Variable

Resources
Content resources
relevant to thematic unit
Large index cards
Poster board
Markers
Tape

This hands-on project allows students to become experts in a content area by stimulating interest, providing for in-class and out-of-class research and planning, and creating an alternative method for oral and written presentation. The poster session serves as the culminating activity for a thematic unit.

Procedure

1. Introduce the activity by outlining the poster session criteria (see Appendix A) and general procedures.
2. Have the students look through content resources relevant to the thematic unit (e.g., books, magazines, pamphlets, videos) to identify an area of interest and a topic. Pair students with similar interests.
3. Give the students opportunities to build expertise. Encourage the students to gather additional resources relevant to their topic via library searches, interviews, and letters of inquiry.
4. Ask the students to use the Poster Session Planning Guide (see Appendix B) to prepare for a student-teacher conference.
5. Hold student-teacher conferences to discuss topics and narrow down the focus of the poster session, using the Guide as a point of departure.
6. Prepare the students to present their posters and view their class-mates' posters by creating an information gap:
   ● First, assist the presenters: Give each pair of students a large index card and piece of tape. Have them write their names and the title of their poster session at the top of the index card. Then ask the students to tape their card to their desks. Next, tell the students to circulate individually from card to card, read the topic written on the card, and write one question they hope will be answered

during the poster session. At the end of this activity, each index card should contain one question from each classmate. Finally, return the index cards to each pair of presenters, who will use the questions while preparing for the poster session.

- Then assist the viewers: Hand out a complete list of poster session topics on a grid with three columns labeled *What you already know, What you want to know,* and *What you have learned from the poster session* (see Appendix C). Have the students fill in the first two columns before doing Step 7.

7. On the day of the poster sessions, allow one student from each pair to circulate during the first half of the viewing period. Allow the other student from each pair to circulate during the second half of the viewing period. Have the students fill in the third column on their grids while circulating.

8. Evaluate the poster sessions according to the criteria outlined in Step 1.

Caveats and Options

1. Arrange for students who prepare poster sessions with potential overlap to discuss approaches for presenting similar information.
2. Have the students display the index cards during the poster session as a guide for asking questions.
3. Invite—and have students invite—other students, parents, school administrators, and staff to view the poster sessions.
4. Have the students prepare a research paper or other writing assignment in conjunction with their poster session.

Appendix A: Poster Session Criteria

The goal of the poster session is to:

1. Present information
   - with a title
   - with key information presented clearly and concisely
   - with the use of visuals, recordings, and other materials that reinforce key information

2. Introduce classmates to relevant content
   - that highlights at least three aspects of the topic
   - that identifies a controversy or issue
   - that can be synthesized into a cohesive whole
3. Help classmates understand content
   - by answering questions thoroughly or suggesting references in which classmates can find answers
   - by demonstrating overall effort and an understanding of the topic
   - by answering questions with enthusiasm

Appendix B: Poster Session Planning Guide

1. Make a list of the different issues and controversies that people have researched on your topic.
2. List the title of your poster session. Consider the message or main idea you want to communicate to visitors.
3. List the key information to be presented in your poster session.
4. List any visuals, recordings, or other materials you will use for the poster session. Make a sketch of your poster session.
5. Make a list of materials and equipment you will need (e.g., markers, tape, videocassette recorder).
6. Predict and write three to five questions that visitors may ask about the information in your poster session. How will you answer these questions?

Appendix C: Poster Session Viewing Guide

Poster session topic	What you already know	What you want to know	What you have learned from the poster session

Contributors

Mona Esposito is a graduate of the MA-TESL program at Northern Arizona University (NAU), Flagstaff, in the United States. Her interests include curriculum design and materials development. Kaye Marshall, a graduate of the MA-TESL program at NAU, has had ESL and EFL teaching experience in English for academic purposes, adult literacy, and refugee programs. Fredricka L. Stoller is Associate Professor in the TESL and Applied Linguistics programs and Director of the Program in Intensive English at NAU.

Cross-Cultural Mathematical Consciousness-Raising

Levels
Intermediate +

Aims
Learn differences in mathematical procedures and terms in various languages

Class Time
2–3 hours

Preparation Time
30 minutes

Resources
Handout
Blank paper
Chart with problems, language groups represented in the class, and space for solutions
Markers
Notebooks
Audio recorders
Audiotapes

This activity was designed after a classroom research project revealed that cultural differences existed in solving mathematics word problems. Bilingual students tended to become confused and frustrated when teachers assumed that they had failed to learn the mathematical concepts when in fact the students and teachers were not conscious that two systems were at work. The activity is designed to aid bilingual students in recognizing and being able to apply culturally appropriate procedures in the correct context.

Procedure

1. Put on a handout three math word problems that require different procedures to which the students have been exposed.
2. Divide the students into groups by L1.
3. Instruct the students to solve the word problems in as many different ways as they can.
4. Have each group of students record on audiotape their discussion in English about their answers to the problems and the steps they took to arrive at the answers. Save these recordings for later use as a listening/transcribing exercise.
5. Direct each group to choose a recorder who will report to the class on the steps the group took to solve the problems.
6. Ask the student recorders to report their group's procedures to the class.
7. Record on a large chart (see the Appendix) the various solutions and procedures by L1 group and the English procedure for solving the problem as recommended by the math text, the answer key, or another resource that accompanied the original problems.

8. Ask the students to look for any differences in the answers to the problems.
9. Discuss any trends (by the L1 group) that surface from the chart display. Avoid endorsing one way as superior to the others.
10. Encourage the students to give their ideas about why differences in steps, procedures, or answers may exist.
11. Have the students record their ideas in a math journal.
12. Point out any differences between the students' way of solving the problems and the school's or program's criteria for solving them. Draw an analogy between culturally appropriate forms of greeting in several languages and differences in math reasoning and procedures.
13. Encourage the students to recognize and use the culturally appropriate math definitions and procedures in the corresponding math contexts.
14. Have the students write in their math journals what they learned from this experience, what they still want to know, and whether they thought the experience was useful for them.

Caveats and Options

1. Use this activity as an in-service training activity to expose teachers to the idea that math is not as international a language as is sometimes assumed.
2. Use the recorded tapes to expand the lesson: (a) Have the groups exchange tapes, or (b) have the students transcribe selected parts of the tapes and use the data to write a report about the findings of this experiment in cross-cultural mathematics.

References and Further Reading

Cocking, R. R., & Mestre, J. P. (Eds.). (1988). *Linguistic and cultural influences on learning mathematics*. Hillsdale, NJ: Erlbaum.

Dale, T. C., & Cuevas, G. J. (1992). Integrating mathematics and language learning. In P. Richard-Amato & M. A. Snow (Eds.), *The multicultural classroom: Readings for content-area teachers* (pp. 330–348). White Plains, NY: Longman.

Freeman, R. (1995, November). *Beyond the key-word approach*. Paper presented at the WAESOL Conference, Bellevue, WA.

Appendix:
Sample Chart

Math problem	First language				
	Japanese	Chinese	Spanish	Korean	English
1					
2					
3					

Contributor

Randi Freeman won the 1995 TESOL/Regents Prentice-Hall/Larry Anger Fellowship for Graduate Studies for her research on math word-problem solving in the ESOL context. She teaches at Central Washington State University, in the United States.

Getting Into the Content

Levels
Intermediate +

Aims
Make a personal
connection to a topic
Participate in
discussions

Class Time
25–30 minutes

Preparation Time
45 minutes

Resources
Index cards
Discussion wheel for
each group
Handout
One wristwatch per
group

This discussion activity elicits attitudes, reactions, and background knowledge regarding a particular subject before introducing the unit's theme. Each group member has a specific role for each round. Because the roles are rotated, each student has the opportunity to take on multiple roles during the discussion.

Procedure

1. Create four to six questions that will bring out students' personal connections to the topic to be presented and any knowledge they may have of it (see Appendix A). Make up one packet of questions per group.
2. Create a handout with an explanation of the roles and some useful phrases designed to aid the discussion (see Appendix B). The phrases will vary according to the proficiency of the students. For example, you may wish to target particular grammatical structures or focus on certain turn-taking strategies.
3. Make one copy of the discussion wheel (see Appendix C) per group.
4. Seat the students in groups of three or four, preferably at tables.
5. Distribute one handout to each student and go over the roles:
   - The leader, who manages the discussion
   - The notetaker, who keeps track of what is said
   - The timekeeper, who monitors the time and the amount of participation by each member

   Discuss the phrases at the bottom of the handout.
6. Distribute one discussion wheel and one packet of questions to each group. Make sure each group has a wristwatch. Ask the students not to write on either the question cards or the discussion wheels.

7. Explain how the wheel works:
   - The wheel is placed in the center of each group of three or four students (a group of three will have only one note-taker per round; a group of four will have two). For the first round, each member takes on the role on the wheel that is pointing toward him or her.
   - The designated discussion leader for that round picks up the top card only and reads it aloud to the group, which discusses the question on the card. Only one card at a time should be revealed.
   - At the end of 3 minutes, the timekeeper signals that the round is over and rotates the wheel clockwise one space. The new discussion leader draws the next card from the pile, and the discussion continues until all questions have been answered.

8. During the discussion, monitor each group and make notes of speaking errors that you wish to comment on later.

9. Ask the groups to report a summary of their responses to the class. Record the main points on the blackboard. Highlight the points that seem most essential in previewing and understanding the new content.

10. Provide feedback on the speaking errors that you noted in Step 8 orally with written support on the blackboard. Focus on patterns of errors and on those related to teaching points that have already been covered in class.

11. Collect the question packets and discussion wheels for future use.

Caveats and Options

1. This activity works equally well as a prelistening exercise (e.g., to introduce a university lecture on the history of the American family) and as a prereading one (e.g., to introduce the novel *The Joy Luck Club*, Tan, 1990).

2. If duplicating handouts is difficult, write the explanation of roles and useful phrases on the blackboard or on butcher paper for the whole class to view.

References and Further Reading

Brown, G. & Yule, G. (1989). *Teaching the spoken language.* Cambridge: Cambridge University Press.

Klippel, F. (1984). *Keep talking: Communicative fluency activities for language teaching.* Cambridge: Cambridge University Press.

Tan, A. (1990). *The joy luck club.* New York: Putnam.

Ur, P. (1981). *Discussions that work: Task-centred fluency practice.* Cambridge: Cambridge University Press.

Appendix A: Sample Discussion Questions

History of the American Family Pre-Unit Discussion Questions

DISCUSSION QUESTION 1
Describe the ideal family. How many members are there? Who are they? What sorts of things do they do together?

DISCUSSION QUESTION 2
What is the ideal role for the husband/father in the family? Is this view changing in your culture? If so, how?

DISCUSSION QUESTION 3
What is the ideal role for the wife/mother in the family? Is this view changing in your culture? If so, how?

DISCUSSION QUESTION 4
What are the ideal roles for sons and daughters in the family? Is this view changing in your culture? If so, how?

DISCUSSION QUESTION 5
How has family life changed from your grandparents' time, to your parents' time, to yours?

Appendix B: Sample Discussion Handout

History of the American Family Pre-Unit Discussion

A. Explanation of Roles Within Each Small Group

Discussion leader	Note taker	Timekeeper
1. Take the top card only and read the question aloud to the group. Make sure everyone understands the topic. 2. *Then either* ● Answer the question yourself (in a timely fashion), ● Ask one of your group members to answer, or ● Encourage someone to volunteer. 3. Make sure all group members participate more or less equally. 4. Keep the discussion on topic and encourage specific examples. 5. If necessary, thank "big talkers" for their contribution and encourage "shy talkers" to add something from their culture.	1. Find out what countries your group members are from. 2. Keep a record of the discussion by taking notes on important points. Make sure you know which viewpoint belongs to which culture.	1. Keep track of the time for each discussion question. Allow a maximum of 3 minutes per question. 2. Make a note of each member's participation. Did everyone participate relatively equally? 3. At the end of the 3-minute round, rotate the discussion wheel one space clockwise so that each member takes on a new role.

B. For All Discussion Participants

1. Listen carefully to others. (How can you show that you are listening carefully?)
2. Ask the leader to reread the question if you do not understand it. (If no one understands, ask the teacher!)

Useful Phrases

What about your culture or family?

What is your opinion?

Could you give us an example of that?

I'm not sure I understood you.

Could you repeat that?

Are you saying that _____?

Do you mean that _____?

That's really interesting.

Oh, it's quite different in my country.

Actually, the role of fathers in my culture is quite similar to their role in yours, [name of group member].

I have an example that will illustrate my point.

In my culture/country, it is typical for parents to

_____.

Appendix C: Discussion Wheel

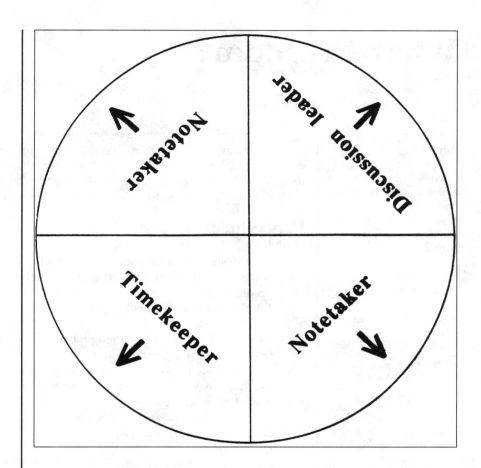

Contributor

Janet Goodwin is a Lecturer in the ESL Service Courses at the University of California, Los Angeles, in the United States, where she specializes in oral skills and content-based instruction.

What Problem?

Level
Any

Aims
Become aware of litter
and garbage
Propose solutions to the
problem of excess
garbage

Class Time
Two class sessions

Preparation Time
Minimal

Resources
Paper or worksheet

Before people can be moved to help solve a problem, they must first be aware that the problem exists. The following activity, designed for a content-based environmental English course, sharpens students' critical thinking skills by requiring them to consider the complex nature of environmental problems, for which there are no easy solutions.

Procedure

1. Ask the students if they know the meaning of the word *litter*; if not, define it and discuss whether they feel it is an environmental problem.
2. Tell the students they will go on a nature hike to observe the amount of litter on the ground.
3. Have the students choose an item that they will watch for on the hike (e.g., soda cans, cigarette butts).
4. Ask the students to predict how many of the items they will see on the hike. Have them write the estimate on a piece of paper or worksheet (see the Appendix).
5. Start the hike (choose an area you know to have a litter problem). Make sure the students are actually counting the items they have chosen.
6. Have the students compare the amount they estimated with the actual number they found. Discuss any discrepancies between the predictions and the actual numbers and among students who counted the same item.
7. Have the students list ways to reduce litter and garbage in general.

Caveats and Options

1. Use the activity as an out-of-class assignment that students do on their way to or from school or as a log in which the students keep track of the quantity of an item they throw away in a week.
2. To counterbalance the passive nature of this activity (looking at the garbage rather than picking it up), arrange a cleanup session later in the unit. In fact, students often propose a cleanup day and are more enthused about it than when the teacher imposes it.

Appendix: Reduce Garbage Campaign

Directions: Think of three things each group could do to reduce the amount of garbage produced.

1. Government

   a. _____

   b. _____

   c. _____

2. Product manufacturers

   a. _____

   b. _____

   c. _____

3. Stores

   a. _____

   b. _____

   c. _____

4. Schools/campuses

    a. _____

    b. _____

    c. _____

5. Consumers

    a. _____

    b. _____

    c. _____

Contributor

Char Heitman holds a BA in TESOL and Spanish from the University of Northern Iowa and an MA in Linguistics from the University of Iowa, in the United States. She taught English in Japan for 4 years and currently teaches in the Intensive English Program at the University of Iowa.

Flowers in the States

Levels
Any

Aims
Remember the names,
two-letter abbreviations,
and locations of the
states in the U.S.

Class Time
3 hours over 2 days
(beginners)
2 hours (intermediate
and advanced students)

Preparation Time
Variable

Resources
Large map of the U.S.
and blank maps with
state borders
A state flower
Illustrations of state
flowers
Pushpins or thumbtacks
List of state flowers and
two-letter state
abbreviations

This activity uses flowers to help immigrant students (e.g., those preparing for clerical positions) learn the names of the states.

Procedure

1. Ask the students to bring catalogues and travel brochures to class. Give the students a few days to collect the brochures. Collect your own in case some students do not bring any to class.
2. Bring any state flower to class. Your choice will be limited by the seasonal availability of flowers; the scarlet carnation (Ohio) is available almost year round, as is the rose (New York).
3. Get the students to talk about the flower (e.g., its color, its scent), their favorite flowers, and meanings attached to flowers. Monitor yourself carefully: Give the students the words they are searching for, but do not give your own preferences. Elicit as much information as possible from the students. Allow 10–15 minutes for this part of the activity.
4. Introduce the idea of flower as emblem. The students will probably respond by giving examples from their respective cultures.
5. Organize the students into groups of three to five.
6. Hand out lists of state flowers (see the Appendix). Acknowledge anybody who has seen any of them.
7. For beginners, read the names of the states.
8. Instruct the students to find as many flowers in the travel brochures as possible in 15 minutes.
9. Mount the large map on a bulletin board. Have the students share the illustrations they have found and pin them to the map.
10. Hand out the list of two-letter state abbreviations. Answer any questions that come up, and respond to observations.

11. For homework, hand out the small maps and have the students fill in as many state names and abbreviations as they can remember. Allow some time at the beginning of the next lesson for the students to compare their map with the large one.

Caveats and Options

1. If there is time, let the students explore the travel brochures. Encourage them to talk and daydream about where they would like to travel.
2. Learning the names of the states is a long-term goal, and students will remember only some of them. However, this activity may help them look more attentively at weather charts and other maps of the United States.
3. Many flowers have medicinal uses. You may be surprised by what your students tell you about flowers!

References and Further Reading

Gordon, L. (1977). *Green magic*. New York: Viking Press.

Appendix: U.S. State Flowers

STATE	FLOWER	STATE	FLOWER
Alabama	Goldenrod	Montana	Bitter Root
Alaska	Forget-me-not	Nebraska	Goldenrod
Arizona	Giant Cactus	Nevada	Sagebrush
Arkansas	Apple Blossom	New Hampshire	Purple Lilac
California	California Poppy	New Jersey	Violet
Colorado	Blue Columbine	New Mexico	Yucca
Connecticut	Mountain Laurel	New York	Rose
Delaware	Peach Blossom	North Carolina	Dogwood
District of Columbia	American Beauty Rose	North Dakota	Prairie Rose
Florida	Orange Blossom	Ohio	Scarlet Carnation

STATE	FLOWER	STATE	FLOWER
Georgia	Cherokee Rose	Oklahoma	Mistletoe
Idaho	Lewis Mock-Orange	Oregon	Oregon Holly Grape
Hawaii	Hibiscus	Pennsylvania	Mountain Laurel
Illinois	Native Wood Violet	Rhode Island	Violet
Indiana	Zinnia	South Carolina	Yellow Jessamine
Iowa	Wild Rose	South Dakota	American Pasqueflower
Kansas	Sunflower	Tennessee	Iris
Kentucky	Goldenrod	Texas	Texas Bluebonnet
Louisiana	Southern Magnolia	Utah	Sego Lily
Maine	Pine Cone	Vermont	Red Clover
Maryland	Black-Eyed Susan	Virginia	Flowering Dogwood
Massachusetts	Trailing Arbutus	Washington	Coast Rhododendron
Michigan	Apple Blossom	West Virginia	Great Rhododendron
Minnesota	Showy Lady Slipper	Wisconsin	Native Violet
Mississippi	Southern Magnolia	Wyoming	Indian Paintbrush
Missouri	Downy Hawthorn		

(Gordon, 1977, p. 177)

Contributor

Barbara Huppauf specializes in vocational English and workplace literacy. She worked for the Adult Migrant Education Services and the College of Technical and Further Education in Sydney, Australia, and now teaches for the American Language Institute at New York University and for the New York Association for New Americans, in the United States.

Interpreting Tables and Figures

Levels
Intermediate +

Aims
Interpret tables and
figures

Class Time
45 minutes

Preparation Time
30 minutes

Resources
Handouts
Butcher paper
Markers

Interpreting visual representations will help students understand complex relationships.

Procedure

1. Have the students work in groups of four. Give each group a copy of the handout Interpreting Tables (see Appendix A). Have the groups take turns looking at the two tables and asking and answering the questions on the handout.
2. Distribute butcher paper and markers. Tell the groups to look at the handout again and, this time, to create a visual representation for them.
3. Direct the groups to post the visual representations on the blackboard.
4. Have the groups look at the handout Interpreting Figures (see Appendix B) and take turns answering the questions on the handout.

Caveats and Options

1. This activity lends itself to sheltered and adjunct courses. Originally, the activity was used in an ESL/animal biology adjunct class in which students were required to create visual representations of data collected.
2. Locate course-related information displayed in table or figure form. Ask students working in groups to create legends for the tables or figures.

References and Further Reading

Brinton, D. M., Snow, M. A., & Wesche, M. B. (1989). Content-based second language instruction. Boston: Heinle & Heinle.

Snow, M. A. (1994). (Ed.). *Project LEAP: Learning-English-for-Academic-Purposes. Training manual, year three*. Los Angeles: California State University/Fund for the Improvement of Postsecondary Education.

Appendix A: Interpreting Tables

Background: A group of biology students conducted a study at California State University, Los Angeles (CSLA). The students made observations to determine the significance of physical appearance in the mating selection of Homo sapiens.

Instructions: Look at Table 1 and answer the following questions:
- What does the table tell you about the observed and expected number of common male–common female pairs at CSLA?
- What can you say about the observed and expected percentage of unusual male–unusual female pairs?

TABLE 1. Male-female pair survey of students at CSLA.

Pair type	Number of pairs		Total percentage	
	Observed	Expected	Observed	Expected
Common male–common female	142	150	61.2	64.7
Unusual male–common female	34	41	14.6*	17.6
Common male–unusual female	34	32	14.6*	13.9
Unusual male–unusual female	22	9	9.5*	3.8
Total	232	232	99.9	100

*Significantly different from the value expected at $p < .05$.

Background: The biology students made a second table containing information about the number of common and unusual males and females observed at CSLA.

Instructions: Look at Table 2 and do the following.

1. Give it a title.
2. Answer the following questions:
   - How does the percentage of common males compare with the percentage of common females?
   - How does the number of unusual males compare with the number of unusual females?

TABLE 2.

	Common	Unusual	Total
Number of males	602	164	766
Percentage of total males	78.6	21.4	100
Number of females	640	138	778
Percentage of total females	82.3	17.7	100
Total	1242	302	1544

Appendix B: Interpreting Figures

Background: A different group of biology students at CSLA investigated circadian body rhythms during "normal" rest and activity periods. "Normal" rest periods were from 2200–2400 to 0600–0800 hours. "Normal" activity periods were from 0600–0800 to 2200–2400 hours. As part of their experiment, students (a) measured their pulse to determine their heart rate and (b) added numbers to determine their adding speed.

FIGURE 1. Biological Rhythm Effects on Pulse Rate

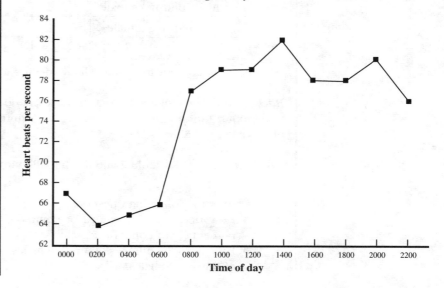

Instructions:

1. Look at Figure 1:
   - How fast does the heart beat at 0200 and 1400 hours? What does this tell you about the heartbeat at rest and activity periods?
   - How fast does the heart beat at 2200 hours? Can you explain why the heart beats that way at that time?
2. Look at Figure 2:
   - Compare the adding speeds at 0200 and 1000 hours. What does this tell you about adding speed at rest and activity periods?
   - Look at the adding speed of people at 2200 hours. Can you explain why that happens?

FIGURE 2. Adding Speed Affected by Biological Rhythms

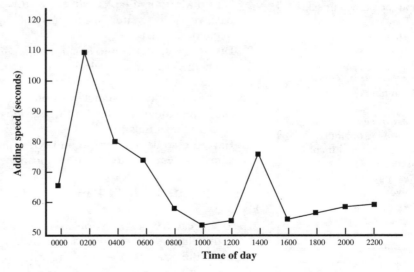

Contributors

Lía D. Kamhi-Stein is Assistant Professor at California State University, Los Angeles, and was a Language Specialist for Project LEAP (Learning-English-for-Academic-Purposes), in the United States. Marguerite Ann Snow is Associate Professor at California State University, Los Angeles, where she conducts faculty training across the disciplines as Director of Project LEAP.

Pumpkins: Resource for Inquiry

Levels
Intermediate; young
learners

Aims
Develop observational,
prediction, estimation,
and measurement skills

Class Time
60 minutes

Preparation Time
20 minutes

Resources
Pumpkins of similar
size (about 4-6 inches
in diameter)
Heavy, serrated plastic
knives
Tablespoons
Measuring tapes
(metric preferred)
Balance scales
Magnifying glasses
Paper towels
Trash bags
Empty wastebasket or
bucket

This multisensory, hands-on activity focuses on the development of students' inquiry skills and their acquisition of scientific concepts. The pumpkin is a great resource for cultural and scientific inquiry.

Procedure

1. Set up a resource table with paper towels, measuring tapes, spoons, balance scales, water bucket, magnifying glasses, knives, and other needed materials.
2. Divide the students into small groups. Give each group a pumpkin.
3. Have the students develop oral and written ideas related to their pumpkins.
4. Have the students interact with other groups to expand on ideas.
5. Have the students return to their groups and explore ideas with the resource materials provided.
6. Have the students develop and write down their ideas and conclusions for demonstration and publication.

Caveats and Options

1. As a preactivity exploration, ask the students questions, such as how many different ways they can measure a pumpkin.
2. Have the students measure the volume of the pumpkins using the water displacement method. Consult science and mathematics textbooks for the middle grades for instructions on this method.
3. As follow-up, have the students compare pumpkins of different sizes, pumpkins with squash, and pumpkins with other vegetables.

References and Further Reading

Baker, A., & Baker, J. (1990). *Mathematics in process.* Portsmouth, NH: Heinemann.

Cliatt, M. J. P., & Shaw, J. M. (1992). *Helping children explore science.* New York: Macmillan.

Appendix

Ideas that have been developed by students:

1. Convergent
   - What are the diameter and circumference of the sample pumpkins?
   - What do you estimate to be the weight of your pumpkin?
   - How many creases does your pumpkin have? Is the number of creases the same for other pumpkins?
   - What is the history of the pumpkin as food and as a cultural symbol?
2. Divergent
   - What uses can you think of for pumpkins?
   - How does the pumpkin compare with other squashes?
   - Create recipes for pumpkins.
   - What animals would enjoy pumpkin seeds?

Contributors

Dorit Kaufman directs the TESOL certification program at the Department of Linguistics, and Wallace Nelson is the Coordinator of Science Teaching and Certification in the Center for Science, Mathematics, and Technology Education, both at the State University of New York at Stony Brook, in the United States.

What's a Button?

Levels
Intermediate; young learners

Aims
Develop observation, classification, and pattern identification skills

Class Time
40 minutes

Preparation Time
15 minutes

Resources
Assorted buttons of different sizes, shapes, and colors (at least five per student)
Overhead projector, large newsprint sheets, or chalkboard

Caveats and Options

This multisensory, hands-on activity involves developing students' awareness of the power of their five senses and their ability to identify property words. The focus of this activity is on the development of observation and classification skills. Students are encouraged to think about the observations they make.

Procedure

1. Have the students become aware of their five senses: touch, smell, taste, hearing, and seeing. Give examples of words that allude to the five senses (e.g., *rough to the touch, peppermint smell and taste, music—hearing, colors—seeing*).
2. Have the students select five buttons from the pile of assorted buttons.
3. Elicit from the students identifying property words for their buttons, with the goal of generating as many words as possible, one word at a time. As students say their words, repeat them and write them for all to see. Keep a record of the words for students' future reference.
4. Work with the students to develop a property-word chart (see the Appendix).
5. Use the buttons to develop data collection, graphing, storytelling, and other creative language arts skills.

1. Do the activity with leaves, seeds, small animals, and so on.
2. Refer to science and mathematics textbooks for the middle grades for information on classification and the five senses (see References and Further Reading).

References and Further Reading

Babcock, D. (Ed.). (1988). *Elementary science program*. Spenceport, NY: Board of Cooperative Educational Services.

Neuman, D. B. (1993). *Experiencing elementary science*. Belmont, CA: Wadsworth.

The University of the State of New York, State Education Department. (1985). *New York State elementary mathematics syllabus*. Albany, NY: Author. (ERIC Document Reproduction Service No. ED 067 238)

The University of the State of New York, State Education Department. (1985). *New York State elementary science syllabus*. Albany, NY: Author. (ERIC Document Reproduction Service No. ED 256 611 SLC #WH)

Appendix: Model Word-Property Chart

Color	Shape	Size	Texture	Weight	Other words
black	round	big	slippery	light	lovely
yellow	square	tiny	rough	heavy	colorful
green	oval	wide	bumpy	dense	useful
red	flat	huge	smooth	massive	shiny

Contributors

Dorit Kaufman directs the TESOL certification program at the Department of Linguistics, and Wallace Nelson is the Coordinator of Science Teaching and Certification in the Center for Science, Mathematics, and Technology Education, both at the State University of New York at Stony Brook, in the United States.

Popping Corn

Levels
Intermediate; young
learners

Aims
Develop observation,
problem-solving, and
measurement skills

Class Time
60 minutes

Preparation Time
20 minutes

Resources
Electric popcorn
popper with removable
top
Popcorn and oil
Large newsprint sheets

This multisensory, hands-on activity develops inquiry skills: observing, predicting, using numbers, recording data, and communicating ideas and information.

Procedure

1. Cover the floor with newspaper or plastic sheets and place the popcorn popper (the flat-dish type works best) in the center of the room. Seat the students in a circle at a safe distance around the popcorn popper.
2. Engage the students in observation, exploration, and prediction. The following are sample questions:
   - What happens to popcorn when it is heated?
   - What will happen to the popcorn if the top is not placed on the popper?
   - What do you think you will see after the popcorn has popped?
3. Have the students draw a prediction chart showing how far from the popper most of the popcorn will fall.
4. Have each student take some popcorn kernels and assign them identifying property words. Develop a property-word chart such as the following:

Shape	Color	Size	Texture
round	brown	small	smooth

5. Have the students place their kernels in the popcorn popper and add oil.
6. Pop the popcorn without the lid and have the students observe the process.
7. After the popcorn has popped, have students develop more words to describe what they have just observed.

142

8. Have the students ask measuring questions (*how far? how high? how many?*).
9. Have the students develop ideas for data tables.
10. Have the students chart the data collected and compare them with their preactivity predictions.

Caveats and Options

1. Use the popcorn experience to develop data-collecting, graphing, storytelling, and other creative language arts skills.
2. Be sure to review safety procedures related to this activity. Do the activity only in appropriately sized classrooms.
3. Be sure to practice this activity before doing it with students.
4. Use property words before, during, and after the activity, and write them so that they are visible to all students all the time.
5. This activity was adapted from a presentation by Dewey Dykstra at the 1991 Association of Constructivist Teaching Conference, Northampton, Massachusetts.

References and Further Reading

Education Development Center. (1994). *The language of numbers*. Portsmouth, NH: Heinemann.

Grennon Brooks, J., & Brooks, M. (1993). *The case for constructivist classrooms*. Alexandria, VA: Association for Supervision and Curriculum Development.

The University of the State of New York, State Education Department. (1985). *New York State elementary mathematics syllabus*. Albany, NY: Author. (ERIC Document Reproduction Service No. ED 067 238)

The University of the State of New York, State Education Department. (1985). *New York State elementary science syllabus*. Albany, NY: Author. (ERIC Document Reproduction Service No. ED 256 611 SLC #WH)

Contributors

Dorit Kaufman directs the TESOL certification program at the Department of Linguistics, and Wallace Nelson is the Coordinator of Science Teaching and Certification in the Center for Science, Mathematics, and Technology Education at the State University of New York at Stony Brook, in the United States.

Learning What Learners Learn: Action Logging

Level
Any; teachers/
researchers

Aims
Build two-way teacher-
student communication
about classroom
learning

Class Time
5 minutes

Preparation Time
None

Resources
Handout

Action logging is a gentle form of action research that allows teachers to continually improve their courses. It allows them to get regular feedback from their students on their comprehension of content and its perceived value so that they can do a better job of adjusting the material to their students.

Procedure

1. Prepare a handout like the one in the Appendix.
2. If you wish, write in outline form on the blackboard each class's content to make it easier for students to understand, take notes on, and write about the different topics later.
3. Have the students write descriptions of each class in a notebook, listing lesson segments and ideas and discussing the content. This allows them to reformulate (reconstruct from their notes) the information they understood and to consolidate more of the input.
4. Set a time for collecting the notebooks.
5. Read the notebooks, writing comments where appropriate.
6. Return the notebooks in the next class.

Caveats and Options

1. Instead of having the students write the action logs outside of class, give the students the last 5 minutes of class time to write all or some of the log.
2. After a few classes, ask the students to exchange action logs in class and read what their partners have written about the course. This allows collaborative learning not only of the content but also of the process of action logging, as students learn how others are doing it.
3. Periodically, ask the students to take a partner's action log home to read in order to review the class from someone else's perspective.

Reference and Further Reading

Murphey, T. (1993). Why don't teachers learn what learners learn? Taking the guesswork out with action logging. *English Teaching Forum, 31*(1), 6-10.

Appendix: Action Log Requirements

After every class, as soon as possible (so you remember well what happens), write a short description of the class: (a) Say briefly what we did and (b) comment about what you learned and what you liked. List the different activities and segments. You may want to take short notes in class to remind you. Comment on activities you especially liked and could learn from, and on those you did not like and you think could be improved. I need your feedback so that I can teach you better. I read your Action Logs. I like your suggestions and will try to use them if possible. If you have anything else that influences your learning that you think I should know, please tell me (for example, outside problems).

Here is an example of an entry for the course Alternative Learning Forms:

April 8 (written April 8, 21:00)*
1) DID: Today we listened to a story, did shadowing, reformulation, speed reading and sang a song.
2) COMMENT: Shadowing seems especially interesting. I'm going to try it in my other classes. I didn't understand some of the points in speed reading:
What is chunking? Sometimes Mr. Murphey spoke too fast. Please speak slower. My partners were Yuki and Hiroko** and it was fun to get to know them. We got a lot of homework, but it looks like fun. I'm looking forward to the rest of the classes. Oh, and I like singing.

*Always put the date of the class and the time you write.
**Always use people's names when you refer to partners.

Contributor

Tim Murphey teaches and learns at Nanzan University, Nagoya, Japan. He is interested in alternative learning forms and has published books with Longman, Oxford University Press, and Peter Lang.

Graffiti Session

Levels
Intermediate +

Aims
Tap prior knowledge on
a topic
Collaborate in a creative
way
Discuss background
knowledge, ideas, and
opinions generated by
class members

Class Time
30–45 minutes

Preparation Time
15 minutes

Resources
Poster-sized butcher-
block paper or poster
board
Tape, tacks, or magnets
Colored marker for each
student

This technique introduces a topic that students have some prior knowledge of or that they can imagine and give an opinion on. It is a type of brainstorming in which students get out of their seats, move around, and talk and work together creatively.

Procedure

1. Introduce the term *graffiti* by using a visual or by demonstrating the term. Provide several examples in Western culture and elicit student comments on the use of graffiti and examples in their own countries.
2. Tell the students that they will create a "graffiti poster" on a particular topic that they will be discussing over several classes or throughout the entire term.
3. Ask them to think about what they already know about the topic.
4. Encourage them to write or draw their ideas in graffiti style: vertically, horizontally, diagonally, big letters, tiny letters, sketches, funny pictures, and so on.
5. Put up the poster paper on the wall. Write the topic or question at the top.
6. Ask the students to stand up, take a marker, and write or draw at least two responses or ideas on the paper.
7. Tell them to stand back after writing, look at what others are writing or drawing, and write again.
8. After the students have written or drawn all their ideas, ask them to sit down and review the graffiti board together.
9. Use the poster as a springboard for discussion.

Caveats and Options

1. This activity works well in intensive English for academic purposes programs and is especially suitable in college adjunct classes. For example, at the beginning of the term in a philosophy adjunct course that focused on the topic of animal rights, the students made a graffiti

poster of their ideas on the differences between humans and animals or the qualities that make a human human. In a speech communication adjunct course, the activity was used to introduce the elements involved in giving an effective speech or oral presentation (see the Appendix).

2. If the topic will be discussed over several weeks or throughout the term, have the students create a follow-up graffiti poster on the same topic to show how learning has changed their ideas.

3. Leave the poster(s) up in the classroom to serve as a record of the students' prior knowledge and collaborative effort.

References and Further Reading

Kessler, C. (Ed.). (1992). *Cooperative language learning: A teacher's resource book.* Englewood Cliffs, NJ: Prentice-Hall Regents.

Willing, K. (1989). *Teaching how to learn—learning strategies in ESL: A teacher's guide.* Sydney, Australia: National Centre for English Language Teaching and Research.

Appendix

A student graffiti poster used in a speech communication adjunct course follows.

Contributor

Julie Sagliano is a Lecturer at Miyazaki International College, Japan, where she teaches ESL in adjunct and English courses.

Terms in Motion

Levels
Intermediate +

Aims
Review key terms and
their definitions
Self-evaluate
understanding of key
terms
Warm up by engaging in
physical activity
Form pairs for follow-up
activities

Class Time
10–15 minutes

Preparation Time
15 minutes

Resources
Blank index cards

This warm-up activity reinforces important content concepts introduced in a previous lesson. At the same time, it provides a positive and lively opening for the lesson and a smooth transition from one class to the next.

Procedure

1. Review key terms and definitions presented in the lecture from a previous class.
2. Select a number of key terms and their respective definitions equal to the total number of students in the class.
3. Write one term or definition on each index card.
4. Distribute a term or definition randomly to each student. If the class contains an unequal number of students, participate in the activity.
5. Direct the students to read and memorize the word(s) on their index cards.
6. Collect the index cards.
7. Have the students stand up and find the classmate who has a matching term or definition by moving around the room from person to person and saying the memorized term or definition aloud.
8. Direct the pairs to check with you when they find a potential match. If the term matches the definition, direct the pair to sit together and work on an appropriate follow-up activity (see Caveats and Options 5). If the match is incorrect, direct the students to continue their search.

Caveats and Options

1. This activity is particularly effective in early-morning or after-lunch adjunct classes when students are sleepy and need a warm-up. It also encourages students to use all four skills in an integrative manner.

2. Note which students are having difficulty understanding the terminology in lectures.
3. Substitute terms from reading assignments.
4. Use the activity to provide practice in classifying terms:
   - Select three or more common terms from the lecture or reading for each classification.
   - Have the students locate the other members of their group and then determine the principle of classification.
5. Have pairs of students who finish early discuss and write a formal definition of their term, complete with their own examples or those given in the last class. Allow an additional 10 minutes for this optional activity.
6. Assist students who are having problems finding a match.

References and Further Reading

King, M., Fagan, B., Bratt, T., & Baer, R. (1987). Social studies instruction. In P. A. Richard-Amato & M. A. Snow (Eds.), *The multicultural classroom: Readings for content-area instruction* (pp. 287–299). New York: Longman.

Shrum, J. L., & Glisan, E. W. (1994). *Teacher's handbook: Contextualized language instruction*. Boston: Heinle & Heinle.

Wright, A., Betteridge, D., & Buckby, M. (1984). *Games for language learning*. Cambridge: Cambridge University Press.

Contributor

Michael Sagliano is an English Lecturer teaching adjunct courses at Miyazaki International College in Japan.

Today's Contestants Are . . .

Levels
Intermediate +

Aims
Review content material
before exams
Work cooperatively
Follow instructions

Class Time
1–1½ hours

Preparation Time
1 hour

Resources
Three or more handouts
Blackboard

This game-show activity helps put students at ease and in a positive frame of mind before taking content exams. It provides the adjunct teacher with an effective way to reexamine key concepts in an active and enjoyable classroom environment.

Procedure

1. Select key concepts from content material presented in past lectures, readings, and other materials.
2. Prepare handouts containing questions, lists of words, and other activities for each of the three game-show rounds as follows (see the examples in the Appendix):
   - On the handout for the first game round, list five sets of three or four interrelated causes and effects in random order.
   - On the second-round handout, write sets of three common words in a category and add one inappropriate word that does not belong with the others.
   - On the third-round handout, list 10 true-or-false statements based on class content and some statements on ideas not taught in the class.

   Provide written instructions for the completion of each task.
3. Divide the class into teams of two or three students each. Have the students create team names and write them on the blackboard.
4. Have the students decide which team goes first, second, third, and so on.
5. Explain to the students that the game will last for a designated number of rounds in which each team will compete with the others for the most points based on correct team answers.

6. Act the part of the game host by being overly enthusiastic, interviewing the "contestants," and previewing the prizes.
7. For Round 1, distribute a copy of the first handout to each team.
8. Direct the students to complete the handout according to your instructions. Encourage team members to work together to complete the questions on the handout as quickly as possible.
9. Elicit the correct answer to each question on the handout after all teams are finished.
10. Have the students mark and total the number of correct answers and write the point total on the blackboard under their team's name.
11. Review the point total under each team name. Encourage keen competition in future game rounds.
12. Repeat Steps 8–11 for Rounds 2 and 3.
13. Total the number of points won by each team during the game and announce the winner.

Caveats and Options

1. This activity was devised to review material in a political science adjunct course. The excerpts in the Appendix are from handouts used for exam preparation in this course.
2. Choose content for the rounds that is appropriate for your course. Complex cause-and-effect relationships are especially prevalent in readings in the social sciences.
3. Adjust the content of the game to the students' proficiency level.
4. Certificates, oddities, and cafeteria and campus event tickets are examples of possible game prizes.

References and Further Reading

Cantoni-Harvey, G. (1987). *Content-area language instruction: Approaches and strategies*. Reading, MA: Addison-Wesley.

Shoemaker, C. L., & Shoemaker, F. F. (1991). *Interactive techniques for the ESL classroom*. New York: Newbury House.

Sion, C. (Ed.). (1985). *Recipes for tired teachers: Well-seasoned activities for the ESOL classroom*. Reading, MA: Addison-Wesley.

Appendix: Sample Game Handouts

1. Strangers

Directions: Cross out the "stranger" (i.e., the word that is not a member of the group).

Set A
toxic
poisonous
healthy
harmful

Set B
monoculture
irrigation
mechanization
salinization

Set C
farming
arable land
erosion
agriculture

Set D
developing
democratic
advanced
industrialized

2. Connections

Directions: For each set of causes and effects, put a number in each blank to show which event is first (1), second (2), third (3), and fourth (4).

Set A

_____ The international market increases its trade in timber.

_____ The amount of forest land decreases.

_____ Logging companies cut down forests.

_____ Wealthy countries desire timber.

Set B

_____ Chemicals enter the food chain.

_____ Toxic chemicals are released into the ocean.

_____ Human health is harmed.

_____ Ships carry toxic chemicals.

Set C

_____ Nuclear waste is produced.

_____ Radioactivity in the ocean rises.

_____ Nuclear power plants are constructed.

_____ Waste is dumped into the oceans.

3. Recollections

Directions: Information in each of the statements below may be true, false, or not presented in the lectures, discussions, and lectures in this class. For each of the statements below, circle *true*, *false*, or *not presented*.

a. The world population is currently leveling off.

　　TRUE　　FALSE　　NOT PRESENTED

b. Japan is the world's biggest consumer nation.

　　TRUE　　FALSE　　NOT PRESENTED

c. The greenhouse effect began in 1945.

　　TRUE　　FALSE　　NOT PRESENTED

d. Chlorofluorocarbons (CFCs) are used in televisions and radios.

   TRUE   FALSE   NOT PRESENTED

e. The world's population triples every 35 years.

   TRUE   FALSE   NOT PRESENTED

Contributor

Michael Sagliano is an English Lecturer teaching adjunct courses at Miyazaki International College in Japan.

Discuss and Draw

Levels
Intermediate +

Aims
Comprehend and
synthesize concepts and
ideas in a text

Class Time
1 hour

Preparation Time
10 minutes–1 hour to
search for suitable text

Resources
Source text
Butcher paper,
approximately 3 ft x 4 ft
Adhesive tape
Markers

This cooperative learning activity, suitable for any content area, provides students with an opportunity to engage in an active discussion of a text. Drawing a visual representation of the text develops the ability to analyze the text for key concepts and ideas and fosters a holistic understanding of the text. The activity also assists students in writing summaries and studying for exams.

Procedure

1. Assign the students a source text (e.g., an article from a periodical, a chapter from a textbook) to read for homework before coming to class.
2. Seat the students in small groups of three to five students each, preferably at tables.
3. Distribute a sheet of butcher paper and a marker to each group.
4. Ask the students to discuss the text they have read and draw a visual (e.g., a pictorial image, graph, flowchart, or matrix) representing and connecting the key concepts and ideas of the text.
5. Give the students a time frame to work within.
6. Tell the students to tape their group's visual representation on the wall when they have finished.
7. Conduct a "gallery session" by having the students walk around the classroom to examine others' work.

Caveats and Options

1. Prepare the students for the activity by showing them examples of visual representations from various sources.
2. During the gallery session, direct the students to write questions and feedback on work done by other groups. Put up a blank sheet of paper next to each group's visual representation for this purpose.

3. Instead of holding a gallery session, ask each group to elect a student to present the group's drawing orally. Follow each presentation by a brief question-and-answer and discussion session involving all students.

4. This activity lends itself well to English for specific purposes courses. In one business administration class, the students read a management case study and produced a visual representation of the core problem and various solutions for a class presentation. In a science class, the students read an article on the causes of the greenhouse effect and participated in this activity to practice discussion skills.

References and Further Reading

Jones, B. F., Pierce, J., & Hunter, B. (1988). Teaching students to construct graphic representations. *Educational Leadership, 46*(4), 20–25.

Appendix: Sample Student Artwork

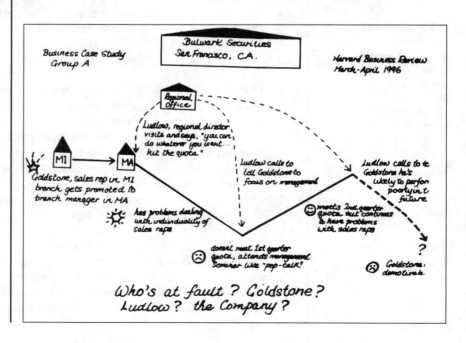

Facts	What's Done	Who's fault?
Goldstone, sales rep, untrained in management is promoted to branch manager in another state	Goldstone gets trial training Ludlow, his boss gives directive to keep the quota	Ludlow? Goldstone? Company?
Goldstone doesn't know how to manage sales reps (they do what they want)	Goldstone tries to deal with it alone. Ludlow doesn't contact him to see how he's doing.	Ludlow? Goldstone? Company?
Goldstone's first quarter quota is not met	Ludlow calls and scolds Goldstone, tells him to focus on management Goldstone attends management workshop	Ludlow? Goldstone? Company?
Goldstone's second quarter quota is met but management problem is unsolved	Ludlow calls and scolds Goldstone. tells him he'll probably do poorly in the future	Ludlow? Goldstone? Company?
Goldstone is unhappy	?	?

Business Case Study - Group C   Harvard Business Review 3-4/96

Contributor

Keiko Tanaka is Assistant Professor at California State University, Hayward, in the United States, where she coordinates the TESOL and ESL programs.

Content Pursuit

Levels
Intermediate +

Aims
Review adjunct course
material
Prepare for a test on
adjunct course content

Class Time
30–50 minutes

Preparation Time
45 minutes

Resources
Dice
Question cards

This activity is a twist on the game *Trivial Pursuit*. Many ESL students are not always aware of what they do not know. They may think that they are prepared for a test in their academic classes when they are not, or they may have knowledge of course content but not know how to verbalize what they have studied. The competitive nature of this game adds incentive for the students to take the review session seriously while helping them see the gaps in their knowledge.

Procedure

1. Have the students review at home the material that they have been studying for their next test.
2. Divide the material being reviewed into six natural categories. For example, material from a psychology course might be divided into the following categories: (a) important people, (b) key concepts, (c) theories, (d) dates and places, (e) vocabulary and terms, and (f) other.
3. Develop a set of questions from the course content for each of the six categories created (see the Appendix). Write each question on a card, putting the answer to each question on the back of the card.
4. Seat the students in groups of four, preferably at tables.
5. Provide each group with a set of cards for all six categories and a die.
6. In turns, have the students roll the die. The number on the die determines the category of question that the student rolling the die must answer. The person on the roller's left selects a card from the appropriate category and reads it aloud. A correct answer earns the student one point. The other group members determine whether or not an answer matches the correct answer given on the back of the card.

7. Have the students take turns rolling the die and answering questions until the questions are exhausted or someone in the group has earned a set number of points.

Caveats and Options

1. Students often have difficulty with the design of tests given in academic content classes. By writing the questions for each category in the same format that will appear on their tests (e.g., multiple choice, fill-in-the-blank, short answer), students will get some practice with these different formats.
2. Give higher point values to questions that are more difficult. Shuffle the more challenging questions randomly into the set of cards in a category, or give the students the option of choosing a "standard" or "challenging" question.
3. Group the students into teams of two or three players and allow them to discuss possible answers before responding to the question. Give guidelines to keep one person from dominating the group and to ensure that all members participate.
4. Give the students the responsibility for developing their own questions for these reviews. Ask each student to write 5–10 different questions that they might expect to see on a test. Collect the questions and write them on the cards. This option helps the students think about what they may be asked to know for a test.
5. Have the groups keep track of the questions that are missed. Review these questions with the whole class.

Appendix: Sample Content Pursuit Questions

The following Content Pursuit questions may be used to prepare students for a test in a marketing course.

Vocabulary and Terms

1. What does the term *product homogeneity* mean?
   a. A product that cannot be varied
   b. A product that can be varied
   c. A product that is differentiated

Marketing Strategies

1. Describe the *concentrated marketing strategy*.
2. Two factors that need to be considered when choosing a market-coverage strategy are company resources and product homogeneity. What is another factor?

People

1. Who is credited with having defined the three market-coverage strategies used by businesses in the United States?

Contributor

Thom Upton is Assistant Professor and Director of ESL at the University of Wisconsin–Eau Claire, in the United States.

The Language of Art,
the Art of Language

Levels
Beginning–intermediate

Aims
Describe works of art
using vocabulary of the
visual artist
Produce and describe
one's own artwork

Class Time
1 hour

Preparation Time
Variable

Resources
Art reproductions or
slides
Blank paper
Overhead projector
(optional)

This introductory lesson provides students with concrete experiences with *line*, one of the design elements in art. By physically becoming different types of line, recognizing lines in works of art, and practicing and then producing their own work, students have numerous opportunities to see and describe this element.

Procedure

Responding Physically as Kinds of Lines

1. Depending on their age and willingness, have the students stand at their desks or remain seated. (Those standing will use their whole body to become a line. Those seated can use their arms.)
2. While giving verbal instructions, model them. Then draw the type of line and write the word on the blackboard or on butcher paper.

Verbal instructions	Physical movements
● Pretend your body (arm) is a line.	● Model, draw, write *line*.
● Be (Make) a vertical line.	● Model, draw, write *vertical*.
● Be (Make) a horizontal line.	● Model, draw, write *horizontal*.
● Be (Make) a diagonal line.	● Model, draw, write *diagonal*.
● Be (Make) a curved line.	● Model, draw, write *curved*.
● Be (Make) a zigzag line.	● Model, draw, write *zigzag*.

3. Randomly repeat the instructions. Gradually stop modeling. Instead, point to the graphic and word. Encourage the students to observe others and to vary their own responses.

Identifying the Elements of Line

4. Display art reproductions or slides. Depending on the proficiency of the class, either point to a line and ask the students to identify the type, or ask the students to identify a line and describe it so that others can distinguish it.
5. If using art reproductions, provide one each to groups of three to four students. Ask the students to identify the types of line.
6. Circulate. For more advanced students, suggest adding characteristics such as *long-short, wide-thin, rough-smooth*; the direction in which the line is moving; and the type of curve—*gradual, wavy, spiral*.

Producing Lines and Works of Art

7. Collect the reproductions. Distribute one piece of blank paper to each student.
8. Ask the students to fold the paper in sixths. Model the folding.
9. On an overhead transparency or on the blackboard, draw each type of line while saying, "These are vertical lines. I am drawing vertical lines. Draw vertical lines in the first section of your paper." Do not label the lines at this point. After drawing all five types of lines, point to each and ask the students to name the type. Add the names as the students say them, and direct the students to write the names on their paper.
10. Distribute a second piece of blank paper. Ask the students to create their own drawing using the types of lines learned.

Describing Their Creations

11. When the students have finished drawing, ask small groups or pairs to share their drawings, describing the lines they used. Circulate and make suggestions for additional descriptors as necessary.
12. Ask if anyone would like to share a creation with the whole group.
13. For homework, ask the students to observe their environment and report on the types of lines they find and the places they find them.

Caveats and Options

1. Because students' abilities in language and in artistic ability vary, provide opportunities for whole-group, small-group, and individual expression in both language and art.
2. In Step 4, group students in twos and threes. Point to a line and ask the groups to discuss what it is. Then call on several groups to respond. In this way, all students, not just the one or two most proficient or vocal students, have the opportunity to talk.
3. For the whole-group sharing at the end, have the small groups select one of their members to describe their drawings. Because the students have had an opportunity to practice in their small groups, they can be less inhibited about talking to the whole group.
4. The affirmation of the artistic experience allows some quiet students to express themselves when normally they would not. Some may bring in other pieces of work they have done and share those with the group.
5. Use this lesson as the first in a series that introduces all the elements of design—line, color, value, shape, form, texture. As more lessons are added, the students begin to describe their own and others' work both objectively by talking about the elements and subjectively by adding their feelings and interpretations of the works.

References and Further Reading

Baker, R. (1971). *All about art: An introduction to the basics of art.* New Haven, CT: Fine Arts Publications.

The Big A. (1987). *Teacher's idea book.* Seattle, WA: KCTS/Seattle, Department of Project and Teleservices Marketing.

California Department of Education. (1989). *Visual and performing arts framework.* Sacramento, CA: Author.

Selleck, J. (1974). *Elements of design: Line.* Worcester, MA: Davis. [one of a series by the publisher on elements and principles of design]

Appendix: Sample Student Paper

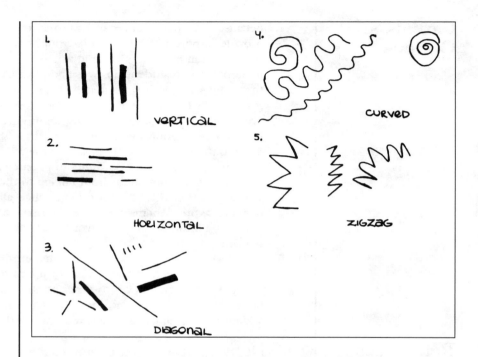

Contributor

Kathryn Z. Weed, Assistant Professor at California State University, San Bernardino, in the United States, teaches courses describing English language learners to preservice teacher candidates and K–12 teachers.

Part IV: Data Gathering

Shao-chieh Chang at Northern Virginia Community College, Alexandria, Virginia USA.

Listening for Information Emphasis Cues in Academic Lectures

Level
Advanced

Aims
Recognize emphasis
cues in lectures
Determine important
information
Take concise, organized
notes of the emphasized
information

Class Time
1 hour

Preparation Time
45 minutes

Resources
Handout with emphasis
cues and information
types
Overhead projector and
transparencies
Audio- or videotaped
segments of a lecture

International students often ignore cues for important information and try to focus on information without distinguishing its relevance. If they are sensitized to the use of salience cues in lectures, they can learn to distinguish important information in lectures and take effective notes on it. The activity assumes that cues have been introduced in previous lectures.

Procedure

1. Locate an appropriate audiotaped or videotaped lecture clip of 4-7 minutes in length. It should extend from one (sub)topic announcement to the next (sub)topic announcement in the lecture.
2. Preview the clip for the types of information and the emphasis cues for each of the types of information. Prepare a handout with a table like the one in the Appendix.
3. In class, review types of emphasis cues in a large-group discussion, asking for definitions and examples.
4. Play the tape segment and have the students mark the emphasis cues and information types on the table.
5. Have the students compare their answers. Write their suggestions on an overhead transparency.
6. Replay the tape segment and have the students check their answers.
7. In a large group, discuss the information types and the emphasis cues for each.
8. Replay the tape segment to resolve any differences in opinion about the emphasis cues and information types, and have the students take notes about the clip.

9. Have the students compare their notes and, in groups of three to five, write a summary of the information in the clip and the way the lecturer emphasized the main points.

Caveats and Options

1. If the clip is new to the students, do any introductory schema building and review of content that is necessary.
2. This activity lends itself particularly well to adjunct or sheltered classes that can be audio- or videotaped.
3. The activity can be adapted to any field of study, but the tapes must be from authentic lectures. Because of this, be sure to observe permission regulations.
4. This activity is particularly effective near the beginning of a term.
5. Commercially available video- and audiotapes are usually not appropriate because they are not used in "live," authentic teaching situations in which the students and the professor have a stake in the information transfer.

References and Further Reading

Bame, J. (1995, April). *Emphasis in lecture discourse.* Paper presented at the annual ITESOL Convention, Twin Falls, ID.

Flowerdew, J. L. (1992). Salience in the performance of one speech act: The case of definitions. *Discourse Processes, 15,* 165–181.

Taglicht, J. (1984). *Message and emphasis: On focus and scope in English.* London: Longman.

Appendix

Infor- mation type	Emphasis cues							
	Pauses	Longer words	Restate-ment	Para-phrase	Buzz-words	Kine-sics	Visuals	Loud-ness
Topic announce-ment								
Directions								
Definitions								
Facts								
Charac-teristics								
Theories								
Background information								
Process steps								
Advantages								
Disad-vantages								
Examples								

Contributor

Jim Bame is a Principal Lecturer at Utah State University, in the United States. His interests are interactional and transactional conversation analysis, task-based language learning, and discourse analysis.

Navigating a Syllabus

Levels
Intermediate +

Aims
Become familiar with a
university syllabus and
classroom expectations

Class Time
15–30 minutes

Preparation Time
30 minutes

Resources
Syllabi from mainstream
classes
Overhead projector and
transparency (optional)

This activity gives international students an introduction to a course syllabus: its format and the expectations and policies it conveys. Students scan the syllabi for information and discuss course expectations.

Procedure

1. Obtain course syllabi from as many different departments as possible (e.g., biology, math, economics; see the Appendix). Syllabi are usually available from the department secretary or chair; otherwise, contact the professors.
2. Delete each professor's name and make sets of copies for small-group work (e.g., three or four different syllabi for groups of three to four students).
3. If possible, photocopy one syllabus onto an overhead transparency for your presentation.
4. Prepare a list of questions to ask the students and make one copy per group. Ask questions like the following:
   - What is the name of the course?
   - When does the course meet?
   - Is the course a lecture or a lab?
   - Are there any required textbooks? What are the titles?
   - How many tests are there? Do you know when the first test is? What kind of test will it be?
   - Is attendance required?
5. Break the class up into groups of three to four students and hand out sets of syllabi.
6. Take the students step-by-step through one syllabus, paying attention to the content and format (textbooks, tests, papers, policies). Use the overhead projector if available.

7. Hand out the lists of questions, one per group (or write the questions on the blackboard). Ask the students to work in groups to scan each syllabus for the information.

If possible, choose a set of syllabi representative of a typical course load for one semester. The students will have a better picture of what they can expect during one semester.

Caveats and Options

Appendix: Syllabus

SPANISH 1020
Instructor:
Semester: Spring 1995 (January 16–May 12)
Class Hours: Monday-Wednesday-Friday, 8:00–9:00
Office Hours: Monday-Wednesday-Friday, 9:00–10:00
                    Other hours available by appointment.
                    My office is in the Campus Center.
Office Phone: 244-4942 (direct line)

I. Course Description/Learning Objectives

This is a continuation of the Spanish 1010 course. You will learn different language functions (e.g., talking about past activities and experiences, describing, expressing opinions, comparing and contrasting), basic vocabulary (e.g., food, clothing, leisure-time activities), and simple grammatical structures (e.g., past tenses, object pronouns, prepositions). Speaking and listening form an important part of the course work.

II. Required Textbooks

(available at the Covenant Bookstore)
Intercambios: Textbook (Hendrickson: Heinle & Heinle, 1991)
                   Workbook/Laboratory Manual (blue)
                   Worksheet Portfolio (green)

III. Methods of Evaluating Student Progress

1. Six unit tests	50%
2. Attendance/participation/oral work	20%
3. Writing assignments/homework/lab work	15%
4. Language projects	10%
5. Attendance at one cultural function	5%

IV. Other Course Information

1. Attendance is required and forms a major part (10%) of your grade. If you cannot attend, you are expected to find out the assignment. Tests cannot be made up except by prior arrangement; if you are unable to come on the day of a test, call me before 8:00 a.m.

2. Credit (as opposed to a grade) is given for homework completed (homework turned in late will receive partial or no credit). *Homework* includes both written and listening exercises from the textbook and laboratory manual, in addition to other projects assigned in class. Some listening exercises to be done in the language laboratory will be assigned; cassette tapes are on reserve in the library.

3. Several special projects (worth 20 points each) will be assigned to help you expand your knowledge of Spanish. These may include scanning a Spanish-language newspaper or ad, watching or listening to excerpts from Spanish TV, or finding Spanish products in a supermarket.

4. The scope of the cultural event will be announced later in the course.

5. I am happy to help you outside of class (please note my office location and hours). If you need additional help, there are free tutorial sessions in the language laboratory (Carlson Tower, 4th floor), Monday-Tuesday-Wednesday, 3:30–5:00 p.m.

V. Preliminary Course Syllabus (subject to change)

Lección 1
Describing leisure-time activities
Talking about past activities
Preterite tense of regular verbs
Negative sentences
Test, *Lección 1*

Lección 2
Expressing likes and dislikes
Ordering a meal in a restaurant
Narrating past experiences
Preterite tense of irregular verbs
Imperfect tense
Test, *Lección 2*

Lección 3
Describing one's activities
Expressing likes and dislikes
Direct and indirect object pronouns
Gustar
Test, *Lección 3*

Lección 4
Specifying preferences
Comparing and contrasting
Expressing opinions
Demonstrative adjectives
Comparatives and superlatives
Test, *Lección 4*

Lección 5
Expressing opinions
Stating preferences
Expressing likes and dislikes
Por/para
Test, *Lección 5*

Lección 6
Expressing opinions
Making requests
Giving advice and orders
Test, *Lección 6*

Contributor

   Dennis Bricault is Director of ESL Programs and Instructor of Spanish at North Park College, Chicago, in the United States. His teaching and administrative experience spans 15 years in Spain, Hungary, and the United States.

Journal Treasure Hunt

Levels
Intermediate +

Aims
Become familiar with
the journal section of a
university library
Learn the elements of a
bibliographic reference
and their order

Class Time
1 hour

Preparation Time
45 minutes

Resources
Library with a good
journal section
Incomplete bibliography

T his exercise requires students to fill in information missing from entries in a bibliography; it is useful for getting students to use journals as part of their research while allowing them to become familiar with the form of references and bibliographies.

Procedure

1. Before taking the students to the library, teach the various parts of a bibliographic reference, raising the issue of the variety of styles.
2. Find or write a bibliography, blanking out pieces of information in each entry such as the author's name or initials, the volume number, or the title (see the Appendix). The remaining information should be sufficient for the student to find the reference in the appropriate journal and complete the reference.
3. Give one copy of the incomplete bibliography to each pair of students. Before the pairs of students go to the library, have them work in pairs and make notes in the margin as to what information is missing.
4. Have the whole class go to the library. Start the students off on different pages of the bibliography so that they are not all looking for the same reference at the same time.
5. When the students have finished the exercise, have them join up with another pair to check their information.

Caveats and Options

This activity comes from a research methods course designed for ESL graduate students hoping to enter British universities for higher degrees in the social sciences. It is a required course that aims to assist students in completing an independent study project in their area of interest. This "minidissertation" is expected to follow the academic conventions of the field in which they will do their graduate studies.

References and Further Reading

Brown, J. D. (1988). *Understanding research in second language learning*. New York: Cambridge University Press.

Dunleavy, P. (1986). *Studying for a degree*. London: Macmillan.

Appendix: Incomplete Bibliography

Directions: In pairs, identify which parts of the bibliography are missing. Then, using the journal section of the library, find the missing information.

Barker, M., Child, C., Gallois, C., Jones, E., & Callan, V. J. (1991). Difficulties of overseas students in social and academic situations. *Australian Journal of Psychology, 43*(2) ░░░░ .

Cenoz, ░░░░ , & Valencia, ░░░░ . (1993). Ethnolinguistic vitality, social networks and motivation in SLA: Some data from Basque. *Language, Culture and Curriculum, 6*(2) ░░░░ .

Hall, J. K. ░░░░ . The role of oral practices in the accomplishment of our everyday lives: The sociocultural dimensions of interaction with implications for the learning of another. *Applied Linguistics, 14*(2) ░░░░ .

░░░░░░░░ . (1994). Student culture and English language education: An international perspective. *Language, Culture and Curriculum, 7*(2), 125–144.

Krashen, S., & Seliger, H. (1975). The essential characteristics of formal instruction. *TESOL Quarterly,* ░░░░ 173–183.

░░░░░░░ . (1990). The advanced learner at large in the L2 community: Developments in spoken performance. *IRAL, 28* ░░░░ 309–324.

Levelt, W. J. M. (1978). ░░░░░░░░ . *Studies in Second Language Acquisition, 1,* 53–70.

Lightbown, ░░░░ . ░░░░ . Great expectations: Second-language acquisition research and classroom teaching. *Applied Linguistics, 6*(2), 173–189.

Long, M. ░░░░ Does second language instruction make a difference? A review of research. *TESOL Quarterly, 17,* 359–382.

Long, M. (1993). Assessment strategies for second language acquisition theories. *Applied Linguistics* ░░░░ , (3), ░░░░ .

Ogberg, K. (1960). ░░░░░░░ . *Practical Anthropology, 7,* 177–182.

Oxford, R., & ░░░░ , J. (1994). Language learning motivation: Expanding the theoretical framework. *The Modern Language Journal, 78*(1), ░░░░ .

Pennebaker, J. W., Colder, M, & Sharp, L. K. (1990). Accelerating the coping process. *Journal of Personality and Social Psychology*, ▓▓▓ , 528–537.

Pica, T. (1983). Adults' acquisition of English as a second language under different conditions of exposure. *Language Learning, 33* ▓▓▓ .

▓▓▓▓▓▓▓▓ . ▓▓▓▓ . Research on negotiation: What does it reveal about second language learning conditions, processes and outcomes? *Language Learning, 44*(3), 377–566.

Poole, D. ▓▓▓▓ . Language socialization in the second language classroom. *Language Learning, 42* ▓▓▓ 593–616.

Roberts, C. ▓▓▓▓ . Cultural studies and student exchange: Living the ethnographic life. *Language, Culture and Curriculum: Special Issue— Culture and Language Learning in Higher Education, 6*(1), ▓▓▓▓ .

Tomasello, M., & Herron, C. (1988). ▓▓▓▓▓▓▓▓▓▓▓ . *Applied Psycholinguistics, 9,* 237–246.

Tomasello, M., & Herron, C. ▓▓▓▓ . ▓▓▓▓▓▓ . *Studies in Second Language Acquisition, 11,* 384–395.

VanPatten, B., & Cadierno, T. (1993). Language processing and second language acquisition: A role for instruction. *The Modern Language Journal,* ▓▓▓ (1), 43–57.

Westwood, M. J., & Barker, M. (1990). Academic achievement and social adaption among international students: A comparison of groups study of the peer-pairing programme. *International Journal of Intercultural Relations, 14,* ▓▓▓ .

Whetten, C., & Song, C. (1992). International students in America's universities: An opportunity, a challenge. *International Education, 21*(2), ▓▓▓ .

White, ▓▓▓ , Spada, ▓▓▓ , Lightbown, ▓▓▓ , & Ranta, ▓▓▓ . (1991). Input enhancement and L2 question formation. *Applied Linguistics, 12*(4), 416–432.

Woods, E. G. (1993). British studies in English language teaching. *Language, Culture and Curriculum: Special Issue—Culture and Language Learning in Higher Education, 6*(1), ▓▓▓ .

Contributor

Angela Creese is an English for academic purposes Lecturer in the Foundation Diploma for Post Graduate Studies at the School of Oriental and African Studies, London University, in the United Kingdom.

Methoding the Research

Levels
Intermediate +

Aims
Become familiar with
the form and function
of a literature review
Categorize according to
predetermined systems
Decide how to apply
referencing styles in
academic writing tasks

Class Time
1½ hours

Preparation Time
1 hour

Resources
Jigsaw reading texts
Five journal articles
Grid worksheet

This activity requires students to examine the genre of the literature review and familiarize themselves with referencing conventions. It is suitable for students who are taking a content-based course or doing independent research.

Procedure

Part 1

1. Familiarize yourself with the style of a literature review, a style manual (e.g., Chicago, Modern Language Association, American Psychological Association) and referencing conventions (e.g., footnoting, endnoting).
2. Find five journal articles that contain examples of the referencing styles outlined above.
3. After making sure the students are familiar with the function and various forms of a literature review, have them do the jigsaw readings and complete the exercises (see Appendixes A and B).

Part 2

4. Seat the students in groups of three.
5. Distribute the grid worksheet (see Appendix C) and one journal article per group.
6. Direct the students to classify the articles according to the categories on the grid worksheet.
7. Discuss the students' decisions in a whole-class forum.
8. For homework, ask the students to find a journal article in their own field and repeat the exercise.

Caveats and Options

1. This activity comes from a research methods course designed for ESL graduate students hoping to enter British universities for higher degrees in the social sciences. It is a required course that aims to assist students in completing an independent study project in their area of interest. This "minidissertation" is expected to follow the academic conventions of the field in which they will do their graduate studies.
2. One copy of each article is sufficient. After a group has finished with one article, have the group pass it onto the next group.

References and Further Reading

Brown, J. D. (1988). *Understanding research in second language learning*. New York: Cambridge University Press.
Dunleavy, P. (1986). *Studying for a degree*. London: Macmillan.

Appendix A: Jigsaw Reading

Student A: Read the following text and be prepared to answer questions on it.

> Literature reviews are based on a systematic reading of existing academic writing on a particular topic. While a routine essay often relies on no more than half a dozen secondary sources, literature reviews are based on many times this number. The aim is to survey and report on a reasonably large or complex field of work, in the process developing some themes to make the review distinctive. Most students encounter plenty of possible topics during their course on which they would not mind conducting some more intensive research. Familiarity with professional academics' review articles means that defining a style is straightforward. Two big problems remain—how to conduct a reasonably comprehensive search for relevant documentation, and how to give your review a distinctive theme or angle of its own.[1]

---

[1]From *Understanding Research in Second Language Learning* (p. 46), by J. D. Brown, 1988, New York: Cambridge University Press. Copyright 1988 by Cambridge University Press. Reprinted with permission.

Appendix B: Jigsaw Reading

Now find out the following information from your partner:

1. Is the literature review section of a dissertation usually titled?
2. What three things should a literature review do?
3. What is an author who is approaching a new area of work unable to do?

Student B: Read the following text and be prepared to answer questions on it.

> This section (usually untitled) should be a discussion of the previous research that is relevant to the study. Such a discussion should, at a minimum, provide (1) the background or rationale for the study, (2) a demonstration of how previous research is related to the study, and (3) a framework for viewing the study. However, an author who is broaching an unexplored area of research cannot cite previous works. In this case, the author should at least explain the route by which this new area was reached. In either case, the author must give you enough information so that you can tell where the study fits into the field.[2]

Now find out the following information from your partner:

1. What are literature reviews based on?
2. What is the aim of a literature review?
3. What two problems are associated with doing a literature review?

[2]From *Studying for a Degree* (p. 112), by P. Dunleavy, 1986, London: Macmillan. Copyright 1986 by Macmillan. Reprinted with permission.

Appendix C: Literature Review Grid

Article	Refer-encing system	Length of article and number of refer-ences	Position of literature review in the article—at the beginning or the end?	Where are the research question(s) in relation to the literature review (before or after)? What are the research questions?
Long, M. (1990). The least a second language theory needs to explain. *TESOL Quarterly*, 24, 649–666.				

Contributor

Angela Creese is an English for academic purposes Lecturer in the Foundation Diploma for Post Graduate Studies at the School of Oriental and African Studies, London University, in the United Kingdom.

Discussing Data

Levels
High intermediate +

Aims
Select key data to
include in a report

Class Time
1 hour

Preparation Time
30 minutes

Resources
Data in the form of
charts, graphs, tables,
and diagrams

This activity introduces students to the key aspects of writing up data: (a) reporting and synthesizing data (using such expressions as *the majority of respondents ..., although ...*) (b) commenting on data (using such expressions as *of interest, surprisingly*), and (c) interpreting data (using such expressions as *This may be due to the fact that ...*).

Procedure

1. Divide the students into groups of three to five students.
2. Give each group the same set of data.
3. Ask each group of students to circle what they consider to be significant information.
4. Conduct a brief class discussion on why each group has highlighted particular data and whether or not it should be included in a minireport.
5. Elicit from the students useful phrases for reporting and commenting on data. Include expressions of comparison and contrast for synthesizing data. Make a list of these on the blackboard for reference.
6. Have each group of students write one sentence for one or two pieces of data, and check that they can use the phrases.
7. Sensitize the students to interpreting data by asking one or two groups to suggest what could be inferred from a piece of highlighted data.
8. Provide additional useful phrases for interpreting data (e.g., *This could be accounted for ...*). Draw the students' attention to the use of modals and hedging in interpreting data.

9. Ask each group of students to write a paragraph reporting and discussing the data.

10. Have each group comment on the other groups' work to decide which has written the best minireport.

Caveats and Options

1. This activity is particularly useful for students in the humanities and social sciences, who often have to conduct surveys and write up the results as part of their studies. However, it is also relevant for science-based students, as the same principles apply to the writing of laboratory reports, for example.

2. Simplify the activity by conducting it as two separate activities. For less proficient students, assign the reporting of data as one writing exercise and the discussion as a follow-up activity.

References and Further Reading

Jordan, R. R. (1990) *Academic writing course*. London: Collins.

Contributor

Lynne Flowerdew is a Senior Language Instructor at the Hong Kong University of Science and Technology, where she coordinates a technical communication skills course.

Read All About It! Witch Hunts: The American Curse

Levels
Intermediate +

Aims
Learn about witches in
U.S. history
Make a personal
connection with events
in a historical novel
Find information in
newspapers

Class Time
Two 1-hour sessions

Preparation Time
30 minutes–1 hour

Resources
Scratch paper
Newspapers
Encyclopedias
Dictionaries
Poster board
Scissors
Glue sticks
On-line reference
materials (optional)

This activity requires the students to gather preliminary background information about witches and witch hunts in U.S. history before reading a historical novel. Students then find examples or evidence of current-day witch hunts in newspapers.

Procedure

1. Ask the students to break into groups of three to five students.
2. Provide the students with paper and ask them to brainstorm their ideas about witches.
3. Make available encyclopedias, computerized encyclopedias, dictionaries, and other resources. Have the groups look up the words *witch* and *witch hunt* in three different reference sources.
4. Ask the groups to write down any additional information they find on witches or witch hunts.
5. Direct the groups to choose a spokesperson to report their findings to the rest of the class.
6. For homework ask the students to find an example of a modern-day witch hunt (in any part of the world) in a newspaper and bring the article to the next class meeting (see the Appendix).
7. At the next class meeting, ask the students to find others in the class who have articles about the same modern-day witch hunt.
8. Distribute scissors, glue sticks, and poster board. Have the students construct posters of articles about modern-day witch hunts.

Caveats and Options

1. This activity is intended as an introduction to the content on colonial America presented in the novel *The Witch of Blackbird Pond* by

Elizabeth George Speare. It was designed as part of a larger, cross-disciplinary content-based course.

2. As a natural extension of this activity, have the students talk or write about why they think their chosen articles are examples of modern-day witch hunts.

References and Further Reading

Richard-Amato, P., & Snow, M. A. (Eds.). (1992). *The multicultural classroom: Readings for content-area teachers*. White Plains, NY: Longman.

Speare, E. G. (1958). *The witch of Blackbird Pond*. Boston: Houghton Mifflin.

Appendix: Sample Homework Assignment

> ### Current Events Tie-In
>
> Assignment for Homework:
>
> You have looked at witch hunts in U.S. history, but they haven't stopped. Witch hunts still go on all the time, all over the world, especially when people are afraid of those who are different or when people use others' fear to gain power for themselves. Some other examples of modern-day witch hunts were:
> - America's Communist hunts
> - The persecution of Jews by the Nazis during World War II in Europe
> - Proposition 187 in California
> - The breakup of the former Yugoslavia
>
> Find an article in a newspaper or magazine that you think is about a witch hunt going on today. Bring it to class.

Contributor

Randi Freeman has taught ESL/EFL in Sweden and the United States. She has an MA in TESOL from the Monterey Institute of International Studies and teaches at Central Washington State University in the United States.

A Fact-Finding Mission

Levels
Any

Aims
Increase knowledge of
content area
Gather information
quickly from
unsimplified materials
Teach content material
to classmates
Gain reading confidence

Class Time
60–90 minutes

Preparation Time
60–90 minutes

Resources
Visuals and reading
materials related to the
subject
Handout

Introducing a new subject to students can be challenging if the students lack both the background knowledge and the vocabulary related to the subject. One way to enliven this introduction is to put the students in charge of gathering many facts related to the topic and then have them share the information they find with their classmates. If provided with resources and a list of questions to answer as a group, the students can, in a very short time, amass a large amount of information and gain a solid foundation in the content area.

Procedure

1. Gather books, magazines, newspapers, pictures, and other reading materials and visuals related to the topic to be studied, preferably one per student. Be sure the difficulty level of the materials corresponds to the English level of the students.
2. If you choose books, scan through them to locate sections that pertain to the specific topic, and give these page numbers to the students.
3. Prepare a set of questions for the students to answer. The answers to all the questions need not be in all the materials as long as the answer to each question is in at least one. Make one copy of the handout for each student.
4. In class, lead the students in a short prereading discussion to find out how much they know about the topic. Write down on the blackboard any key points they mention. This discussion is not intended to be a thorough explanation of the subject; its purpose is to briefly introduce the topic and activate the students' prior knowledge of the topic, if they have any.

5. Introduce key content-related vocabulary to prepare the students for their information search. If possible, reinforce these words with visuals.

6. Pass out a copy of the questions to each student.

7. Pass out a resource to each student. (If your class is large or resources are limited, have the students work in pairs or small groups.) If possible, match the difficulty level of the resource with the reading ability of the student.

8. Tell the students to scan through the resources to look for answers to the questions. Make sure they know they may not be able to locate an answer for every question. Set the time allowed for this activity based on the length and density of the materials and the number of questions.

9. Walk around the room while the students are working to check on their progress, give guidance, answer questions, and avoid giving the activity the appearance of a test.

10. When the students finish the worksheet, have them sit in a circle and discuss the answers. Because the students will have answered different questions, they will all need to explain their answers clearly, listen to one another's answers, and ask clarifying questions. To ensure a high-quality discussion:

   ● Encourage the students to add to one another's answers, as the resources will vary in the amount of information they provide.

   ● Encourage the students to show and explain any visuals they encountered in their materials.

   ● Ask additional questions during the discussion if you know the students have read, but failed to comment on, an important point.

   ● Have the students write down the information they learn from their classmates.

Caveats and Options

1. The success of the activity depends largely on the quality of materials you bring to class and on the questions you provide. By bringing in a variety of resources, you can individualize this activity so that all the students are working at their reading level and are increasing their level of content knowledge.

2. Excellent sources for beginning and intermediate students in the United States are school textbooks, school libraries, and the children's section of public libraries.

3. Do all of this activity in class. Do not assign it as homework for these reasons:
   - The students may feel impelled to read their materials word for word and translate all the words they do not know. This defeats one of the goals of the activity, which is to demonstrate to the students how much they can learn from unsimplified material in a short time.
   - You will not be available to help the students if they have questions.

4. This activity works well with virtually any topic. If the students have no prior knowledge of the topic, expand the prereading activities and establish links between the content and topics the students are already familiar with.

5. If you teach advanced students, send them to the library to check out materials on the topic, write several questions based on their materials, and bring their materials and questions to class. In class, have them exchange materials and questions and look for the answers to the questions their classmates wrote.

Contributor

Carolyn Heacock is a Teacher Trainer and Curriculum Coordinator for ESL reading courses at the University of Kansas, in the United States. She is also the Co-Director of the ESL computer lab.

Synthesizing From the Start

Levels
Intermediate +

Aims
Become aware of the
importance of
synthesizing information
from multiple sources
Analyze course
information using a
graphic organizer

Class Time
15–20 minutes

Preparation Time
15–20 minutes

Resources
Content course syllabus
Videotaped segment of
introductory lecture
Handout with
information grid

The type of information grid used in this exercise increases students' awareness of the importance of obtaining information from multiple sources. It is geared toward students in U.S. universities, who are responsible for understanding course material via course readings and lectures. The activity is also useful for students abroad who are interested in attending an English-medium university.

Procedure

1. Have the students read the academic course syllabus (see Appendix A).
2. Show the students the videotaped segment of the professor's introductory lecture.
3. Distribute the information grid to the students (see Appendix B).
4. Have the students decide if the information in the left-hand column was written in the course syllabus or discussed by the professor in the lecture and check the appropriate column on the grid.
5. Ask the students to discuss their answers with classmates in small groups and come to a consensus.
6. Go over the grid with the class. Discuss duplication of information as well as the way the professor chose to emphasize certain points during the lecture segment.
7. Discuss the necessity of processing information from multiple sources, such as readings and lectures, especially in preparing for tests.

Caveats and Options

1. This activity is especially useful at the beginning of the academic year but may be unnecessary once the students are accustomed to first-day procedures.

2. This activity is adaptable for use throughout the course as a study guide to help students synthesize course content. Use different information from course readings and videotaped lectures in the left-hand column. Paraphrasing activities also work well with this activity.

3. This type of activity is also useful when discussing test-taking strategies.

References and Further Reading

Brinton, D., Goodwin, J., & Ranks, L. (1994). Helping language minority students read and write analytically: The journey into, through, and beyond. In F. Peitzman & G. Gadda (Eds.), *With different eyes: Insights into teaching language minority students across the disciplines* (pp. 57–88). White Plains, NY: Longman.

Appendix A: History Course Syllabus

History 160
M W F 12:00–12:50
Knudsen 1220B

Professor Laslett
6288 Bunche Hall
Office Hours:
Monday 10–12
Wednesday 2–4

The Immigrant in America

This is a general introduction to U.S. immigration history, suitable for a breadth requirement of a history major. No prerequisites needed. The course examines, in the context of U.S. social history, the reasons for migration, the passage to America, and the occupational and cultural contributions of, prejudice toward, and assimilation of a wide range of immigrant groups from the early 19th century to the present day. Insight is also gained into the problems of immigration into southern California today.

Requirements: 40% of the grade is based on either the midterm (Monday, May 10) or a 15-page paper based on the student's own ethnic heritage. The paper consists of interviews with family members plus readings; consultation with the instructor is required. 60% of the grade is based on the final examination (Friday, June 18, 11:30–2:30).

Readings: All are required and can be purchased at the student bookstore.
　　J. Laslett, *U.S. Immigration History* (APS)
　　Bodnar, *The Transplanted* (Europeans)
　　J. Houston, *Farewell to Manzanar* (Japanese Americans)
　　L. Chavez, *Shadowed Lives, Undocumented Immigrants* (Mexican Americans)
　　Academic Publishing Service (APS) Course Reading Packet

WEEK 1	*Conceptual Frameworks & Reasons for Migration*
Readings	Bodnar, chapter 1; Chavez, pp. 3–6; Handlin, "Peasant Origins" (APS)
Issues	Definition of terms; role of capitalism in prompting migration and immigration from Europe, Asia, and Mexico; other reasons for migration

WEEK 2	*Process of Migration—Misconceptions of Handlin Thesis*
Readings	Bodnar, chapter 2; Handlin, "Peasant Origins" (APS); Vecoli, "Contadini in Chicago" (APS)
Issues	Methods of migration; role of family in migration process; immigrants not "helpless, bewildered people"

WEEK 3	*European Old Immigrants, 1820–1890*
Readings	Bodnar, chapters 3–7 FILM: Friday, April 30, *Inheritance* (part 1)
Issues	Arrival, distribution, and occupations of North Europeans in American society; upward social mobility and class system; role of AF of L and Democratic party

WEEK 4	*European New Immigrants, 1880–1917*
Readings	Bodnar, chapters 3–7
Issues	Arrival, distribution, and occupations of south and east Europeans in American society; factory and mine labor; residential patterns' role in politics and Progressivism; socializing role of (a) pardon and (b) Catholic church

WEEK 5	*Early Mexicans and the Asians in West, 1848–1917*
Readings	Bodnar, Chapters 3–7; Saxton, "Indispensable Enemy" (APS) MIDTERM: Monday, May 10 FILM: Friday, May 14, *Sewing Woman*
Issues	Indigenous Mexican Americans of the Southwest deprived of land, etc.; beginnings of immigration into California; gold rush, mining, railroads and Chinese; legal restraints on Asians; reasons for hatred of Asian immigrants
WEEK 6	*Nativism and Restrictionism, 1917–1924*
Readings	Higham, "Strangers in the Land" (APS), Bodnar, Chapters 6, 8–9, 11
Issues	Movement for restriction gathers strength; eugenics and racism; First World War, Russian revolution, and East Europeans; Immigration Restriction Acts, 1921, 1924; consequences of restriction
WEEK 7	*Depression and World War II, 1929–1945*
Readings	Houston, *Farewell to Manzanar* FILM: Friday, May 21, *Inheritance* (part 2)
Issues	Impact of Great Depression on immigrant workers; "revolving door" and Mexicans; role of new Europeans in rise of CIO and Communist Party; impact of New Deal; fighting for the United States; Japanese internment program
WEEK 8	*Recent Immigration Policy*
Readings	Chavez, Chapters 2–8, 10
Issues	Changes in immigration policy since World War II and their consequences; attempt to rescue Jews; Immigration Reform & Control Act (1986); Europeans and Third World immigrants; political or economic refugees?

WEEK 9	*Problems of Undocumented Workers*
Readings	Chavez, chapters 2–8, 10
	FILM: Friday, June 4, *La Raza: Survival*
Issues	Similarities and differences in the experiences and treatment of undocumented Hispanic immigrants from those of earlier immigrants; how the problems of recent immigrants can or should be alleviated
WEEK 10	*Assimilation, Acculturation, or Accommodation?*
Readings	Gordon, "Nature of Assimilation" (APS)
Issues	Gordon's assimilation model; adequacy of Gordon's model; alternate models (melting pot, cultural pluralism, separatist models)

Appendix B: Information Grid

ESL 33C—Module I
The Immigrant in America
Introduction to History 160—Dr. Laslett

Instructions: After reading the syllabus for History 160 and listening to the segment of Dr. Laslett's introductory lecture, look at this list of course information and decide if the information is contained in the course syllabus, in the lecture, or in both. Put a check mark (✓) in the appropriate column(s). After completing the information grid, discuss your answers with your classmates.

Information	Syllabus	Lecture
Prerequisites needed		
Percentages of grade		
Required textbooks		
Sources for paper		
Length of paper		
Date paper is due		
Date of final exam		
Types of test questions		
Weekly topics		
Film titles		

Contributor

Linda Jensen, who specializes in reading and content-based instruction, is a Lecturer in the Department of TESL & Applied Linguistics at the University of California, Los Angeles, in the United States.

A Scaffolding Approach to Library Research

Levels
Intermediate +

Aims
Learn to use computer
databases and indexes
Use the results of library
research in a writing
assignment

Class Time
1½ hours

Preparation Time
2–3 hours

Resources
Library assignment
handout

This hands-on activity helps ESL students use the electronic library and provides them with on-line research strategies applicable to their content courses.

Procedure

1. Select a paper topic that students will enjoy working on for the duration of the term.
2. Prior to the beginning of the term, ask a library subject specialist to (a) help you design a library assignment that is integrated into your paper requirement (see the Appendix), (b) help you select a number of journals appropriate for the writing assignment required in your class, and (c) hold a bibliographic instructional session in your class that, in contrast to the traditional library tour, provides the students with hands-on activities. Ask the librarian to:
   - Provide the students with *scaffolds*: The librarian models successful database research strategies by engaging the students in activities that gradually move from librarian to student control and giving the students an opportunity to apply the strategies with their classmates.
   - Define any library-related terminology.
3. In class, hold the bibliographic instructional session.
4. A week after the bibliographic instructional session, have the students turn in the library assignment requiring the identification of a specified number of sources to be used in the eventual paper assignment.

Caveats and Options

1. This activity lends itself to courses that include multistep writing assignments. For example, in an animal biology course, the students turned in and received feedback on the library assignment after

participating in the bibliographic instructional session (see the Appendix), returned to the library and revised their library search, and completed a draft of selected sections of the paper (e.g., Introduction and Literature Cited, Methodology).

2. For the library assignment and the subsequent paper assignment, give the students a list of key subject headings and descriptors (e.g., *rapid eye movement, jet lag*), databases to be used (e.g., LEXIS/NEXIS, CARL in the United States), and names of print indexes (e.g., *General Science Index*).

3. Find out whether your school library subscribes to computer databases such as LEXIS/NEXIS, CARL, or OCLC in the United States. LEXIS/NEXIS is an excellent resource because it provides full-text retrieval of magazines, newspapers, and journals pertaining to business, law, and medicine.

References and Further Reading

Kamhi-Stein, L. D., & Stein, A. (1995). Electronic databases and information services: Integrating their use into the requirements of your syllabus. *Instructionally Speaking, 6*(2), 5–6.

Snow, M. A. (1994a). Collaboration across disciplines in postsecondary education: Attitudinal challenges. *The CATESOL Journal, 7*, 59–64.

Snow, M. A. (1994b). (Ed.). *Project LEAP: Learning-English-for-Academic-Purposes. Training manual, year three*. Los Angeles: California State University, Los Angeles/Fund for the Improvement of Postsecondary Education.

Appendix: Sample Library Assignment

Biological Rhythms

Directions: Listed below are some of the subject headings/descriptors related to your biological rhythms assignment. Use them to complete the library assignment due on _____.

Subject Headings (Topics/Descriptors):

Aviation—physiological aspects
Jet lag
Dreams
Sleep (REM)
Slow-wave sleep (SWS)

Rapid eye movement
Air pilots—work load
Periodicity
Sleep-wake cycle
Moon—biological effect

Important: Feel free to combine subject headings related to your biological rhythms assignment. Combining subject headings will allow you to locate more articles on your topic.

1. Locate your subject heading (topic) in the *General Science Index* or the *Applied Science and Technology Index.*
2. Photocopy the page listing references on your topic. Attach a copy of that page.
3. Go to the second floor, Library North. Make sure that the library owns the journal/magazine you identified in Step 2, and
   - Photocopy the title page of the article (the first page).
   - Attach the title page.
   - Complete the information requested below:
     Title of the article:_____
     Author(s) of the article:_____
     Journal title:_____
     Volume:_____ Number:_____
     Pages:_____
     Month:_____ Day:_____ Year:_____

4. Use computer indexes on CD-ROM to locate abstracts (summaries) of articles in journals, magazines, and newspapers. Locate references/citations for your subject heading/topic. Then:
   - Print out the list of references.
   - Attach the CD-ROM printout.

5. Use CARL (in the United States) to locate abstracts of journals and magazines found in the library's collection and complete the following:

   Key words used for the search:_____

   Titles of three articles from acceptable journals:
   - _____
   - _____
   - _____

6. Use LEXIS (in the United States) to locate the full text of magazines, newspapers, or medical journals related to the topic and complete the following:

   Key words used for the search:_____

   Number of articles on the topic:_____

   Titles of three articles from acceptable journals (the articles should be different from those identified in Step 5):
   - _____
   - _____
   - _____

Contributors

Lía D. Kamhi-Stein is Assistant Professor and was a Language Specialist for Project LEAP: Learning-English-for-Academic-Purposes; Beverly Krilowicz is Associate Professor in Biology; Alan Stein is Coordinator of Bibliographic Instruction and conducts faculty and student training on the uses of on-line databases and the Internet; and Marguerite Ann Snow is Associate Professor and conducts faculty training across the disciplines as director of Project LEAP, all at California State University, Los Angeles, in the United States.

Serial Question Exchange for Review

Level
Advanced

Aims
Review and consolidate material from texts and lectures
Prepare for a quiz

Class Time
1 hour

Preparation Time
10 minutes

Resources
Strips of paper

In this activity, students review the content in a section of a textbook in a lively and interactive manner. As the students move from one partner to the next, they become proficient in answering questions on the content assigned.

Procedure

1. Have the students choose (or allot them) approximately the same number of different sections of a chapter in the content-area textbook to specialize in.
2. Ask each student to compose three or four questions, each on a separate strip of paper, that will elicit important content information to help them understand the material at hand. Tell them not to write the answers but to write down notes that may be helpful in answering the questions.
3. Have the students form pairs and ask each other questions. Tell the questioners to help their partner answer the question in full through discussion and prompting (e.g., *Can you expand on that? Can you explain that in more detail? Do you recall ...?, How about ...?*).
4. After the partners have both asked and answered questions, have the partners exchange questions (i.e., Student A takes Student B's questions and vice versa.).
5. Have the students, with the new questions in hand, find a new partner and continue this series of activities.
6. Repeat Steps 3–5 until all the students have answered all the questions and the students have covered the material in the entire chapter.
7. Collect the questions and choose some of them for a quiz.

Contributor

Elizabeth Lange teaches English at Temple University Japan.

Cities Alive!

Levels
Intermediate +

Aims
Gain an accurate view
of life in an English-
speaking country
Learn differences
between various cities
Learn and practice
vocabulary related to
various aspects of city
life
Communicate orally in
English about something
of interest
Read for specific
information

Class Time
2 hours

Preparation Time
15 minutes

Resources
Book or books on U.S.
cities
Different readings for
each student in a group

Teachers in EFL settings often find that students have stereotyped, Hollywood-influenced views of life in the United States. This cooperative jigsaw learning activity, designed for a theme-based unit on U.S. geography or culture and lifestyle, gives depth to students' understanding of the everyday concerns of Americans and some of the differences of life in different cities. It makes U.S. cities come alive for the students.

Procedure

1. Make cooperative learning groups of three to five students each.
2. For homework, give each student in a group a different city to read about in a book or books on U.S. cities (see References and Further Reading). Select readings of about the same length, or select shorter readings for weaker students. Try to choose cities that are different from each other.
3. Discuss primary vocabulary and then preview the reading format and various sections of the readings.
4. With the readings, give an assignment describing what information the students should report to their group mates in the next class. For example:
   - Describe the weather in your city.
   - List the pros and cons of the "quality of life" in your city.
   - List the strengths and weaknesses of business and commercial life in your city.
5. In the next class, have the students meet first with other students who have read about the same cities and discuss their answers to the assignment.
6. Have the students return to their original groups and tell each other what they wrote about their city in the assignment. They can

supplement their prepared answers with information from others who read about the same city.

7. Have the students continue in the same groups and discuss the following questions:
   - What is each city best for? Worst for? (Give them a list of items—perhaps corresponding to the reading sections—such as wages, employment opportunities, taxes, politics, weather, transportation, education, health care, public safety, cultural attractions, sports and recreation, and cost of living.)
   - In which city they would you prefer to live? Why?
8. Have the class as a whole discuss the questions above.

Caveats and Options

1. Adapt the readings and discussion questions to a lower skill level.
2. To give the activity more of a language focus, concentrate more on vocabulary.
3. Have the students write papers about the city they read about, perhaps comparing their work with other students' work on the same city.

References and Further Reading

Marlin, J. T. (1988). *Cities of opportunity*. New York: Master Media.

Contributor

Margo Menconi teaches adults English in Bratsk, Russia. Her master's thesis research involved comparing aspects of the content method of instruction with three English programs in Siberia.

Pictures to Paragraphs

Levels
High intermediate +

Aims
Determine subtopics
and information relevant
to a topic
Sort information by
subtopic
Organize subtopics for
expository writing

Class Time
30 minutes–1 hour

Preparation Time
Variable

Resources
Students' notes
Pictures, including some
duplicates, of aspects of
a topic students have
taken notes on
Pictures not relevant to
the topic
Captions for pictures,
about 10 in. x 3 in.
Markers

Information on a large topic suitable for expository essays or research papers is often found scattered in different source materials. This exercise makes clear the nature of choosing information relevant to a particular thesis statement and helps students identify and manipulate the concepts of category, hierarchy, and subordination, which are crucial to organizing expository prose. This technique utilizes both visual and kinesthetic modes of learning and provides practice in (re)categorizing and (re)organizing to provide a prewriting framework (outline).

Procedure

1. After the students have collected information on a topic, such as *albatrosses*, choose a thesis statement or focal point for the exercise, such as *dangers to albatrosses*.
2. Put various pictures of albatrosses and their environment (mounted on poster board and laminated, if you wish) into one large pile.
3. Hold up each picture separately and ask the students to decide if it represents a danger to albatrosses or not; put those that do in one pile, and put the others aside (you may also make a pile of pictures students are uncertain about).
4. If the students recall a piece of information, such as a particular danger, that is not represented in a picture, make a quick sketch on a piece of paper or make a picture caption by writing one or two key words on a strip of paper and adding it to the picture pile.
5. Ask the students to direct you to put the pictures and captions in the "relevant" pile into groups according to whether they are examples of the same idea, are part of (subordinate to) other pictures, or include (are superordinate to) other pictures or captions. (A chalkboard ledge is an easy sorting place that is visible to everyone.)

6. Ask the students to move the pictures and caption slips around physically until they are satisfied that they have made the most inclusive and consistent arrangement of main and subordinate categories. For example, the category *type of danger* includes subcategories such as *natural dangers*, *nonnatural dangers*, *military dangers*, *nonmilitary dangers*, *dangers to chicks*, and *dangers to adults*.
7. To help the transition from pictures to language, replace each picture with a caption on a strip of paper. Tape these to the chalkboard or wall in hierarchical, linear outline fashion (see the Appendix). This outline serves as the basis for the students' written compositions.
8. Have the students write the first draft of their essays.
9. Have the students check their own or each other's work by making an outline of their drafts, seeing if they match the outline, and determining whether the drafts or the outline needs to be reorganized.

Caveats and Options

1. For any topic, start with a few pictures and build up your collection gradually. You should have at least six or seven to start with.
2. Do not use numbering systems for outlines; vertical lines connecting categories at the same organizational levels emphasize the representation of hierarchy.
3. For more practice, use the same topic but pick a different way of categorizing the information. For example, instead of *natural dangers* versus *nonnatural dangers*, use *present dangers* versus *past dangers*. Use the same pieces of paper, moving them to fit the new organization.
4. Go back to the original whole set of pictures and repeat the process on another topic, such as *life-cycle of the albatross*. The students will select some of the same and some different pictures to include. For example, all of the dangers that might happen to a chick will be included briefly with other aspects of the chick's life.
5. Use a "zoom-lens" technique to practice expansion and contraction of supporting detail, depending on the scope of the topic. For example, after the students have outlined and written on all the dangers together, ask them to outline another composition on one danger alone, such as *natural predators*. The focus will shift so that more depth and detail will be included than in the first task.

References and Further Reading

Winer, L. (1994). Teaching classification in ESOL writing. *TESL Canada Journal, 11*, 85–98.

Appendix: Two Possible Outlines for the Same Topic

1. Dangers to Albatrosses
   Natural Dangers
     predators
       sharks
       small birds
         eat eggs
       big birds
         eat chicks
     floods
     wind
   Nonnatural Dangers
     egg hunting
     pollution
       lead paint poisoning
       litter
         plastic toys
           choking
         plastic six-pack
           drink-can rings
             strangulation
       elimination of nesting sites
         bulldozed and buried
     collisions with planes

2. Dangers to Albatrosses
   Past Dangers
     egg hunting
     lead paint poisoning
     elimination of nesting sites
       bulldozed and buried
   Present Dangers
     predators
       sharks
       small birds
         eat eggs
       big birds
         eat chicks
     floods
     wind
     litter
       plastic toys
         choking
       plastic six-pack
         drink-can rings
           strangulation
     airplanes

Contributor

Lise Winer teaches in the TESOL and Applied Linguistics programs at Southern Illinois University, Carbondale, Illinois, in the United States.

Part V: Text Analysis and Construction

Marco A. Solano and Hoang Mai Kim at Northern Virginia Community College, Alexandria, Virginia USA.

Picture This!

Levels
Intermediate +

Aims
Actively use new
vocabulary

Class Time
20 minutes with familiar
words

Preparation Time
15 minutes

Resources
Vocabulary lists
(optional)

This activity gives students the chance to practice new vocabulary that is already somewhat familiar in a meaningful way while reinforcing what they are learning in their content class. It helps students make the transition from passive knowledge of vocabulary to active use.

Procedure

1. Choose a topic related to the content being studied. The topic can be represented in the form of a picture, table, or graph but does not have to be. For example, in an ESL/humanities adjunct class, the topic could be a picture of a sculpture, building, or painting; a piece of music; a musician; a poem; or a historical period.

2. Identify 5–10 words that the students have studied and discussed previously in relation to the content of the class and that could be used to describe the picture or discuss the topic. Type up a list of these words.

3. Tell the students what the topic is (or give them a picture if the topic is a painting or sculpture). Pass out the list of review words or write them on the blackboard.

4. Divide the students into pairs.

5. Instruct them to describe the picture or discuss the topic by taking turns at using as many words as possible from their list.

6. Circulate among the students and answer questions or give hints about using the words correctly.

7. When the students are finished, review the words and the ways they can be used.

Caveats and Options

1. Have the students work in pairs or small groups with different topics or pictures and lists of words. Circulate the topics and word lists from group to group as a way of reviewing and practicing more words, or have each group report on its topic to the class.
2. Give individual assignments for homework. The next day, have the students report on their topics or pictures using the prescribed words.
3. Group work and reports for any of the variations of the activity can be either oral or written.
4. Use the activity as a vocabulary test. Give the students the topic or picture and list of words and instruct them to write a paragraph about the topic using the words. In some cases, it may be possible to have the students compare or contrast two topics (e.g., two historical periods, two works of art) using the given words.

Contributor

Maureen Andrade is an Instructor at Brigham Young University, Hawaii, in the United States. Her interests include curriculum design, content-based instruction, and teaching writing.

A Day in the Life

Levels
Intermediate +

Aims
Develop content-specific
vocabulary
Develop vocabulary
related to emotions
Relate issues in content-
area sources to real-life
situations
Discuss feelings about a
problematic societal
issue
Write informally about
this issue

Class Time
45 minutes (main
activity)
30 minutes (optional
activity)

Preparation Time
1–2 hours
30 minutes (optional
vocabulary handout)

Resources
Sets of related mounted
pictures or illustrations
(one per group)
Vocabulary development
worksheet (optional)
Learner's dictionary
(optional)

In this in-class experiential writing and read-around activity, students write a "day-in-the-life" journal entry based on a picture or photograph of an individual in a societal situation (e.g., at war, homeless). When used in conjunction with the vocabulary development worksheet, the activity provides students with a means of better expressing their own feelings (as well as the feelings of those affected) about a problematic societal issue.

Procedure

1. Form groups of four to five students. Give each group a set of 8–10 pictures or illustrations that relate to the topic of the unit being taught (e.g., Depression-era photographs for a unit on U.S. history in the 1930s; photographs of homeless people for a unit on the causes and social consequences of homelessness; photographs of individuals leaving burning buildings, looting, and defending their businesses for a unit on urban uprisings).

2. (optional) Distribute a vocabulary development worksheet (see Appendix A) and ask students to complete it, using a learner's dictionary to look up any unfamiliar words. While students are engaged in this activity, circulate and answer additional questions.

3. Ask the students to discuss the pictures (i.e., the circumstances in which they believe the individual to be, their reactions to the picture) and to silently select the picture that moves them the most.

4. Have the students write a brief "day-in-the-life" journal entry, assuming the persona of the individual depicted in their favorite picture. Instruct them to write in the first person and ask them not to overtly mention which picture they have chosen. (See Appendix B for sample journal entries.)

5. Collect the journal entries and redistribute them to different students.

6. Place one set of the pictures at the front of the room where the students can clearly see them (e.g., set them on the blackboard tray or affix them to the black- or whiteboard).

7. Have the students silently read their peer's product. Then ask for student volunteers to read a journal entry aloud. Have other students identify the picture of the person whose experience is being shared.

8. If you wish, ask the students to comment on the journal entry that they liked best.

9. Have the students collectively brainstorm the main issues that surfaced. Write these on the blackboard and have the students make connections to the source materials they have studied in the unit.

Caveats and Options

1. This activity works best once the students have already been exposed to a range of source materials in the unit (e.g., readings, video or film clips). The true purpose of A Day in the Life is to make the issues come alive for the students and have them recognize that what may appear to be dry information in an academic reading exists in the real world and affects human beings very much like themselves.

2. The start-up time for the read-around may seem unusually long. It often takes the students time to gather the courage to read aloud. Be patient. Once the activity gets going, more and more students volunteer.

3. Photography books and popular photography magazines are good sources for the picture sets, as are newspapers or magazines and illustrations from content-area textbooks.

4. To preserve the picture or photograph sets, mount them on colored cardboard. Laminate them or place them in protective plastic sheets.

References and Further Reading

Hagen, C. (1985). *American photographers of the Depression: Farm Security Administration photographs 1935–1942*. New York: Pantheon Books.

Appendix A: Student Vocabulary Development Handout

The Many Faces of America's Homeless

Directions: The mounted pictures that you have received illustrate the many faces of America's homeless—men, women, young, old, mentally stable, mentally ill, families, single people, Black, White.

1. Look at the pictures. What emotions can you see on the faces of the homeless? Put a check next to the words that you think apply. Then compare your answers with those of the other members of your group. Be prepared to explain why you answered as you did.

_____ affection		_____ hatred	
_____ anger		_____ hope	
_____ care		_____ humiliation	
_____ courage		_____ love	
_____ defiance		_____ need	
_____ depression		_____ outrage	
_____ determination		_____ pity	
_____ fear		_____ pride	
_____ greed		_____ rejection	
_____ guilt		_____ terror	

2. Now look at the pictures again. What emotions do you feel looking at these faces of America's homeless? Put a check next to the words that apply. Then compare your answers with those of the other members of your group.

_____ admiration		_____ frustration	
_____ anger		_____ guilt	
_____ awe		_____ hope	
_____ care		_____ outrage	
_____ curiosity		_____ pain	
_____ depression		_____ pity	
_____ disbelief		_____ repulsion	
_____ disgust		_____ respect	
_____ fascination		_____ sympathy	
_____ fear		_____ terror	

Appendix B: Student Products

3. Silently select the picture that you think best represents the plight of the homeless. Put yourself in the "shoes" of the individual in the picture you selected in Step 3 above. Write a diary entry for the day on which the picture was taken.

A Day in the Life of an Elderly Homeless Couple

> On April 20, 1995 after my husband & I walked hundred of miles looking for places to stay, I was very exhausted. I was cold, hungry, and tired. When I saw the bench on the sidewalk, I gave my husband a look; he knew it right away what exactly I wanted to do. Yes! It's to take a nap. Unfortunately, there was only one bench because I was sure that he would like to lie down too. But it was so sweet of him to tell me that he was alright and not tired. He could sit and watch me sleep.

A Day in the Life of an Unemployed Homeless Man

> I am a homeless. However I had no intention to become one of them. I lost my job due to unreasonable decision of my boss. This incident suddently deprived all my energy to get up early morning and find a new job. I stopped functioning as a man who use to be what I was. I stopped calling up my girl friend. Worse enough, I found myself broke. I started to go around aimlessly and started finding something to eat. Today, I found the canned food in a trash can near the station. I know I look miserable. But I don't care anymore. I discard my life.

A Day in the Life of an Elderly Homeless Woman

> Well at least today, I found fresh fruit. That's a treat after days of ramaging through garbage and only finding hard crusty bread which hurts my delaying teeth. I guess that I shouldn't complain because there are days that I can't find anything. My stomach aches from hunger. The endless hunger becomes my only existence. If I'm not hungry then I am so weak because of the lack of food. Sometimes when I remember my dreams, I recall the days of ice cream sunades with hot fudge and crunchy walnuts. I love a good medium rare lamp chops with a crisp baked potato and fresh steamed string beans.

A Day in the Life of a Homeless Vietnam Veteran

> Here I am once again thanking God that I am still alive. I've seen many of my friends die, die to the cold winter and the lack of food. Today was a very special day for me because I met a new friend. We have both lead similar life styles, but now we see ourselves as homeless poor souls who are desperately seeking the path that will bring us more blessings. I feel like an owl because I cannot sleep at night; I am scare. The sun is my only protection. The nights seem to be the most terrible nightmare that anybody could encounter. At times I feel like an eagle flying anywhere without any special journey in life. Somebody gave me $1.00 dollar today. This made my day. I finally have enough to buy something that I always want to eat, a piece of french bread. People look at me and feel horrified, but they do not know me. I am a human being just like any one of them. Life has been a dreadful process. I am glad I am alive today. Thank you God.

Contributor

Donna M. Brinton is Academic Coordinator of ESL Service Courses and a Lecturer in the Department of TESL & Applied Linguistics at the University of California, Los Angeles, in the United States.

What Does the Lecturer-Reader Want?

Levels
Intermediate +

Aims
Work out what a
content-area instructor
expects in a writing
assignment
Determine what a
writing assignment
requires
Adopt a communicative,
rhetorical approach to
essay writing

Class Time
2 hours over one or two
sessions

Preparation Time
1 hour

Resources
Blackboard or overhead
projector
Content course
assignments or essay
questions
Practice handouts

This activity is part of a program of lessons to wean students from a "knowledge-telling" approach to school writing and encourage them to take into account the audience's needs, the purpose of the writing, and the conventions operating in the discipline. The goal of this activity is to train students to abandon their preoccupation with topic information and turn their attention instead to the rhetorical situation defined by the lecturer-evaluator's intention and the tutor-reader's expectations in terms of specific rhetorical acts (e.g., discuss interpretations, make judgments about validity, measure significance, define criteria for evaluation).

Procedure

Demonstration

1. Write on the blackboard or project by means of an overhead projector a question from a content course assignment or examination paper that requires students to take a position and involves them in making judgments (e.g., *assess the influence of* X *on* Y, *critically evaluate* X, or *analyze* Y *using* X *framework*).
2. Explain the aim of the exercise: to identify in concrete and specific language what the lecturer-reader expects students to *do*, not just *say* in the essay. Explain the notion of communicative acts in academic writing and the moves involved, using an example (e.g., the act *compare* is not performed when we merely tell everything we know about the two items to be compared; the criteria used for comparing must be set out).
3. Explain the terms *instruction words* and *value words* as they apply to content course assignments. Ask the students to pick out the instruction words and value words in the question (e.g., *assess*, *influence*).

4. Show the students how to discover, by means of questions and tentative answers, the speech acts and argument moves required by the question. Encourage them to express what they assume is expected by the lecturer-reader and to verbalize their doubts. Guide the students to consider the assignment question's specific requirements not in terms of topic information but in terms of thinking and argument processes (e.g., ask, "How do we assess something?" "How can we measure influence?" "How do we demonstrate little influence or a great deal of influence?"). Write up three or four sets of questions and answers (Q and A) on the blackboard as they emerge.

Practice

5. Distribute practice handouts with the demonstration question from a content course and a few pairs of Q and A resulting from an analysis of lecturer-reader expectations (see the Appendix). Have the students form groups of three and continue the task analysis in the handout by discussing what the next likely Q is and how to answer it in a way that shows attention to *how* rather than to *what*, to argument and rhetorical strategies rather than to topic information alone.

6. Have the groups report their results to the whole class. Commend efforts that indicate attention to the speech acts and line of argument expected by the assignment; point out questions and answers that seem to focus exclusively on topic information. Direct the students' attention to argument strategies, the lecturer's intended purpose in setting the assignment, and the lecturer-reader's response to the topic information offered (e.g., ask, "What is the purpose of telling me this information?").

7. Homework: Direct the students to select an essay question or topic from a content course, analyze the instruction and value words therein, and identify the speech acts and argument moves expected by the lecturer-reader. The result should be a series of Q and A showing an understanding of what argumentative acts the essay question requires the students to perform.

Caveats and Options

1. Topic information words in an essay question can distract students from the rhetorical acts expected, especially if they denote unfamiliar knowledge or controversial issues. One solution is to take the instruction or value word out of the question and place it in a simpler context. For example, with the word *assess*, say to the class, "If you're asked to assess your parents' influence in your life, how would you do it? How would you prove 'little influence' or 'much influence'?"

2. Some essay assignments consist of only a topic with no instruction words (e.g., *logging and its ecological implications*). Guide the students to identify the questions and subquestions implied in the topic and decide what speech acts their lecturer-reader expects by drawing attention to the course objectives and advising them to note in reading material from the discipline the kinds of arguments appropriate for discourse in that discipline.

3. When students generate topic knowledge instead of Qs and As about argument moves, redirect their attention to the rhetorical problem posed by the assignment question; ask them to consider how the content knowledge will be used to develop the argument expected by the lecturer-reader and what role it will play in convincing the reader that the student's thesis is reasonable.

4. In a class of students from diverse disciplinary backgrounds, have the students pair off with someone from another discipline to discuss the output of the homework in Step 7. Working with a classmate in a different discipline ensures that the discussion does not focus on right or wrong topic information. Each student tells the other the rationale for the proposed speech acts in the essay. The partner listens and asks questions about how the lecturer-reader's expectations are being met (e.g., "Does the lecturer want a comparison? What criteria will you use?").

References and Further Reading

Bereiter, C., & Scardamalia, M. (1987). *The psychology of written composition*. Hillsdale, NJ: Erlbaum.

Appendix: Task Analysis

Essay question: *Assess the influence of Eastern religions on Western culture*.

Here are two excerpts from a student's analysis of the lecturer's expectations in the question. Discuss in your group what the next set of Q and A in each excerpt could be.

Excerpt 1

Q: What does the R (reader) expect me to do in *assess*?
A: To measure the extent of the influence. To say there is a lot of influence, or not much influence.

Q: What influence? On what?
A: The influence of the teachings perhaps of Buddhism, Hinduism, Zen, etc. on Western culture.

Q:_____
A:_____

Excerpt 2

Q: How do I show that there has been little or much influence? Describe Buddhist centers in the West, meditation practices, books on Zen—is this enough?
A:_____

Q:_____
A:_____

Contributor

Antonia Chandrasegaran is a Lecturer at Murdoch University in Perth, Australia. She teaches academic writing and reading skills in academic English and foundation courses.

Music Video Is the Story

Levels
Intermediate

Aims
Build vocabulary
Express creative ideas
Explore current popular
cultural themes

Class Time
30–40 minutes

Preparation Time
20–30 minutes

Resources
Music video with story
line
Handout with lyrics

This activity provides an entertaining and familiar structure for the fostering of creative ideas in writing and discussion. The focus is primarily vocabulary building and expansion or exploration of ideas.

Procedure

1. Locate a music video that has a clear story line and that the students have not seen.
2. Transcribe the song lyrics.
3. Play the video for the class without the sound.
4. Have the students write down all their ideas of what the video story is about.
5. Have the students share their ideas.
6. Allow the students to write one paragraph or one page about the video story.
7. Play the video with the sound as many times as the students wish.
8. Have the students identify key words and themes from the lyrics heard.
9. Hand out the written lyrics. Compare the students' stories with the actual video story line.

Caveats and Options

1. Select a video that matches the content of your course (e.g., relationships, the family, teens, U.S. culture). I used this activity in Contemporary American Society, Communication Activities, and Music ESL content courses at all levels. Try *Mmm Mmm Mmm Mmm* by the Crash Test Dummies for cross-cultural understanding and communication issues.
2. Make this activity more grammar oriented by creating a cloze test from the lyrics. Try *Tom's Diner* by Suzanne Vega.

3. Adding a video and music activity to the classroom repertoire is refreshing and enjoyable. The end result need not be a piece of writing; discussing and retelling the story keep the students engaged in the learning process.

References and Further Reading

Connell, E. L., Harrison, M. R., Hulse, M. L., Kling, J. M., Tickle, A., & Turner, J. (1995, March). *Building a content-based program: A dynamic dialogue*. Colloquium presented at the 29th Annual TESOL Convention, Long Beach, CA.

Hulse, M. L. (1994, March). *Developing a content course: A template*. Paper presented at the 28th Annual TESOL Convention, Baltimore, MD.

Contributor

Eve L. Connell is an ESL Instructor at the Monterey Institute of International Studies (MIIS) and Monterey Peninsula College as well as a Public Speaking and Business English Specialist for the MA Programs at MIIS, in the United States.

Building a Life

Levels
High intermediate +

Aims
Practice combining
sentences containing
main ideas and
background information
Recognize the
communicative purpose
of main and subordinate
clauses
Avoid plagiarism by
taking succinct reading
notes

Class Time
80 minutes over two
classes

Preparation Time
1 hour

Resources
Handout: time line

This activity allows students to practice combining sentences in a context where main ideas (conveyed in independent clauses) are distinguished from background information (grammatically subordinated). It further allows students to understand the "rule" that in sentences the "most important" information occurs in the main clause and the "less important" information occurs in the subordinate clause. Finally, the activity assists students in taking reading notes that can be the basis for original, content-based academic writing that does not sound plagiarized.

Procedure

1. Select a famous person and consult an encyclopedia or brief biography to prepare a time line that includes 10–15 major events in his or her life (see Appendix A). Leave enough space between the items on the time line for students to write down additional information about the key names, places, and concepts after consulting a secondary source.

Day 1

2. Distribute the time line. Have the students circle the name, place, or concept that is the key to understanding the significance of each element on the time line (see Appendix B).

3. For homework have the students find and write down relevant background information about all of the items identified and circled during the class discussion. Suggest that the best source for relevant information will be a book or encyclopedia article on the famous person or a native speaker who knows the cultural significance of an item. Instruct the students to write words and phrases, not complete sentences, and not to repeat information already given in the time line.

Day 2

4. Assign each item on the time line to a different pair of students. Ask each pair to compare the information they gathered, select the most relevant background information, and compose two simple sentences to write on the blackboard:
   - A simple sentence stating the information from their time line item
   - A simple sentence containing the selected relevant background information (see Appendix B).

5. Using one set of sentences on the blackboard, demonstrate the process of sentence combining by transforming one of the sentences into an adjective clause. This will be a foolproof way of demonstrating adjective clause formation because the task itself requires a name, place, or concept in the first sentence to appear in the second sentence. Show how either sentence can become the subordinate adjective clause, and discuss the basis for deciding which clause to subordinate: The life of the famous person is the *primary focus* and should therefore be in the main clause (see Appendix C).

6. Have the whole class work individually or in pairs or groups to combine their sentences on the blackboard, using adjective clauses.

7. Have the students who wrote the original sentences on the blackboard present their combined sentence to the class, explaining their choice about which sentence to subordinate as well as the correct structure and punctuation of the adjective clause.

8. As a follow-up assignment, have the students write a summary of the life of the famous person by working from their time lines, which have now been expanded with background information. Instruct them to try to use adjective clauses to include information that the reader will need to better understand the significance of the facts that they decide to include in this summary.

Caveats and Options

1. The time line itself and the finished homework assignment serve as models of effective note-taking, which requires extracting information from the language in which it is embedded. These notes provide the basis for subsequent writing on the topic in the student's own language.

2. This activity is also an exercise in asking significant questions and in recognizing what makes information significant. It helps students understand the difference between relevant and irrelevant information. For example, Martin Luther King, Jr., was born in Atlanta, Georgia, in 1929. That Atlanta is a southern city and that in 1929 it was, as other southern cities in the United States, segregated are relevant facts. It is also true that Atlanta was the site of the 1996 Olympics, but this fact is not relevant to the subject at hand.

3. To extend this activity and make it more content focused, begin by having the students work from an encyclopedia article to create the initial time line. At the next class meeting, divide the students into groups to compare time lines, check for accuracy of information, and identify key names, places, and concepts.

4. When reviewing the formation of adjective clauses, review the distinction between restrictive and nonrestrictive clauses and related punctuation rules. The clauses produced by this exercise will be largely nonrestrictive.

5. With an advanced-level class, review the grammar of reduced adjective clauses so that the students will have a wider set of options to choose from as they combine sentences.

6. Some sentences, although grammatically correct, will be overembedded and sound awkward. Help the students understand the importance of keeping the focus of the sentence on the idea in the main clause. Congratulate them on correct structure even as you help them acquire a sense of how much embedding is too much.

References and Further Reading

Chase, N. D., Gibson, S. U., & Carson, J. G. (1994). An examination of reading demands across four college courses. *Journal of Developmental Education, 18*, 10–17.

Darby, J. (1990). *Martin Luther King, Jr.* Minneapolis, MN: Lerner.

Gajdusek, L. (1995, May). *Plagiarism: A behavior or a learning issue?* Paper presented at the 1995 Georgia TESOL Conference, Athens, GA.

Gajdusek, L., & Grant, L. (1995, October). *Revising the process: Dyadic interaction and oral drafts in the ESL classroom.* Paper presented at the Southeast Regional TESOL Conference, Memphis, TN.

Shih, M. (1986). Content-based approaches to teaching academic writing. *TESOL Quarterly, 20*, 617–648.

Appendix A: Time Line, as Given to Students

TIME LINE OF EVENTS IN THE LIFE OF MARTIN LUTHER KING, JR.

1929:	Born January 15, in Atlanta, GA (father and grandfather Baptist ministers; middle-class African American family)
1944–1948:	Attended Morehouse College, Atlanta, GA
1951:	Received Bachelor of Divinity degree from Crozer Theological Seminary (graduated at the head of his class)
1953:	Married Coretta Scott (They had four children.)
1954:	Became pastor of the Dexter Avenue Baptist Church, Montgomery, Alabama
1955:	Received a PhD in theology from Boston University
1955–1956:	Bus boycott in Montgomery; MLK president of the Montgomery Improvement Association
1957:	Southern Christian Leadership Conference (SCLC) formed; MLK president
1958:	First book published, *Stride Toward Freedom: The Montgomery Story*
1959:	Trip to India to study the life and teachings of Mahatma Gandhi
1960:	Moved back to Atlanta as co-pastor with his father of Ebenezer Baptist Church Supported sit-ins organized by Atlanta students to protest segregated lunch counters in a department store. Arrested; charges dropped
1963:	Birmingham, Alabama: Demonstration to end segregated lunch counters and hiring practices. Violence, jailed "Letter From Birmingham Jail" August 28: March on Washington: "I Have a Dream" speech
1964:	Civil Rights Act passed *Time* magazine's Man of the Year Nobel Peace Prize
1965:	Selma, Alabama: Voting rights campaign
1968:	Assassinated April 4, in Memphis, Tennessee James Earl Ray later convicted

Appendix B: Time Line, as Completed by Students

TIME LINE OF EVENTS IN THE LIFE OF MARTIN LUTHER KING, JR.

1929: Born January 15, in Atlanta, GA
(father and grandfather Baptist ministers; middle-class African American family)
southern city with a large African American middle-class community

1944–48: Attended Morehouse College, Atlanta, GA
well-respected college for African American women

1951: Received Bachelor of Divinity degree from Crozer Theological Seminary
(graduated at the head of his class)
located in Chester, PA; a northern, predominantly White school for religious studies

1953: Married Coretta Scott (They had four children.)
from Alabama; studying music in Boston

1954: Became pastor of the Dexter Avenue Baptist Church, Montgomery, Alabama
segregated southern city

1955: Received a PhD in theology from Boston University
prestigious northern university

1955–1956: Bus boycott in Montgomery; MLK president of the Montgomery Improvement Association
refusal by the Black community to ride on city buses as long as they were allowed to sit only at the back. Start— arrest of Rosa Parks

1957: Southern Christian Leadership Conference (SCLC) formed; MLK president
association formed to carry on the struggle for civil rights for African Americans

1958: first book published, *Stride Toward Freedom: The Montgomery Story*
account of the Montgomery bus boycott

1959: Trip to India to study the life and teachings of Mahatma Gandhi
famous Indian leader, used nonviolent protest to win independence for India

1960:	Moved back to Atlanta as co-pastor with his father of Ebenezer Baptist Church
	Supported (sit-ins) organized by Atlanta students to protest segregated lunch counters in a department store. Arrested; charges dropped
	demonstrations for equal rights at segregated facilities
1963:	(Birmingham, Alabama) demonstration to end segregated lunch counters and hiring practices. Violence, jailed
	one of the South's "most segregated cities in 1963"
	"Letter from Birmingham Jail"
	famous justification of the civil rights movement and explanation of the philosophy of nonviolent direct action
	August 28 March on Washington "I Have a Dream" speech
	historic demonstration of national solidarity for the civil rights movement (over 200,000 Blacks and Whites at the Lincoln Mem.)
1964:	Civil Rights Act passed
	legislation prohibiting segregation in public facilities, calling for equal opportunity in education and work
	Time magazine's Man of the Year
	Nobel Peace Prize
	most prestigious acknowledgment of one person's contribution to human peace & dignity; awarded annually in Sweden
1965:	Selma, Alabama, voting rights campaign
	movement to register Black voters so that they could accomplish civil rights reform through the democratic process
1968:	Assassinated April 4, in Memphis, Tennessee
	James Earl Ray later convicted
	White drifter, escaped convict

Appendix C: Examples of Sentence Combining

a. Martin Luther King was born in Atlanta, Georgia, in 1929.
b. In 1929, Atlanta was a segregated southern city with a large, middle-class African American population.

Sentence combining, Choice 1 (focus clear—on the life of MLK):
In 1929, Martin Luther King was born in Atlanta, Georgia, which was a segregated southern city with a large, middle-class African American population.

Sentence combining, Choice 2 (focus weak—on the city, not the person):
In 1929, Atlanta, Georgia, where Martin Luther King was born, was a segregated, southern city with a large, middle-class African American population.

Note: This sentence might be perfectly appropriate in an essay about the history of Atlanta. Context and purpose determine the focus and the choice of the most important information.

Contributor

Linda Gajdusek, Assistant Director of the ESL Program at Georgia State University in the United States, develops materials for teaching grammar as meaning in literary and academic texts.

Reinforcing Content Through Visuals

Levels
Intermediate +

Aims
Describe orally a picture relating to a text
Use vocabulary and expressions from a text in oral production

Class Time
30 minutes

Preparation Time
1 hour

Resources
Pictures or photographs related to sections of a reading
Handout with vocabulary list and text extract

This activity provides a model that encourages students to speak in a meaningful context. The photograph or picture helps contextualize situations found in the reading.

Procedure

1. Ask the students to read over the text as homework.
2. In the next class, divide the students into groups. Distribute a handout containing a different part of the reading to each group and have them read it.
3. Give each group a different picture relevant to the reading passage they have read. Have them pick out words from the reading that describe the picture.
4. Have the students in turn describe the picture in groups, based on the reading and the vocabulary elicited above.
5. Ask the students to summarize their group discussion and select a representative to present the summary to the whole class.
6. Direct each student representative to talk about the group's picture.
7. Ask the students to write a journal entry about their impressions of the picture.

Caveats and Options

1. In an advanced ESL course, the content of which was the history of immigration, the students read *Farewell to Manzanar* (Houston & Houston, 1973), which deals with the Japanese American experience during and after their World War II internment. In a reprinted newspaper published during the war, I found several vivid photographs of the camp that were directly related to the book.

2. Provide prompts for the students while they are describing the picture (see Appendix A). As a follow-up activity, have the students write a journal entry about one of the characters in the photograph (see Appendix B).

3. Divide each group into two parts, giving the picture to half the group and a reading passage to the other half; in this way the second subgroup can help the first prepare for their oral description of the picture by providing the necessary information and vocabulary from the reading.

References and Further Reading

Brinton, D. (1991). The use of media in language teaching. In M. Celce-Murcia (Ed.), *Teaching English as a second or foreign language* (pp. 454–471). Rowley, MA: Newbury House.

Houston, J. W., & Houston, J. D. (1973). *Farewell to Manzanar*. New York: Bantam Books.

Appendix A: Student Handout for *Farewell to Manzanar*

Picture 1: The First Day at the Mess Hall

Directions: First describe the picture; then talk about what the first day at the mess hall was like and how the Japanese felt about their meal.

Vocabulary: *mess halls, Vienna sausage, string beans, steamed rice, apricots*

[relevant part: pp. 14–15]

Picture 2: Barracks

Directions: First describe the picture, using the following vocabulary; then talk about what the barracks were like and how the Japanese divided up their sleeping space.

Vocabulary: *pine planking, knotholes, bare bulb, oil stove, steel army cots, army blankets, mattress covers*

[relevant part: p. 15]

Picture 3: A Long Line at the Mess Hall

Directions: First describe the picture, using the following vocabulary; then talk about how the family took meals and what mess hall hopping was.

Vocabulary: *mess halls, eating as a family, Granny, mess hall hopping, eat in gangs*

[relevant part: pp. 26–27]

Picture 4: Mt. Whitney

Directions: First describe the picture, using the following vocabulary; then talk about why this mountain is significant to the Issei, the first-generation Japanese.

Vocabulary: *watercolors, purple, Whitney, Fujiyama, spiritual sustenance, powerful, inevitable*

[relevant part: pp. 70–71]

Picture 5: Baton

Directions: First describe the picture, using the following vocabulary; then talk about the class Jeannie was interested in and what brought her to it.

Vocabulary: *baton, twirling, broomstick, Nancy, "accepted," unmistakably American*

[relevant part: p. 79]

Picture 6: Odori, Japanese Traditional Dancing

Directions: First describe the picture, using the following vocabulary; then talk about how the old geisha looked and how Reiko and Mitsue teased her.

Vocabulary: *old geisha, aristocratic-looking, occult figure, Reiko, Mitsue, good skin, clothing, stockings, underpants*

[relevant part: pp. 79–81]

Appendix B: Student Journal Entries

1. The First Day at the Mess Hall

> This picture is a very good illustration to expose the a part of real life of Japanese people in Manzanar camp. Even though, unlike the concentration camp in World war II in Germany, which the Jewish people were tortured and taken into the gas room, the life of the Japanese people in the Manzanar is still not comfortable and had to be restrained by American military police. From this picture, two boys, the middle one and right one, awkwardly used the fork to eat their food, because they might not use fork before and they used to eat food by chopsticks at home. The other boy on the left was wondering How the sausage taste like? His cute face expressed a kind of interesting motion. very funny! and lovely!
>
> The author also described in the "Farewell to Manzanar": "The steamed rice had been cooked so long, and on the top of the rice a serving of canned apricots. Among the Japans, of course, rice is never eaten with sweet foods, only with salty or savory foods." But, in that situation nobody dare to complain the food which had been served.

2. Block 41

> In this picture, I can see that Jeannie's family was moved to Block 41. In this concentration camp, they have to follow various kind of rules such as lining up for the food. I thought that they were victim because they were not involved in the war. Also, they were residence in the United States for a long time. For example, Jeannie was an American-born Japanese. She did not know how to speak Japanese, but she and her family were forced to the concentration camp. In addition, the government confesciate all her family's property because they were Japanese.
>
> The government did not examine whether her family were involved in the war or not. After the war end, the government did not give any compensation. Furthermore, they have to move out within a certain period of time. I did not think that the government treat them as an American citizen, even though they reside here for a certain period of time.

3. Two Little Dancers

In this picture, there are two little dancers dressing up in traditional Japanese kimonos and performing the Japanese dance. The movements of the Japanese traditional dance are very subtle and elegant. In order to perform the dance successfully, dancers have to spend a lot of time to practice. In Farewell Manzanar, when the main character - Jeanne reached the age of ten, she was trying to learn some Japanese culture. Therefore, she once went to visit a seventy-year-old teacher who teaches odori. The teacher was a tiny, aristocratic-looking woman. She kneeled in her kimono and spoke in very gentle Japanese. From Jeannes point of view, she felt everything the old teacher did was so exotic to her. Especially when the teacher bowed to her at the end of the class, Jeanne just felt so odd and hurried out of the class. In spite of that, Jeanne was still very curious about the dancing class. She has two rich classmates- Reiko and Mitsue who were also students of the old geisha. Jeanne usually asked these girls about what happened in their dancing class. However, those girls are so insincere. They were always teasing Jeanne when she asked them.

4. Manzanar

This picture gave the feeling of how the Japanese American lived in Manzana. The houses look kind of small that build so close to each other in order to consume space. A road is on the side of the house with electrical wire running along in poles straight beside the house. The dirt road seems to be just dirt unlike many roads exist in America.

In the book of Manzana, Jeanne described her first experience as she started to live in the camp. She and her family complained about how dirty the place was including the dust roaming the whole house from the road near by. Due to many holes in the house, they all covered with dust as they slept.

Aslo from Jeanne description, the camp was very crowded. I used to live in a similar way before I came to America. So I could relate so much to Jeanne's life. When I first saw this picture, it reminds me of the camp that I used to live. It was exactly the same. Live in camp is somewhat alive since there was so many people. At the same time, it's not that clean, exciting, or comfortable. Hearlth is the main subject everyone is concentrated on since the place was too dirty.

I kind of miss the people I used to know, but I don't miss the place that much. Unlike Jeanne, my life is a little better, since I volenteered to be there. I was also very comfortable with many other Cambodians friends, on the other hand Jeanne is affraid of Asians. Reading Jeanne's book and looking at this picture, I started to remember many good and bad things that I used to experience in the camp.

5. A Long Line at the Mess Hall

A picture, "A long Line at the Mess Hall" shows Japanese residents standing in queues awaiting their turn in order to take meals at the mess halls. To maintain human beings' existence, clothes, food, and shelter are very essential. Among these necessities of life, taking meals is regarded as the most important for human beings' living. This picture describes that despite of the importance of food, how the residents had difficulty in taking meals in the mess halls.

In addition, the residents in the camp were deprived of their happiness which they can eat as a family. Mealtime is very important for not only eating but also enjoying talking at table among family members. However, a family of the residents in the mess halls could not help separating for getting better foods and eating their fill. Although Granny was too weak to walk at a distance from the barracks to the mess halls three times a day, she had to put up with such a inconvenience and sometimes, other people instead of granny brought food to her in the barracks.

In the hope of taking better foods and eating their fill at mealtime, most families of the residents scattered all direction-from this mess hall to that mess hall. While adults ate at a table, children got together and ate in gangs at another table. In fact, many children enjoyed running around the mess halls and eating with other children in meal period.

This mess hall hopping in the camp badly affected the idea of dignity or filial piety for the residents. Because many valuable table manners were entirely ignored in the mess halls, it had been very hard to recover their good old customs for the residents in the camp.

Through that I see and describe this picture, I can really recognize that the indignitities of forced detention had given the residents in the camp not only physical pain but also spiritual pain. Furthermore, the lives in the camp seem to have had badly affected mental heritage for the residents.

Contributor

Tetsuo Harada is a doctoral student in the Department of TESL & Applied Linguistics at the University of California, Los Angeles, in the United States, where he teaches an advanced ESL course.

Taking Students Beyond Content

Levels
Intermediate +

Aims
Learn the role of form,
purpose, audience, and
background in reading
and writing

Class Time
2–3 hours

Preparation Time
10–30 minutes

Resources
Two or more familiar
texts of the same genre
Handout

Students tend to consider content the most important factor in under-standing and producing written discourse. Encouraged by their ESL/EFL textbooks, they are most concerned with learning and using vocabulary or understanding and stating "the main idea." In their efforts, they often miss other text elements that are essential to text processing. The purpose of this activity is for students to understand that elements other than content within and outside of texts are essential to text comprehension and production. If they are to read, write, or listen intelligently, they must consider the writer's and readers' purposes, their communities and experiences with texts, and the interactions of these factors with text structure, grammatical form, argumentation, and content in the production of a specific text.

Procedure

1. Selecting a text: Select, or have students select, at least two texts of the same genre (i.e., that are generally identified by the same name) that are familiar to the students and easy for them to read (e.g., flyers or bulletins, newsletters, wedding invitations, advertisements, obituaries). If possible, consider texts in both the students' first languages and English.

2. Analyzing the genre: Create a handout like the one in the Appendix, which assists students in analyzing the genre of automobile advertisements. In groups of no more than four, have the students examine the chosen texts and answer the following questions:
   - Naming: What would you call these readings? Why are they called *X* (e.g., in the Appendix, *automobile advertisements*)? How can we identify the general features or purposes of this type of reading? How are these texts different from (or like) other texts

that you read? (How do advertisements differ from readings in your textbooks or from other genres in newspapers, such as editorials?)

- Locating: Where do you find these texts in English? Do you find similar texts in your native language? (Does your native-language newspaper have a classified section?)
- Analyzing the content: What kinds of information do you expect to find in these texts? (List and classify what you find according to categories of meaning or with other classification criteria.)
- Analyzing the form: How are these texts organized? (In the case of advertisements, why aren't they organized in paragraphs?) What kinds of grammatical items do these texts include? Why do you think certain tenses are used? (Note: The kinds of questions posed here will depend on the chosen genre.)
- Establishing the writer's and reader's purposes: Why would a person write this kind of text? (Or, what is the writer's purpose?) Why do people read this kind of text? What information would they read for? (Or, what do *you* read a text like this for? What information would you look for first?) Is there a relationship between the way in which these texts are organized, the reader's purposes, and the way that the reader processes this text? (Or, are these texts easy to read? Why?) Is there a relationship between the layout and grammar and the readers' and writer's purposes? (Note: This question can lead to a lesson on particular grammatical items and their functions within the text.)
- Examining features of the selected texts: What is particularly notable about the texts you are examining, if anything? How are they different from each other? What kinds of audiences were they written for? How do you know? What kinds of publications might they be found in? Is one text more successful than the other? Why?

3. Producing the genre: After groups of students have examined their chosen texts in some detail, direct them to develop goals for producing their own texts in this genre, specifying their audience(s), their purposes, and the particular structural or lexical choices they must make to be consistent with audience and purpose. (In the case of advertisements, the students wrote texts that attempted to sell a car owned by one of the group members.)

4. Developing criteria for evaluation: Based on the various rhetorical factors considered in the exercise (audience, writer's purposes, basic genre elements, predicted content and form), have the whole class develop criteria and scoring procedures for evaluating the text type being considered.

5. Presenting and evaluating: Have the groups present their texts to other groups, discussing their audiences, their purposes, and the linguistic and organizational choices they have made while other groups evaluate the texts using the criteria developed in Step 4.

Caveats and Options

1. The purpose of beginning this ongoing exercise with familiar texts is to remind the students of what they know implicitly: that content is only one of many elements that make texts successful for specific audiences in particular rhetorical situations. Thus, when examining two textbooks on the same subject, they can consider the authors' purposes and assumptions about readers in light of the text structure and presentation of content. The students are also more aware of rhetorical factors when writing. When examining an essay question for a content class, for example, they consider the ways in which content has been presented in a course, the values of the discipline, the expectations of the particular content instructor, and, not incidentally, possible content and argumentation to use in answering the question.

2. Once the students have analyzed familiar texts, move to other, less familiar texts to which the students are exposed—in the university setting, lab reports, student essays, or genres from certain disciplines, such as short monographs or first-person accounts. Ask the students to notice the various rhetorical elements influencing these texts, considering how these elements play central roles in the creation and processing of discourses within particular situations. Also ask genre-based questions, such as "What are the essential elements of lab reports?" "How can you tell the difference between a lab report and a research article?" Each such exercise takes about 30 minutes.

3. Because many students are more visual than print oriented, try this exercise with films. Before showing a film produced by the Soviet Union during the 1930s, for example, I asked the students to consider

the following when watching: Who produced this film? What were their purposes? Who was the intended audience? What effects did the filmmakers use to achieve their purposes (e.g., music and lighting, photographic angles)? Have the students answer these questions in groups after viewing the film; then discuss how successful the film was in achieving its purposes.

References and Further Reading

Berkenkotter, C., & Huckin, T. N. (1993). Rethinking genre from a sociocognitive perspective. *Written Communication, 10*, 475–509.

Bhatia, V. K. (1993). *Analyzing genre: Language use in professional settings*. London: Longman.

Freedman, A., & Medway, P. (Eds.). (1994). *Learning and teaching genre*. Portsmouth, NH: Heinemann/Boynton Cook.

Johns, A. M. (1994). Using classroom and authentic genres: Student initiation into academic writing. In D. Belcher & G. Braine (Eds.), *Academic writing in a second language: Essays on research and pedagogy* (pp. 277–292). Norwood, NJ: Ablex.

Swales, J. M. (1990). *Genre analysis: English in academic and research settings*. London: Longman.

Appendix: Handout

Below are texts of the same genre taken from a newspaper. In small groups, answer the questions about these texts.

985 AUTOS FOR SALE
CHEVROLET '89 Corvette. Special buy & priced to sell. $9,995. 942-7883 dir.
CHEVROLET '90 Celebrity Wagon V-6 auto, AC, pwr wind/locks. 3rd seat & more. #124516. $5950. WESTCOLL MAZDA 474-1591.

985 AUTOS FOR SALE
CHEVROLET '93 CAVALIER RS auto, ps, air, tilt, low mi. #248662, $9,990. COAST NISSAN 942-1717
CHRYSLER '93 LeBaron Convertible GTC, 6 cyl. leather, all the goodies w/ the premium times. $13,005 #572795 San Diego Nissan/Suzuki 280-2252

CHEVROLET '90 Camaro RS V8 Auto., loaded like new $7995 dir 679-1900

CHEVROLET '91 CAMARO RS V8, loaded, low miles. Sharp! #3CT J289. $8,995
BOB BAKER JEEP EAGLE
CHECK US OUT! 929-0072

CHEVROLET '91 Corsica V-6, auto, air, ps, ob, tilt, pl, am-fm stereo, xlt cond., airbag, 54K mi CHEVROLET '91 Cavalier. $6,495, auto, AC, AW/FM, super clean! #131137
COLONIAL FORD. 477-7443.
$6495. 483-8028.

CHRYSLER '70 Newport convt. new paint top tires, 1 owner, 272-5605

CHRYSLER '78 Le Baron 4 dr. am-fm tape stereo, could use tuneup otherwise runs great, dependable $675 516-9255

CHRYSLER '79 Newport 4 dr, V8, new tires, xlnt, 1 ownr. $1250. Brkr 480-9346.

CHRYSLER '84 LeBaron, 4 dr. 4 cyl. auto, PS, P wndws, dig. AM-FM cass., air. xlnt cond $1995/offer 763-0059.

1. Naming: What are these texts called? Why are they called *X*?
2. Locating: Where do you find these texts in English? Do you find similar texts in your native language newspapers?
3. Analyzing the content: What kinds of information do you expect to find in these texts? Why? (Classify this information.)
4. Analyzing the form: How are these texts organized? What kinds of grammatical items do these texts include? What are the reasons for these organizational choices?
5. Establishing the writer's and readers' purposes: Why would a person write this kind of text? For what reasons does a person read this kind of text? How do you, as a reader, read this text? Do you start at the top? What do you look for first? Second? What is the relationship between form, content, and the readers' and writer's purposes?
6. Examining the features of the selected texts: What is particularly notable about the texts you are examining, if anything? How are they different from each other? What kinds of audiences are they written for? Is one text more successful than the other? Why?

Now it's your turn to write a text:

1. Ask members of your group about the cars that they own. Select one car from the group and, using the owner's description, write an advertisement for it.
2. What makes an auto advertisement good? Why? With the rest of the class, write criteria for a good auto advertisement.
3. Present your group's advertisements to the other groups and listen to their critique. What is particularly good about your advertisement? Why? What could be improved?

Contributor

Ann M. Johns is a Professor of Linguistics and Writing Studies at San Diego State University, in the United States, where she co-directs the linked (adjunct) class program for freshmen and teaches classes in applied linguistics and academic reading and writing. For 8 years she was Co-Editor of English for Specific Purposes: An International Journal.

Making the Most of Office Hours

Levels
Intermediate +; college/
university

Aims
Become more confident
when communicating
with course instructors

Class Time
10–15 minutes

Preparation Time
15 minutes

Resources
Handout with
suggestions

This activity (a) promotes interaction among students and content-course instructors outside of the classroom setting and (b) gives students individual feedback on content-specific and language issues.

Procedure

1. Ask the students whether or not they usually visit their course instructors during their office hours. Have the students discuss why doing so could be beneficial.
2. Require the students to meet with you outside of class at least once during the term.
3. Distribute one copy of the handout Making the Most of Office Hours (see the Appendix) to each student.
4. Seat the students in groups of four, and instruct the groups to study the open-ended questions on the handout and to think of two questions for you—a content question and a language question—based on your lectures or course assignments.
5. Make appointments to have the students meet with you in pairs for 15 minutes during your office hours.

Caveats and Options

1. This activity lends itself to adjunct courses. It was developed for an ESL/Introduction to Political Science adjunct course in response to the content professor's concern that her ESL students failed to take advantage of her office hours. In the political science course, the students were required to meet with the content instructor in return for points toward their final grade. In the ESL course, the students developed the questions and, after meeting with the content instructor, shared some of the information they had obtained with the rest of the ESL class.

2. Suggest that the students prepare an "agenda" prior to meeting with the content instructor. This will help break the ice when meeting with the content instructor for the first time.

References and Further Reading

Brinton, D. M., Snow, M.A., & Wesche, M. B. (1989). *Content-based second language instruction.* Boston: Heinle & Heinle.

Snow, M. A. (1993). (Ed.). *Project LEAP: Learning-English-for-Academic-Purposes. Training manual, year two.* Los Angeles: California State University/Fund for the Improvement of Postsecondary Education.

Snow, M. A., & Kamhi-Stein, L. D. (Eds.). (1996). *Teaching academic literacy skills: Strategies for content faculty.* Los Angeles: California State University/Fund for the Improvement of Postsecondary Education.

Appendix: Making the Most of Office Hours

Meeting with your instructors during their office hours is an important part of the university experience. This activity will help you clarify key concepts and become more confident when talking to your instructors.

When you talk to your instructor, you can use the expressions below:

Useful Expressions

Excuse me, Dr. _____, may I interrupt you?

Excuse me, Dr. _____, could I ask you a question?

Excuse me, but I have a question regarding _____.
Could you clarify that concept for me?

I am still not clear on the concept of _____.

I am sorry, but I did not understand the part about _____.

Before you visit the professor during office hours:

1. Write a question or think about a concern you may have regarding:
   - lecture material
   - the information presented in the textbook.
2. Write a question about a language term that you are unsure of (e.g., the term *watershed*).

3. Prepare a written "agenda." If you get nervous, you can always refer to your notes.
4. By [date], go to your instructor's office and have him or her answer your questions.

Contributors

Lía D. Kamhi-Stein is an Assistant Professor in Educational Foundations and Interdivisional Studies and was a language specialist for Project LEAP: Learning-English-for-Academic-Purposes; Nadine Koch is an Associate Professor in Political Science; and Marguerite Ann Snow is an Associate Professor in Educational Foundations and Interdivisional Studies and conducts faculty training across the disciplines as director of Project LEAP, all at California State University, Los Angeles, in the United States.

The Multistep Writing Assignment

Levels
Intermediate +

Aims
Learn skills needed in the various phases of a writing assignment

Class Time
Variable

Preparation Time
1 hour

Resources
Handout with guidelines on the writing assignment

The "one-shot" writing assignment typically allows little opportunity to teach students how to write for an academic audience. The multistep assignment, on the other hand, guides students through the writing process, teaching students the skills underlying the assignment (e.g., doing library research, interviewing informants, summarizing sources and preparing a literature review, analyzing data, reaching conclusions). Moreover, students benefit along the way from peer and instructor feedback.

Procedure

1. Select a topic that your students will enjoy working with for an extended period of time.
2. Develop guidelines for completing the multistep writing assignment (e.g., the different sections in the paper, the kind of information that the students are expected to present in each section, a list of sources that the students are expected to use, deadlines).
3. Distribute the guidelines for the paper and encourage a discussion on the requirements of the writing assignment. (See Appendixes A–D for examples of multistep writing assignments from various disciplines.)
4. Provide the students with models of well-written sections of papers.
5. During the multistep writing assignment, require the students to do some or all of the following:
   - Participate in a library instructional session
   - Complete a graded library assignment that requires the students to identify sources to be used in their paper
   - Write, turn in, and receive feedback on a draft of one (or more) section(s) of the paper
   - Revise the various drafts and turn in the final paper

Caveats and Options

1. This activity lends itself to theme-based, sheltered, and adjunct courses. It was developed for general education courses that required the students to complete a research paper assignment (Snow, 1993, 1994).
2. Adapt the phases in the writing assignment to your content and scheduling needs. You may want to have the students complete the writing assignment in two or more phases.

References and Further Reading

Brinton, D. M., Snow, M.A., & Wesche, M. B. (1989). *Content-based second language instruction*. Boston: Heinle & Heinle.

Esquivel, L. (1992). *Como agua para chocolate*. New York: Doubleday.

Galarza, E. (1971). *Barrio boy*. Notre Dame, IN: University of Notre Dame Press.

Gillenkirk, J., & Motlow, J. (1987). *Bitter melon: Stories from the last rural Chinese town in America*. Seattle: University of Washington Press.

Kamhi-Stein, L. D., & Stein, A. (1995, Fall). Electronic databases and information services: Integrating their use into the requirements of your syllabus. *Instructionally Speaking, 6*, 5–6.

Mahmoody, M. (1987). *Not without my daughter*. New York: St. Martin's Press.

McMillan, T. (1992). *Waiting to exhale*. New York: Viking Press.

Nash, G. (1990). *The American people: Creating a nation and society* (2nd ed.). New York: Harper & Row.

Snow, M.A. (1993). Discipline-based foreign language teaching: Implications for ESL/EFL. In M. Krueger & F. Ryan (Eds.), *Language and content: Discipline- and content-based approaches to language study*. Lexington, MA: D. C. Heath.

Snow, M. A. (1994). Collaboration across disciplines in postsecondary education: Attitudinal challenges. *The CATESOL Journal, 7*, 59–64.

Snow, M. A., & Kamhi-Stein, L. D. (Eds.). (1996). *Teaching academic literacy skills: Strategies for content faculty*. Los Angeles: California State University and the Fund for the Improvement of Postsecondary Education.

Tan, A. *The joy luck club*. (1988). New York: Putnam.

Zich, A. (1977). *The rising sun*. Alexandria, VA: Time-Life Books.

Appendix A: The Multistep Writing Assignment in Political Science

Topics:

- Campaign finance in the U.S. presidential election
- Campaign ads in the election
- New uses of the media—cable TV, satellite TV, MTV—in the election
- The use of public opinion polls in the election
- The role of independent parties in the election
- Young voters and the election

Phases:

After selecting a topic, you will be asked to write the research paper in two different phases:

Phase 1. Review of the Literature, and a Bibliography. Due on _____. The Review of the Literature consists of the summaries of articles on your assigned topic. In the review of the literature, you have to summarize eight articles in no more than four double-spaced typed pages.

Phase 2. Complete paper. Due on _____. The complete research paper will include four distinct sections:
Section I : Introduction and Statement of the Problem
Section II: Review of the Literature
Section III: Discussion and Conclusion
Section IV: Bibliography

Selecting the articles for the review of the literature:

Select no more than two articles from each of the four sources below:

1. Newspapers

    New York Times, Los Angeles Times, Washington Post, Wall Street Journal, Christian Science Monitor

    You are not allowed to use *USA Today*.

2. Magazines

   Time, Newsweek, U.S. News & World Report

3. TV/Radio News Programs

   Nightline, The Newshour With Jim Lehrer, network news, National Public Radio programs

4. Political Journals

   American Political Science Review, California Journal, Gallup Opinion Poll, New Republic, National Review, National Journal, Public Opinion Quarterly

Appendix B: The Multistep Writing Assignment in Animal Biology

Guidelines for the Scientific Paper

Topic:

Chronobiology: The Study of Biological Rhythms

Phases

The scientific paper will be written in different phases:
Phase 1. Data collection: Personal chronobiology and library exercise. DUE ON _____
Phase 2. First draft of Materials and Methods. DUE ON _____
Phase 3. First draft of Results and Literature Cited. DUE ON _____
Phase 4. First draft of Introduction. DUE ON _____
Phase 5. First draft of Discussion. DUE ON _____
Phase 6. Final version of the complete paper. DUE ON _____

Selecting the Sources

The journal articles cited in your paper should be selected from the following sources: *Scientific American*, *Science News*, *Science* (News and Comment section), *Nature* (News and Comment section), *Psychology Today*, and *Discover*.

Writing the Introduction

1. The Introduction should comprise two to three paragraphs maximum.
2. The Introduction should provide a scientific perspective. How does your topic fit into the context of biology?
3. The Introduction should familiarize the reader with your topic. Tell the reader what the literature has to say about your topic. For this purpose, you need to cite two or three references that contain information pertaining to your topic.
4. The Introduction should resemble a "book report." This means that when you cite the literature, you have to be objective.
5. In the last sentence of the Introduction, you should state your hypothesis or the purpose of the study.

Writing the Materials and Methods Section

1. The Materials and Methods section should detail exactly what you did to collect your data. The detail should be such that, with only your report to follow, a fellow scientist could repeat the experiment.
2. In completing the chronobiology paper, tell the reader that the data, consisting of your pulse measurement, eye-hand coordination, and adding speed, were collected at the time you woke up and went to bed, and at other time points during the 24-hour day. In addition, describe the procedures you followed in measuring your pulse and eye-hand coordination and your adding speed.

Writing the Results Section

The Results section of a scientific paper describes the data collected. The Results section should include:

- A description of the data collected, and
- A visual presentation of the data collected in the form of tables or figures. The same data should not be presented more than once, and your tables and figures should:
    - Be self-explanatory. This means that the reader has to understand the results by looking at the tables or figures only.

— Have a number and a title. If your tables or figures include symbols, you need to explain what they mean.
— Be referred to by name (e.g., *see Fig. 1*) in the text.

Writing the Discussion Section

1. The Discussion section should explain what your results mean.
2. Interpret your results in terms of previous experiments published in the scientific literature. For this purpose, you need to cite five or six journal articles (from the journals listed earlier) on the topic of chronobiology. Decide whether or not your findings support the literature on the topic you are investigating.
3. In one paragraph, explain any errors you may have made in the data collection process. Explain how the experiment could be improved.
4. The last paragraph in the Discussion section should include a general conclusion.

Writing the Literature Cited Section

1. Abumrad, N. N., D. Rabin, M. P. Diamond, and W. W. Lacy. Use of a heated superficial hand vein as an alternative site for the measurement of amino acid concentrations and for the study of glucose and alanine kinetics in man. *Metab. Clin. Exp.* 30:936–940, 1981.
2. Bergstrom, J., P. Furst, L. O. Noree, and E. Vinnars. Intracellular free amino acid concentration in human muscle tissue. *J. Appl. Physiol.* 36:693–697, 1974.

Below is an explanation of how you should arrange your references.

1. Number the references (as in the examples above).
2. List the references in alphabetical order. Start with the first author's last name and initials (e.g., Abumrad, N. N.). Continue with the second author's initials and last name (e.g., D. Rabin).
3. Include the title of the article in lowercase. (Use of a heated superficial hand vein as an alternative site for the measurement of amino acid concentrations and for the study of glucose and alanine kinetics in man.)

Appendix C: The Multistep Writing Assignment in U. S. History

4. Include the title of the journal in italics or underlined, capitalizing the first letter in each word (*Metab. Clin. Exp.*). Include the volume number (30:), page numbers (936–940), and year of publication (1981).

Based on lectures, *Barrio Boy*, the "Ping Lee" reading from *Bitter Melon*, and chapter 19 of Nash, answer the following question in a well-thought-out essay:

> Can we speak of an immigrant experience or must we speak of immigrant experiences? Were the experiences of different immigrant groups more similar than different, or more different than similar? (3 or more typed pages)

1. In order to answer the question, make two lists:
   - Evidence that shows similar experiences
   - Evidence that shows different experiences
2. Turn in the lists (one page—does not have to be typed).
3. There is no one specific right answer, although the evidence can be applied correctly or incorrectly. You have data to support both sides of the question, but you must decide which side is more convincing to you. To convince the reader of your choice, you must not ignore the evidence and arguments supporting the alternative positions.
   - Remember, all good papers have a thesis.
   - Be general when you talk about immigrant experiences.
   - Be specific when you discuss Galarza's family, for example.
   - Use as many different kinds of examples to support your thesis as you can, but do not describe the examples. For example, when you mention the extended family, do not discuss each family member. You may assume that I have read the material and know the details of the examples.
4. Plagiarism is "the unauthorized use or close imitation of the language and thoughts of another author and the representation of them as one's own original work" (*Random House Dictionary of the English Language*, s.v. "plagiarism"). Since this is an exam, you may use ideas from all of the assigned readings without footnotes,

but you may not copy the authors' exact words without footnotes. If you quote, write the author's last name and the page number in parentheses after the quotation, for example (Nash, p. 400). Please do not change one or two words and call the sentence yours.

5. Please write your name on a separate cover sheet. Staple the pages together. No fancy binders, please.

Steps in Answering the Take-Home Assignment in U.S. History

1. Ask yourself what the question requires. What must be included? What must be excluded? Try out some possible theses. Figure out different ways to organize your paper.
2. Gather the following information:
   - Look over the lecture(s) and write down all of the useful categories of information, such as *extended family*.
   - As you read *Barrio Boy* and "Ping Lee," compare their experiences and the categories in the lectures.
   - Finally, look over chapter 19 of Nash for examples of different and similar immigrant experiences.
3. You should have a relatively long list, 20–25 items. You may have to group the items into categories. For example, all of the information on families may go in a single category and may end up in one paragraph.
4. Now you have to decide whether you think the immigrant experiences were more different or more similar. Your answer will be your thesis.
5. Outline your paper.
   - State your thesis in the introductory paragraph.
   - In the next few paragraphs present your evidence on either the similarities or the differences. In the last few paragraphs discuss the opposing view.
   - Restate your thesis in the concluding paragraph.
6. Does your outline organize your evidence to support your thesis?
7. Write the paper.

8. Edit the paper.
- Write an outline from your paper. Did your paper follow your original outline? Did it answer the question?
- Make sure that you have your thesis in the introduction, the conclusion, and the beginning of each of the two major sections of your paper.
- Check the topic sentence in each paragraph to see if it, in fact, does introduce the remainder of the paragraph.
- Check for errors—for example, in grammar and spelling. Be alert for the mistakes that you commonly make.

Appendix D: The Multistep Writing Assignment in Cultural Anthropology

Read either *Rising Sun* (Japanese culture), *The Joy Luck Club* (Chinese culture), *Waiting to Exhale* (African American culture), *Not Without My Daughter* (Iranian culture), or *Like Water for Chocolate* (Mexican culture). Make sure you choose a novel about an ethnic group other than your own. Take notes on what you learned about that culture from the novel. Next, interview at least three people who are members of the ethnic group portrayed in the novel regarding how accurately the novel depicts the cultures described. Then write a five- to eight-page (typed, double-spaced) paper discussing the above two issues. Papers will be graded on content, appearance, and writing style.

Objectives

1. To give students practice in reading works of popular fiction that focus on various ethnic groups and in evaluating the accuracy of the cultural information presented.
2. To give students experience in collecting data utilizing a primary anthropological technique—interviewing.
3. To give students the opportunity to learn about another ethnic group by talking to several members of that group.

Thus, the assignment has three basic parts:

1. Present cultural information from the novel about the group discussed. The information should be organized according to the topics covered in class (e.g., the information learned about their values,

world view, kinship system, marriage and family practices, economic system, religious beliefs). Do not simply list points, but present an organized description of the culture.

2. Interview several (three to five) members of that ethnic group (refer to them as *informants*). Look specifically for the points covered in the novel. Discuss how the information presented by the novelist is supported or contradicted by the informants.

3. Evaluate how accurately the novelist presented the cultural material. If there are discrepancies—i.e., differences between what the novelist had to say and what the informants said—analyze why they exist. Was the novelist biased? Was he or she presenting individual rather than cultural behavior? Was the information simply related to a plot? Were the informants biased? If so, in what way? Do the different informants give the same or contradictory information? If it is contradictory, why?

How to Do the Assignment

1. Read the novel.
   - As you read, underline any information given about the culture. (See the sample sheets at the end of this handout for the kinds of cultural data to note.)
2. Select your informants.
   - Choose three to five people who are members of the ethnic group you are reading about. Try to get both first- and second-generation informants. Consider interviewing other members of the class who are from the culture depicted in the novel.
3. Make a list of cultural elements.
   - Copy the passages you underlined in Step 1 onto several sheets of paper. Be sure to note the number of the page where you found the information near each point you list.
   - Next, organize your notes into topics (e.g., values, religion, death and dying). We will be doing an in-class exercise to help you with the process of categorization.
   - Go over your list. For each item you have listed, ask yourself, "What does this say about [Mexican, Chinese, etc.] culture?"

Write it down on another sheet of paper; you will need it in Step 6. If it doesn't say anything about the culture, then it may just be about the character or plot of the novel. In that case, do not include it in your list of cultural elements.

4. Write a one-page (typed, double-spaced) description of the culture (Cultural Description).
   - Do not include any quotations; just give the most important information you learned about the culture. Write it in essay form. Turn it in.

5. Turn in your revised list of cultural elements along with your one-page description of the culture.
   - See the handout entitled Sample List of Cultural Elements.

6. Rephrase the description of each cultural item in your own words.
   - List each bit of information you get about the culture on a separate sheet of paper. (Look at the description of the culture that you wrote in Step 4. This will help you write the statements.) For example, "On page 94 of *Like Water for Chocolate*, it states, 'Only Tita, whose mission it was to serve her until death, was allowed to be present during this ritual, to see her mother naked.'" The cultural information here is that female modesty is very important in Mexican culture.
   - Turn your statements into questions for the interview. For example, you might ask, "Is modesty important for women in your culture? Can you give me some examples?"
   - List each question at the top of a separate sheet of paper, which you will use to write your informants' answers during the interviews.

7. Interview your informants.
   - Ask them the questions you wrote about the cultural elements in Step 6. Be sure to have them give you specific examples that support their view. (Again, write the responses of each informant to the same topic on the same page, but be sure to note whom you are interviewing.)

8. Turn in your list of informants' views.
   - See the handout entitled Sample List of Informants' Views.

9. Write the first draft of your paper.

10. Write the second draft of your paper. Turn it in.
11. Write the final draft of your paper.
   ● Integrate the suggestions I made on your second draft. Take it to the Writing Center for help if necessary.
12. Turn in your paper.

How to Write the Paper

1. The introduction of your paper should state the name of the book you selected and the culture described. Give the name of the novelist, his or her ethnic background, and his or her "credentials" to describe that culture. (You may be able to get this information from the book jacket, or you may need to find a newspaper or magazine interview with the author.)

2. You should then state the sources you used to evaluate the cultural material—the names of the people you interviewed. (You may use pseudonyms to protect their privacy. Do not use initials, however; they are not as easy to read and do not indicate gender.) Be sure to provide relevant background information about your informants: for example, their age, gender, how long they lived in their native country, how long they have been in the United States, whether they live in an ethnically diverse community or a homogeneous one, how well you know them, why you chose them. In addition, state your research methodology: Did you tape-record the interviews? Take notes? Write notes from memory? Did your informants appear to be comfortable? Were they telling the truth? The purpose of this information is to help your reader assess the validity of your informants' statements.

3. Then state the major topics you will discuss (e.g., values, marriage and family patterns, religious beliefs). Much of the material you used in your one-page cultural description will be used here.

4. In the body of your paper (Parts 1 and 2 from Objectives), present what the novelist had to say about each topic (e.g., religious beliefs) and then compare that with what the informants had to say on that same point. (Note: Select five to eight of the most important or interesting cultural elements to write about in your paper.)

5. The conclusion (Part 3 from Objectives) of your paper should discuss how accurately (or inaccurately) the novelist presented the culture. Analyze any discrepancies.

Target Audience

An intelligent college student who is taking this course but has not read the novel.

Citations

When you cite information from the novel, either state the author's name followed by the page number (e.g., Crichton states . . . (p. 74).) or refer to the title of the book (e.g., In *Rising Sun* . . .). If it is a direct quotation, use quotation marks. If you are paraphrasing, you do not need quotation marks.

When you cite information from your sources, be sure to provide the source.

Example from *Rising Sun*:

Connor, the main character in *Rising Sun,* mentions the ethnocentrism of the Japanese several times. For example, he states that "everyone who is not Japanese is a barbarian . . . a stinking, vulgar, stupid barbarian. They're polite about it because they know that you can't help the misfortune of not being born Japanese" (p. 20). My informant agreed that the Japanese are ethnocentric, stating, "They are a very nationalistic people, although they will be polite to your face."

Please note the following:

1. Book titles are always capitalized and underlined or italicized (e.g., The Joy Luck Club or *The Joy Luck Club*).
2. The punctuation mark (e.g., a period) goes after the page number, not after the quotation—for example, "They're polite about it because they know that you can't help the misfortune of not being born Japanese" (p. 20).

Evaluation Criteria

The paper will be worth a maximum of 50 points. It will be evaluated on the following points:

1. How completely you present the cultural data included in the novel and how well it is organized/categorized (30%)
2. How well you relate the data from the informants to the material from the novel
3. Presentation of background data on the informants (10%)
4. How well you discuss the accuracy of the novel (20%)
5. Your overall organization, writing style, grammar, spelling, and presentation of your research methodology (10%)

Due Dates

April 4: Select your novel. Turn in a sheet of paper with the name of the novel to the instructor.

April 13: Turn in a list of informants you will be using, including a few sentences describing each and why you chose them.

April 25: Bring a list of cultural elements from your novel to class. Turn in a one-page, typed Cultural Description.

April 27: Turn in your notes, organized into anthropological categories, on the cultural information presented in the novel. (See the handout entitled Sample List of Cultural Elements for further details.) This must be typed.

May 11: Turn in a list of informants' views on the same topics. (See the handout entitled Sample List of Informants' Views.) This must be typed, double spaced.

May 18: Turn in a rough draft of your final paper. It must be typed, double spaced. If you make a significant number of grammatical errors, I will make a note to that effect on your draft. You must then take your paper to the Writing Center for help before turning in your final draft.

June 1: Turn in the final paper.

Points will be deducted from your final grade for any late material at the rate of 1 point per day. It is better to turn the paper in early than to take a chance on turning it in late.

REMEMBER TO HAVE FUN AND ENJOY THE NOVEL!

Contributors

Nadine Koch is Associate Professor of Political Science; Beverly Krilowicz is Associate Professor of Biology; Carole Srole is Associate Professor of History and was named CSLA 1995 Outstanding Professor; Geri-Ann Galanti is Assistant Professor of Anthropology; Lía D. Kamhi-Stein is Assistant Professor of Educational Foundations and Interdivisional Studies and was a language specialist for Project LEAP: Learning-English-for-Academic-Purposes; and Marguerite Ann Snow is Associate Professor of Educational Foundations and Interdivisional Studies and conducts faculty training across the disciplines as Director of Project LEAP, all at California State University, Los Angeles, in the United States.

Finding a Critical Voice I (Summary and Evaluation)

Levels
Advanced

Aims
Identify the discourse
structure of review
articles
Differentiate the
functions of summary
and evaluation in a
review article

Class Time
1 hour

Preparation Time
1 hour

Resources
Five review articles from
an academic journal or
journals
Review article
photocopied onto an
overhead transparency
Overhead projector

This activity and the two that follow take the form of a discourse analysis of a number of review articles. The main purpose of this activity is to demonstrate to students the dialogic nature of much academic writing and inquiry. On one side of the dialogue is the represented voice of other writers (summarization); on the other is the critical voice of the reviewer/ student (evaluation). This activity, the first in a sequence of three 1-hour activities, looks at how these two voices are differentiated linguistically. Finding a Critical Voice II focuses further on summarization, and Finding a Critical Voice III focuses on evaluation. At the conclusion of this sequence, students can be asked to write their own review of a text.

Procedure

1. Locate a selection of review articles from a journal or journals related to the students' academic backgrounds. Each article will preferably be no longer than one page and be a review of a single text.
2. Hand out one review to the students to skim. Ask them to identify the purpose of the text. Ask them also to identify (a) the author of the review, (b) the author of the original text, and (c) the title of the original text. (See Finding a Critical Voice III, Appendix A, for sample reviews.)
3. Write the following categories and their designations on the black-board.

> S = summary of the original text
> E = evaluation of the original text
> E+ = a positive evaluation of the original text
> E– = a negative evaluation of the original text
> E? = a neutral or ambiguous evaluation of the original text
> S/E = a combination of summary and evaluation
> O = other information, such as biographical information
>   about the author

4. Display the review on an overhead projector.
5. As a class, study each sentence of the review and assign it to one of the categories above. Ask the students which linguistic devices help them decide on the category, especially how to distinguish summary from evaluation.
6. From the annotations on the overhead transparency, sketch the discourse structure of the review on the blackboard. (See Finding a Critical Voice III, Appendix A, for sample analyses.)
7. Hand out additional review articles to the class. Have the students repeat Steps 5 and 6 in groups of three.
8. After the students have completed Step 7, ask for volunteers to sketch the discourse structure of each review article on the blackboard. Discuss any variations.

Caveats and Options

1. This activity was used with a group of prospective international relations graduate students who had had little experience of evaluative writing. It is most suitable for adjunct classes but can also be used with students from mixed disciplines. It is a useful starting point for students who are not certain what it means to adopt a critical approach in their discipline. The activity also shows how to resolve the seemingly contradictory requirements of academic discourse— expressing an individual point of view while avoiding explicit reference to oneself.
2. Select the review articles carefully, including a mix of favorable and less favorable reviews. Although the reviews should be of a formal academic nature, their content should be as accessible as possible to the students. Therefore, select articles from relatively less specialized journals.
3. Although you do not have to analyze the first sample review on the overhead projector, I have found that this mode is more engaging for the students than reading from a handout.

Contributor

Tim Moore is a Lecturer at Language and Learning Services at Monash University in Australia, where he conducts adjunct programs mainly for humanities students.

Finding a Critical Voice II (Focus on Summary)

Levels
Advanced

Aims
Explore the language of summary
Understand rhetorical purposes and strategies

Class Time
1 hour

Preparation Time
None

Resources
See Finding a Critical Voice I

This activity focuses on sections designated *S* (summary) in the sample reviews in Finding a Critical Voice I. The main purpose is for students to explore the linguistic features of summarization, particularly expressions that have a reporting function (e.g., *Smith argues that . . .*, *Smith recommends that . . .*). Focusing on these reporting expressions will also draw students' attention to some of the rhetorical purposes and strategies of the original texts (i.e., to argue a point, to make recommendations), which will also benefit students in their approach to academic reading.

Procedure

1. On the blackboard, draw the following table:

Author reference	Text reference

2. Display the review article from Finding a Critical Voice I on the overhead projector. Refer the students to the section(s) that have been designated *S* (summary).
3. Ask the students to identify any expressions that refer to the author of the original text or to the text itself. Write these in the table. (See Finding a Critical Voice III, Appendix B, for expressions in sample reviews.)

4. Have the students refer to other review articles from Finding a Critical Voice I and complete the table in groups of three. Ask the students to identify the most commonly used reporting expressions.
5. Get the students to volunteer information to complete the table on the blackboard together. Discuss the features of reporting expressions (see Caveats and Options).

Caveats and Options

Treat any subsequent discussion as an opportunity to explore different aspects (both linguistic and rhetorical) of the reporting expressions identified in this activity. A range of possible tasks and questions follows.

1. English has a very rich vocabulary of reporting verbs and expressions. Ask the students to volunteer any other verbs or expressions they know and to explain the function of these expressions in a summary text (Tadros, 1985). Ask, for example, why they are used so frequently.
2. Discuss the differences between *author-reference* and *text-reference* expressions. Ask which reviews focus more on the author and which on the text, and elicit possible reasons for this variation. Ask whether the verbs that collocate with author subjects are different from those that go with text subjects and whether authors are referred to by full name, by surname only, or by a pronoun. Elicit the terms used to refer to texts (e.g., *book, work, study, chapter*).
3. Have the students try to allocate reporting expressions to other functional categories (Thompson & Ye, 1991). One other possible division could be between processes of saying (e.g., *Smith argues that* . . .) and processes of doing (e.g., *Smith makes several recommendations* . . .). Ask the students how they might apply this analysis to their academic reading (e.g., to identify rhetorical purposes and strategies employed by a writer).
4. Draw the students' attention to the grammatical features of reporting expressions, particularly those which the students are likely to find difficult in their own writing. These features could include (a) transitivity (i.e., which reporting verbs are transitive, intransitive, or both) and (b) verbal-nominal pairs (i.e., which reporting verbs have nominal equivalents, such as *argue* vs. *argument*).

References and Further Reading

Tadros, A. (1985). *Prediction in text* (Discourse Analysis Monograph 10). Birmingham, England: University of Birmingham.

Thompson, G., & Ye, Y. (1991). Evaluation in the reporting verbs used in academic papers. *Applied Linguistics, 12*, 365–382.

Contributor

Tim Moore is a Lecturer at Language and Learning Services at Monash University in Australia, where he conducts adjunct programs mainly for humanities students.

Finding a Critical Voice III (Focus on Evaluation)

Levels
Advanced

Aims
Explore the language of evaluation
Understand criteria for evaluating texts
Write a review of an academic text

Class Time
1 hour

Preparation Time
None

Resources
See Finding a Critical Voice I
Text for students to review

T his activity focuses on sections designated *E* (evaluation) in the sample reviews in Finding a Critical Voice I. The main purpose is for students to explore the special language used by writers to evaluate texts. The activity also draws attention to some of the underlying criteria by which texts are evaluated. At the end of the unit students write their own review of a text.

Procedure

1. Ask the students what makes a good text in their field.
2. On the blackboard, draw the following table:

Positive evaluations	Negative evaluations

3. Display the review article from Finding a Critical Voice I on the overhead projector. Refer the students to the section(s) designated *E* (evaluation).
4. Ask the students to identify any expressions that signal either a positive or a negative evaluation of the original text. Write these in the table.
5. Present and discuss the following evaluative criteria (not an exhaustive list). Add any other criteria mentioned in Step 1.

Criteria Used in the Evaluation of Texts

A. Completeness of work
   - Is the work comprehensive? Does it cover the complexity of the topic being investigated?
   - Are some important issues or areas left out?
B. Usefulness of work
   - Is the work useful? Does it have practical applications? Is it too theoretical?
C. Balance of work
   - Does the work offer an even-handed or biased coverage of the topic? Does it acknowledge other points of view? Is evidence used only in a selective way?
D. Currentness of work
   - Is the work relevant to the present? Have circumstances changed to make the work out of date?

Ask the students to match these criteria with the evaluations in the sample review (see Appendix C).

6. Have the students, in groups of three, repeat Steps 4 and 5 with other review articles to complete the table. Advise the students that not all evaluations will match the criteria given. In subsequent discussion, see if any other evaluative criteria (and questions) can be added to the list generated in Step 4.

7. Distribute a selected text and ask the students to write their own review of it.

Caveats and Options

1. Focus in some detail on the evaluative language noted in Step 4. The students may find it interesting to observe how first-person pronouns are avoided (if indeed they are). Ask the students why many writers avoid personal reference and what rhetorical effect they achieve by doing so.

2. Carefully select the text given to the students to review at the end of the unit to match the students' reading levels and academic interests. Alternatively, have the students select their own text to review. The review can either be written without preparation or after some discussion of the text in class.

Appendix A: Discourse Structure of Sample Reviews

Sample Review 1

North, South, and the environmental crisis. By Rodney R. White. Toronto: University of Toronto press. 1993. 214pp. Index. £32.50; ISBN 0 8020 5952 x. Pb.: £12.00; ISBN 0 8020 6885 5.

O

S

Rodney White is Associate Professor of Geography at the University of Toronto. He has written an elementary introduction to modern-day environmental problems, focusing on those issues that involve some form of international cooperation or resource flows between North and South. The book, therefore, covers global warming, the ozone layer, acid rain, pollution, land use, water supply, waste management, and urban problems.

E−

Lumping these together as international issues is perhaps a little misleading. Only global warming and the ozone layer are genuinely problems of "the global commons"; the rest are either local or regionally defined (such as acid rain). Moreover, the absence of biological diversity as a major issue—if not *the* major issue—is very surprising.

E+

E−

As a guide to the issues and the technological options this is a helpful introduction. It is at its weakest, however, when touching on policy and institutions. The book was written at the time of the Rio Conference of June 1993, and it would have paid to wait six months to cover the Climate Change and Biodiversity Conventions in more detail. As it is they are confined to a postscript. There is a similar and less excusable neglect of the vast economics literature on carbon taxes, tradable emission permits, tradable development rights, and international franchising. The worst omission is any discussion of the Global Environmental Facility which has both been in existence since 1990 and has become the financial mechanism under the Rio Conventions.

E−

Addressing global environmental issues in one book is an ambitious objective, but the end result is that Professor White has produced only half a book. Given the availability of many good surveys of world environmental problems, one could have wished for less emphasis on the problem and more on the solutions. But, as an introduction the book is well worth keeping for reference.

E+

David Pearce, CSERGE, University College London[1]

Sample Review 2

The new global economy and the developing countries: Essays in international economics and development. By Gerald K. Helleiner. Aldershot, Hants: Edward Elgar. 1990 290pp. Index. £40.00. ISBN 1 85278 329 x.

S

In this collection of essays Helleiner discusses the types of external shock which have confronted developing countries in the 1980s and which policy-makers and economists in the industrial world have been unable to alleviate. Though he frequently offers alternatives to existing policies, his

E+

primary contribution is in suggesting future avenues for economic research.

S

While pointing out the importance of sound domestic policies, the author describes how external shocks in the 1980s have retarded the progress of many of the world's developing countries. These countries have suffered from oil price increases, high global interest rates, exchange rate variability, depressed commodity prices, and disruptions in external finance. Such shocks have become more severe because of the greater openness of the economies to increased flows of goods and capital.

S

Helleiner criticizes the response of the industrial countries and of the international financial institutions. Western governments maintain quotas on many commodities while rejecting suggestions by developing countries that they create a commodity stabilization fund. The International Monetary Fund and the World Bank are reproached for focusing too often on short-term measures and for recommending orthodox remedies with no account taken of the particular circumstances of each country. The author suggests instead greater emphasis on long-term solutions which are growth-oriented and on the effects of any policies on income distribution in the afflicted country.

E+

Helleiner is at his best when pointing out the inadequacies of existing theories of international trade and economic development. He provides examples of how market imperfections militate against *laissez-faire* policies such as those advocated by the international financial institutions and he recommends a more interventionist role for national governments in developing countries. He argues forcefully and with conviction, and provides a good survey of the international economic issues relevant to

E–

developing countries. The one drawback of the book is that it is based on essays written mostly in the early 1980s or even earlier. Though many of the arguments remain the same, much of the description in the book is decidedly dated.

Stephen Thomsen, Royal Institute of International Affairs[2]

Appendix B: Reporting Expressions in Sample Reviews

Author reference	Text reference
Review 1 ● *He has written ...*	● *The book, therefore, covers ...*
Review 2 ● *Helleiner discusses ...* ● *... he frequently offers alternatives ...* ● *... pointing out the importance ...* ● *... the author describes ...* ● *Helleiner criticizes ...* ● *... are reproached ...* ● *The author suggests ...*	

Footnotes to Appendix A

[1]From D. Pearce, 1993, [Review of the book *North, South, and the Environmental Crisis*], *International Affairs, 69,* p. 779. Reprinted with permission.

[2]From S. Thomsen, 1991, [Review of the book *The New Global Economy and the Developing Countries: Essays in International Economics and Development*], *International Affairs, 67,* p. 340. Reprinted with permission.

Appendix C: Evaluative Expressions and Criteria in Sample Reviews

Positive evaluations	Negative evaluations
Review 1 ● *. . . a helpful introduction* (Criterion B) ● *. . . the book is well worth keeping for reference* (Criterion B)	● *. . . is a little misleading* (Criterion C) ● *. . . the absence of . . . is very surprising* (Criterion A) ● *. . . it would have paid to wait . . .* (Criterion D) ● *. . . there is a similar and less excusable neglect of . . .* (Criterion A) ● *. . . the worst omission is . . .* (Criterion A) ● *. . . one could have wished for less emphasis on problems and more on solutions.* (Criterion C)
Review 2 ● *Helleiner is at his best when pointing out the inadequacies* (Criterion A/B) ● *He argues forcefully and with conviction* (Criterion A/B) ● *. . . provides a good survey . . .* (Criterion A)	● *The one drawback of the book . . . the book is decidedly dated.* (Criterion D)

Contributor

Tim Moore is a Lecturer at Language and Learning Services at Monash University in Australia, where he conducts adjunct programs mainly for humanities students.

The Power of Persuasion

Levels
Advanced

Aims
Understand and practice
the language of
persuasion
Practice summarizing

Class Time
1 hour

Preparation Time
1 hour

Resources
Film on videotape or
video sound track

The art and power of persuasion form an important component of any content course and thus can be a module for persuasive statements in fields ranging from speeches for political, religious, and social purposes to essays related to the sciences. In this activity students learn the language used to influence the beliefs or actions of the audience with the support of facts, figures, opinions, and examples.

Procedure

1. Have the students view a selected movie on videotape on their own time.
2. Find a powerful but comparatively easy speech in the movie (e.g., the speech by the colonel at the climax in the movie *Scent of a Woman* or the central speech on an important human relations question in *When Harry Met Sally*).
3. Ask the the students to summarize the whole story in the movie (to set the background).
4. Play the first segment of the speech and let the students summarize it.
5. Ask questions to elicit any major missing points.
6. Ask the students to summarize the first segment one more time.
7. Repeat Steps 4-6 with subsequent segments until the speech is finished.
8. Ask the students to summarize the whole speech.
9. Hold a conversation (combined with some questions and answers) on the major techniques (e.g., visual expression, tone, facts) employed by the speaker to move the hearts of the audience and their effectiveness (based on the audience's reaction).

10. Discuss whether the students agree or disagree with the speaker and why.
11. Ask the students what they would have said if they were the speaker.

Caveats and Options

Ask the students to write an opinion essay or deliver a persuasive speech on a controversial topic related to the content area they have been dealing with in class, utilizing the persuasion techniques mobilized in the movie speech.

References and Further Reading

Brinton, D. M., Snow, M. A., & Wesche, M. B. (1989). *Content-based second language instruction.* Boston: Heinle & Heinle.

Contributor

Jong-oe Park has taught English to college students and adults in South Korea and Japan.

Mystery, Mayhem, and Essay Planning

Levels
Advanced

Aims
Understand the structure of an academic essay
Assess and organize evidence to support the chosen solution to a problem
Become aware of deductive reasoning processes

Class Time
30 minutes (analyzing the question)
60 minutes (planning an answer)

Preparation Time
20 minutes +

Resources
Blackboard or overhead projector
Copies of question cards
Copies of background information
Three sets of evidence cards
Copies of planning chart

Many students, despite good research and writing skills, fail to produce an essay with the academic style and linear form of argumentation preferred in English academic writing. Although overseas or immigrant students are often faced with this problem (Crosling, 1993), other nontraditional students (such as students from lower socioeconomic groups and rural and isolated students) may also need to be taught academic argumentation. The global aim of this activity is for students to acquire an understanding of the structure of an academic essay and its major features (see Arnaudet & Barrett, 1984, pp. 2–5) using the exciting and easily accessible genre of the detective murder mystery.

Procedure

Question Analysis

1. On the blackboard or overhead projector, present the students with the "essay question" to be solved: *There is evidence that Mortimer was murdered. How likely is this? Is murder the only possible explanation? Give evidence for your case.*
2. Elicit from the students possible theses (i.e., ways Mortimer may have died: murder, accident, suicide). Ask the students what information they would need to know if they were investigating these options and what questions they would ask for each possible thesis.
3. Note the students' suggestions on the blackboard or overhead projector and ask them to sort them into thematic areas that match the four prepared question cards (see Appendix A): motive, intent, means, and opportunity.
4. Distribute the copies of the question cards and have the students read them, highlighting any points not discussed in the previous step.

Essay Planning

5. Direct the students to read the background information (see Appendix B) and evidence cards (see Appendix C) thoroughly.
6. Organize the students into three groups according to their preferred solution: premeditated murder, accidental death, or suicide.
7. Provide the students with a planning chart (see Appendix D). Instruct each group to organize the evidence for their case, using the themes and questions on the question cards, in order to argue for the solution they are supporting.
8. Monitor the progress of the groups, ensuring that their discussion and decisions are applicable to the group's answer to the question.
9. Ask each group to present its analysis of the evidence in support of its interpretation (i.e., murder, suicide, or accident) to the class.
10. Summarize the procedure used in this activity:
   - Consider all possible solutions/arguments
   - Outline the areas of inquiry
   - Select the most valid argument
   - Gather the information
   - Interpret the information according to the chosen argument
   - Organize the information to support the argument
   - Present the argument and supporting evidence

Caveats and Options

1. The analysis of the structure of academic discourse presented here is based on *story grammar*, first developed to analyze components of folktales and children's stories (Johnson & Mandler, 1980) and later used to segment academic discourse into claims supported by evidence (Cootes, 1993).
2. The language and narrative form of Mystery, Mayhem, and Essay Planning will be more familiar to students from an English-speaking background than to others. Two strategies may make it more accessible to other students: (a) Provide the students with a glossary of unfamiliar words (e.g., *rosy*, *manor*, *butler*) or (b) preteach these words within a discussion of English culture.

3. Use the situation in this activity in other areas of essay-writing instruction. After the students analyze and brainstorm the question and organize the given evidence, ask them to write out their reasons and supporting evidence (topic sentences, connectives, deductive paragraphs, referencing); organize written paragraphs into the body of an essay (paragraphing, relevance, and ordering); and write an introduction, conclusion, and synopsis for the essay.
4. Expand the practice in debating and oral presentation beyond the introductory level given here.
5. Provide the evidence in a variety of formats. Pasting each piece of evidence onto a card, although time consuming, produces more durable resources.

References and Further Reading

Arnaudet, M. L., & Barrett, M. E. (1984). *Approaches to academic reading and writing.* Englewood Cliffs, NJ: Prentice-Hall Regents.

Cootes, S. (1993). Using story grammar to teach essay writing skills. In P. McLean & M. Devlin (Eds.), *Proceedings of the language and learning workshop: University of Melbourne. November 12-13, 1992* (pp. 5-11). Melbourne, Australia: Language and Learning Practitioners Network.

Crosling, G. (1993). Straight or circular? Academic writing and the non-traditional student. *HERDSA News, 15*(1), 10-13.

Johnson, N. S., & Mandler, J. M. (1980). A tale of two structures: Underlying and surface forms in stories. *Poetics, 9,* 51-86.

Mann, R. C., & Mann, P. M. (1990). *Essay writing: Methods and models.* Belmont, CA: Wadsworth.

Troyka, L. Q. (1987). *Simon and Schuster handbook for writers.* Englewood Cliffs, NJ: Prentice Hall.

Appendix A: The Greenhouse Mystery Question Cards

1. MOTIVE
• If Mortimer was murdered, what was the murderer's reason?
Which characters in the story have a motive?
How plausible are the motives?
• If Mortimer committed suicide, what were his reasons?
Is there any evidence to support the idea that Mortimer killed himself?
How plausible is it?
• Does motive apply if the death was an accident?

2. INTENT
• If Mortimer was killed, then was it done on purpose?
Is there evidence of someone planning to murder Mortimer?
What evidence could be used to support your decision?
• Did Mortimer intend to kill himself, or was it an accident?
Is there evidence to suggest what he was thinking and feeling at the time of his death?
• Did someone else accidentally kill Mortimer?
What do the facts suggest?

3. MEANS
• If Mortimer was murdered, how did the murderer do it?
Can you reconstruct the crime using the evidence given?
Who had access to the poison?
• If Mortimer committed suicide, how did he do it?
Is there any evidence to indicate what Mortimer used to do this?
• If Mortimer died by accident, how could this have taken place?

4. OPPORTUNITY
● If Mortimer was murdered, when did the murderer do it?
Which characters in the story had the opportunity to murder Mortimer?
Is there evidence to support this?
● If Mortimer committed suicide, when did he do it?
Can you reconstruct the events leading to his suicide?
● If Mortimer died accidentally, when did his death occur?

Appendix B: The Greenhouse Mystery Background Information

Prudence and her brother Mortimer Duckshott were the only members of their family to survive a fatal fire 20 years ago. The fire partially destroyed the family home—a large country manor, famous for its roses.

While Prudence and Mortimer lived in the same house, they lived separate lives and would only meet over a cup of tea on Sunday afternoons in the greenhouse of the manor. As Mortimer was the elder, he was in control of the finances of the family.

Recently, Prudence started dating a young accountant, Sly Summations; she was hoping to marry him and move into a new home. However, he was poor and her only access to the family fortune was through her brother. So she approached her brother about the money needed for their new home, and Mortimer agreed to give the couple an annual income from the estate.

Everything seemed rosy—until Mortimer was found dead in the greenhouse . . . .

Appendix C: The Greenhouse Mystery Evidence Cards

Extract From Coroner's Report on the Death of Mortimer Duckshott
. . . It appears that the deceased suffered a severe heart attack resulting from ingesting large amounts of As_2O_3—commonly known as white arsenic—a deadly chemical found in rat poison, rose spray, and slug bait and often described as "deadly marzipan" because of its almond taste . . . .

Extract From Police Forensic Laboratory Report:
The Greenhouse Mystery

. . . A test was undertaken of the remaining cake found at the scene of the crime: Traces of white arsenic were found in the icing. The tea remaining in the teapot had no poisonous substances in it, but there were traces of poison in the empty teacup, which had been dropped and spilled over the table. Furthermore, there were two similar sugar bowls on the table; one was found to contain sugar, while the other had pure white arsenic in it . . .

Extract From Police Investigation Report:
The Greenhouse Mystery

ITEM 27: An unsigned typed note found on the desk—underneath the bowl of poison. It reads, "I can no longer pretend. I have kept the secret about the fire for all these years. I've tried to forget. I've tried to pay all our bills. The world is against me—goodbye cruel world." The typeface matches the keys of the typewriter that was on the desk in the greenhouse . . . .

Extract From Statement to Police by Prudence Duckshott

. . . I often had tea and cake with my brother. He had a sweet tooth: he even took four teaspoons of sugar in his tea. Occasionally, I'd bake his favourite cake—Marzipan Cake. I made one on the Saturday night while Sly was visiting. I was making the icing when Mortimer called me on the intercom and said he would now see me. I rushed off to his room straight away. I was ashamed about our argument and desperately wanted to apologize. I had tried earlier that evening to talk to my brother when I had taken him a cup of tea out in the garden shed where he was mixing up some rose spray. As I forgot to put sugar in it, I had to go back for the bowl and take it out to him. He was still too angry to talk to me. I tried again later when I went back to collect the cup, but it and Mortimer were gone. Strangely, the sugar bowl was still there, so I took it back to the greenhouse. It was quite late and dark by then.

Extract From Statement to Police
by Peeves, the Family's Butler

. . . I thought Prudence was planning to stay for afternoon tea—she'd even made a cake—but, at the last minute, she had to go to another appointment. She didn't even stay for a quick bite to eat. So when Sly arrived, she wasn't here, but he didn't mind. He said he wanted to see Mortimer. About ten minutes later, I thought I could hear voices shouting: Mortimer was saying "You'll never get away with it!" and Sly said "I'll tell her anyway, and everyone else!" I returned to the Greenhouse an hour later to clean up. That's when I found the body and the note.

**Extract From Statement to Police by Sly Summations,
Accountant and Fiancée to Ms. Duckshott**

. . . I was there when she made the cake. I saw her make it. She didn't put any poison in it—why would she? He was a rude, nosy, grumpy man who loved his roses more than people, but she was his sister and she loved him. There was a lot Prudence didn't know about him or the estate. Anyway, I investigated his past. It seems he was fond of matches as a boy, and of gambling as a young man. He told people he was broke, and maybe he was— but there was still the fire insurance money. There was a clause in the will that only allowed the last living member to inherit any insurance money. It didn't apply in the case of accidental death, though. They were certainly a strange family . . . .

**Extract From Statement to Police
by the Duckshotts' Family Doctor**

. . . Mortimer often came to see me when he was worried; he was a nice chap, but a bit weak—couldn't stand the sight of blood. He was very concerned about the family reputation; his sister wanted an expensive wedding and they were broke. I don't think Prudence realized how little money they had; probably nobody did. It made him severely depressed. He told me at his last visit that he felt there was no way out. Now Prudence has been having trouble sleeping since the death of her brother and seems greatly, and understandably, perturbed. I've had to prescribe some strong sleeping pills for the poor girl . . . .

Extract From Statement to Police by the Local Greengrocer

. . . Prudence was in here buying some cake ingredients on Saturday afternoon, when Mortimer came in. He seemed quite angry. They started to argue; I couldn't hear it all, but she said something like: "I don't care, I love him anyway," and "You're trying to ruin my only chance of happiness." He stormed out. Prudence stood staring out the window for a while, then asked for some rat poison, which surprised me a bit as they have so many cats up at the manor . . . .

Extract From Statement to Police by Mortimer's Closest Friend, Pongo

. . . He was worried about this accountant fellow, you know; he thought he might be after the girl's inheritance. So Morty did a check on him. Turns out that Sly was a fraud—he even had a wife in the city! Apparently Sly doted on his wife. She would've been a bit expensive to keep, mind you. Anyway, Morty was very confused about it . . . .

Appendix D: Planning Chart

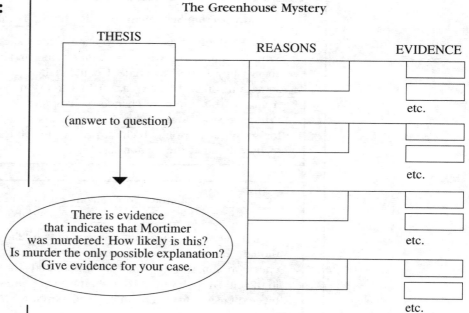

The Greenhouse Mystery

THESIS

REASONS

EVIDENCE

(answer to question)

There is evidence
that indicates that Mortimer
was murdered: How likely is this?
Is murder the only possible explanation?
Give evidence for your case.

etc.

etc.

etc.

etc.

Contributors

Aveline Perez is a linguist who teaches learning skills at both Monash University and the University of Melbourne in Australia. Eliza Romey is a Learning Skills Adviser at Monash University in Australia, with a tutoring background in politics, sociology, and health studies.

Now You See It— Now You Don't

Levels
Intermediate +

Aims
Discuss paraphrasing in native and target cultures
Become aware of elements in paraphrasing
Practice paraphrasing techniques
Help classmates paraphrase sentences and short passages

Class Time
1 hour

Preparation Time
15 minutes

Resources
Overhead projector (OHP)
Overhead transparency of sentences from previous reading

This simple activity uses students' own work to make paraphrasing understandable and accessible. By eliciting paraphrasing techniques from the students themselves, it serves as an introduction to or reinforcement of this important academic skill.

Procedure

1. Discuss these questions or similar ones with the students:
   - What is paraphrasing?
   - When do we paraphrase?
   - Is paraphrasing important in your culture? Explain.
   - Why is paraphrasing important in Western culture?
2. Using the OHP and the prepared transparency, focus the students' attention on a sentence from reading material previously covered in class.
3. Allow about 2 minutes for the students to read the sentence a few times until they understand it. Make sure that they do not take notes and that they use their dictionaries only if necessary.
4. Switch off the OHP and ask the students to write the meaning of the sentence in their own words in their notebooks.
5. Preview the student sentences for several good examples of paraphrasing—all of them using different structural elements (e.g., changing vocabulary, changing the sentence structure, simplifying, changing voice, or changing parts of speech). Try to choose student sentences that illustrate different combinations of these elements.
6. Ask several students to write their sentences on the blackboard.
7. Switch on the OHP.
8. Compare the students' sentences with the original ones. Discuss the differences with the students:

- Have the new sentences kept the original meaning?
- How did the students manage to change the sentence and keep the same meaning?

9. Elicit as many elements involved in paraphrasing as possible. Introduce one or two other elements if appropriate.

10. Repeat Steps 1–8 for one or two more sentences or until all the students have grasped the idea of paraphrasing.

11. Give the students a short paragraph from a previous reading to paraphrase. Encourage them to use a variety of paraphrasing elements in their sentences.

12. Have the students compare their paraphrase with a partner's and then with those of other class members.

Caveats and Options

1. Begin the activity directly with Step 2 of the procedure; do Step 1 as a follow-up cross-cultural discussion.

2. Use the blackboard instead of the OHP.

3. Make sure the sentences on the OHP or blackboard are neither too long nor too short. The following was used in a natural life science adjunct class: *Many of our daily activities may contribute to the greenhouse effect because they involve the burning of fossil fuels, such as coal, gas, and oil.*

4. After classroom practice, give the students a reference sheet that outlines the elements in paraphrasing and gives specific examples of each one. Use sentences from a previous reading covered in the course as illustrations.

References and Further Reading

Damen, L. (1987). *Culture learning: The fifth dimension in the language classroom.* Reading, MA: Addison-Wesley.

Oshima, A., & Hogue, A. (1991). *Writing academic English: A writing and sentence structure handbook* (2nd ed.). Menlo Park, CA: Addison-Wesley.

Wood, N. V. (1991). *College reading and study skills: A guide to improving academic communication* (4th ed.). Fort Worth, TX: Holt, Rinehart & Winston.

Contributor

Julie Sagliano is a Lecturer at Miyazaki International College, Japan, where she teaches EFL in adjunct and English courses.

The 5-Minute Professor

Levels
Intermediate +

Aims
Review lecture material
by examining lecture
notes
Work on a collaborative
lecture
Recognize lecture style
and organization
Ask and answer
questions on content
material

Class Time
30 minutes (first class)
5 minutes per student
(second class)

Preparation Time
30 minutes

Resources
Students' lecture notes
Handout on
organization of prior
lectures

In this activity, students first assess their own note-taking abilities and confirm their comprehension of the main points in a lecture. Next, they become more aware of their professor's lecture organization, style, and delivery. Finally, they practice valuable oral presentation skills.

Procedure

1. Form groups of four students.
2. Have each group review, complete, and combine their notes on a specific lecture. Assign each group a different one.
3. Provide each group with a list of major rhetorical modes and associated signal words used in the lecture by a particular professor. Discuss the unique verbal and nonverbal cues employed by the lecturer.
4. Have the students write a lecture based on their combined notes. Divide lecture responsibilities among the group: Ask one student to write and give the introduction, two students to develop the lecture, and one student to provide the conclusion. Advise the students to incorporate lecture cues and specific expressions normally used by their content teacher.
5. Have the students practice their lecture together outside class.
6. In the next class period, encourage each group member to "become" their content teacher for 5 minutes by acting out the role with gestures, body language, eye contact, voice projection, and audiovisual aids.
7. Have all members of the group present their part of the lecture in turn. Ask questions related to it and encourage inquiries.

Caveats and Options

1. The activity assumes that the adjunct teacher already has ample knowledge of the characteristic lecture styles of the students' professors and specifics on the organization and content of the original lectures.
2. Outside class, confer with student groups to (a) check the written draft of the lecture for organization, completeness, and the use of cohesive devices; (b) give the opportunity to rehearse; and (c) build confidence prior to the oral presentations.
3. If you teach low-level classes, preface the activity with group work to develop schema, lecture-related vocabulary, and essay-writing skills related to specific content.

References and Further Reading

Begler, D., & Murray, N. (1993). *Contemporary topics: Advanced listening comprehension*. New York: Longman.

James, G. (1992). *Interactive listening on campus: Authentic academic mini-lectures*. Boston: Heinle & Heinle.

Reuthen, M. K., (1986). *Comprehending academic lectures*. New York: Macmillan.

Contributor

Michael Sagliano is an English Lecturer teaching adjunct courses at Miyazaki International College in Japan.

Diagram the Discussion

Levels
Intermediate +

Aims
Record information
about a text in a
diagram
Read a text selectively
Discuss a text by
referring to diagrams

Class Time
45 minutes

Preparation Time
Variable

Resources
Handouts with diagrams
or graphic organizers
Text

This activity improves students' comprehension of an article or story and provides students with an outlining strategy useful for both oral and written summaries.

Procedure

1. Locate a feature article in a newspaper or magazine about a particular political, social, or environmental problem or a short story with a variety of relationships and events. Prepare the following handouts:
   - Flowchart of Events (see Appendix A)
   - Relationship Map (see Appendix B)
   - Incident and Explanation Grid (see Appendix C)
   - Points on a Map (a map of important locations mentioned in the story)
   - Characters in Contrast (the differing characteristics of two characters in the story)
   - Family Tree (a diagram of the family history in the story)
2. Assign the first reading of the text as homework for students. Give them a short quiz in the following class to ensure that they have done the reading. Alternately, allow time in class for prereading activities with the text.
3. Divide the students into six groups of four to six students.
4. Hand out a different diagram to each group and briefly explain that the diagrams are going to be used in small-group work. Stress to the students that each diagram calls for a different sort of information. The group discussing the Flowchart of Events has to decide which events should be listed and in what order they occurred. The students working on the Relationship Map have to determine the central character in the text and how this character is related to other people

in the story. In the Incident and Explanation Grid students identify the key events in the story and explain them.

5. After the groups have finished discussing the story and have completed their diagrams, ask them to count off so that they can form new groups consisting of one member from each of the previous groups. Have each student in the new group explain the diagram from the previous group to the new group members.

Caveats and Options

1. The best articles to choose are often those that raise the issue of cross-cultural values. One example is the article "Woman's Suicide Bid With Her Children a Cultural Tragedy" (1985). It is a feature article of about 2,000 words on Fumiko Kimura, a Japanese woman living in the United States who attempted *oyako-shinju*, parent-child suicide, after learning that her husband, Itsuroku, had been having an affair.

2. Many suitable pieces have been anthologized in reading texts, including Gansberg's (1984) famous article, "38 Who Saw Murder Didn't Call the Police," about the stabbing of Kitty Genovese in New York City, and Roger Caras's (1987) "A Bull Terrier Named Mackerel," a comic memoir about the escapades of a neighborhood dog.

3. Choose a reading that has enough material in it for each of the different diagrams to be used purposefully.

4. Use computer software to generate the diagrams quickly and professionally.

5. Use the activity as a prelude to a writing assignment. The Flowchart or the Family Tree could lead to a narrative paragraph; Characters in Contrast, to comparison-and-contrast writing; and Incident and Explanation, to cause-and-effect writing.

6. Create role plays based on the characters in the story.

References and Further Reading

Caras, R. (1987). A bull terrier named Mackerel. In M. A. Miller (Ed.), *Reading and writing short essays* (3rd ed., pp. 108–110). Singapore: McGraw-Hill

Carrell, P. (1987). Content and formal schemata in ESL reading. *TESOL Quarterly, 21*, 461–481.

Ellis, R. (1982). Informal and formal approaches to communicative language teaching. *ELT Journal, 36*, 73–81.

Gansberg, M. (1984). 38 who saw murder and didn't call the police. In G. Goshgarian (Ed.), *The contemporary reader* (pp. 120–123). Boston: Little, Brown.

Mohan, B. (1986). *Language and content*. Menlo Park, CA: Addison-Wesley.

Shih, M. (1992). Beyond comprehension exercises in the ESL academic reading class. *TESOL Quarterly, 26*, 289–318.

Woman's suicide bid with her children a cultural tragedy. (1985, March 9). *The Atlanta Constitution*.

Appendix A: Flowchart

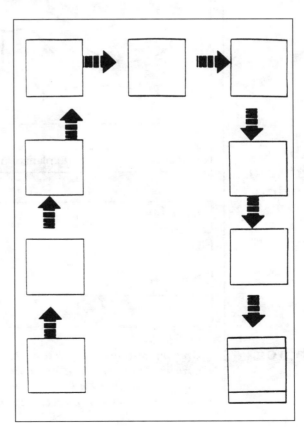

Appendix B: Relationship Map

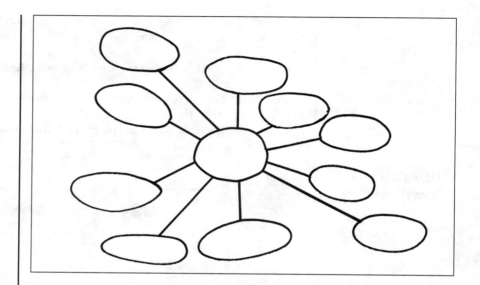

Appendix C: Incident and Explanation Grid

Incident	Explanation
1.	
2.	
3.	
4.	
5.	

Contributor

Gregory Strong is a full-time Lecturer in the English and American Literature Department at Aoyama University, Tokyo, Japan. He has also worked in Canada and China, where he was involved in testing for a Canadian foreign aid project and in teacher training.

Once Upon a Time

Levels
Intermediate +

Aims
Become familiar with
literary terms
Improve reading
comprehension
Discuss and analyze
literary pieces

Class Time
1 1/2 hours

Preparation Time
5 minutes

Resources
Story
Handout with
definitions of literary
terms
Blank paper

This is a two-part activity involving reading and writing. It can be used (a) as an introduction to literary terms, (b) as part of a self-access program in which students choose novels from the library and prepare oral and written reports on them, or (c) as an enrichment activity for a content-based course (assuming the literary work chosen relates to the course content). Using literary terms enables students to become independent readers who can develop their own analyses of literary works. In the second part of the activity, students create a story as a group and extend their ability to understand fiction.

Procedure

1. Choose a story about a paragraph in length, or write one that can be read quickly and easily yet contains each of the literary terms (see Appendix A).
2. Explain the literary terms, give the students a handout with the definitions of each one (see Appendix B), and make sure that the students review the terms as homework (see Caveats and Options 1).
3. In the next class, pass out copies of the story; ask the students to read it and label the parts of the story where the literary terms appear. Explain to the students that one literary term, *theme*, is a more general term that applies to the story in general. Allow about 15 minutes for the reading and analysis.
4. Circulate and encourage slower readers (or those looking up every word) to finish the story and analyze it.
5. Form the students into pairs to check each other's analysis.
6. Ask different pairs of students to describe the way the literary terms are used in the story. List any ambiguous ones on the blackboard for

further discussion. Brainstorm ideas about the theme of the story, asking the students to support their ideas.

7. Have the students use the literary terms or "story grammar" (Dimino, Taylor, & Gersten, 1995) to create a collaborative story. Start by giving each student a blank piece of paper and asking them to write down the names of four characters, real or imaginary, and to give their appearances and ages.

8. Have the first student fold over the paper to hide the names and pass the paper to the student sitting behind.

9. Ask the second student to add a setting and then fold the paper over again.

10. Tell the third student to add a symbol and a brief explanation of it.

11. Ask the next student to describe the conflict.

12. Ask the fifth student to describe an irony.

13. Have the sixth student read all the information on the paper, decide on a point of view, then write a one-paragraph story and title it within 15 minutes.

14. Ask the students to share their stories either with each other in a small group or with the class at large. Discuss possible themes for the stories.

Caveats and Options

1. This activity works best in the third class in a series on literary terms. In the first class, explain the literary terms to the students and ask them to review the terms for homework. In the second class, give a short matching quiz to ensure that the students can distinguish the terms.

2. Choose a story that is neither long nor complex and that has simple vocabulary. The point of the activity is to engage the students in a literary analysis as quickly as possible. In future classes, more difficult reading can be attempted.

3. The students may come up with more than one correct answer. As long as they can support their opinions, their answers should be considered acceptable.

4. This activity works very well as part of a self-access reading program. Set aside an area of the library for graded readers and abridged novels. At regular intervals, have the students choose books and do reports using the literary terms.

References and Further Reading

Bamford, J. (1992). Beyond grammar translation: Teaching students to really read. In P. Wadden (Ed.), *A handbook for teaching English at Japanese colleges and universities* (pp. 63-72). Oxford: Oxford University Press.

Beckson, K., & Ganz, A. (1987). *Literary terms: A dictionary.* New York: Farrar, Straus, Giroux.

Dimino, J., Taylor, R., & Gersten, R. (1995). Synthesis of the research on story grammar as a means to increase comprehension. *Reading and Writing Quarterly, 11*, 53-72.

Appendix A: Sample Story

The Look

Walking down Third Avenue, she hardly noticed the warmth of the summer night, or the smell of the flowers from the nearby park. Lonely, miserable, she felt like leaping from the bridge. It stood a few blocks away, an ugly grey.

Ahead, a young man was jogging toward her, looking straight into her eyes. He was a handsome sportsman. Their eyes met as he passed.

BANG—she turned her head. The young man had hit a telephone pole. She laughed.

That night, she slept well.

Appendix B: Literary Terms

1. *Setting:* the time and location of a story, or the setting of the novel
2. *Point of view:* a story is told from one point of view:
   - First person: sympathetic, unreliable
   - Third person: factual, little insight into characters' minds and emotions
   - Omniscient: insight into the minds and emotions of many characters
3. *Conflict:* a character is in conflict with:
   - Himself, herself, or with someone else
   - A man or woman versus a man or woman
   - A man or woman versus himself or herself
   - A man or woman versus his or her environment
4. *Symbol:* a thing that stands for another thing, person, or idea

5. *Irony:* whenever something happens in a story that is unexpected yet appropriate
6. *Theme:* the main idea, usually a moral or a lesson in a story

Contributor

Gregory Strong is a full-time Lecturer in the English and American Literature Department at Aoyama University, Tokyo, Japan. He has also worked in Canada and China, where he was involved in testing for a Canadian foreign aid project and in teacher training.

Paragraphing and Linking: A Reconstruction Activity

Levels
Intermediate +

Aims
Select appropriate verb tenses and modal verbs to use in reporting research
Use intrasentential linking devices
Group sentences into logical paragraphs

Class Time
1 hour

Preparation Time
1 hour

Resources
Excerpt from text students are familiar with
Text reconstruction handout
Overhead projector
Transparency of text excerpt

This is a consciousness-raising academic text reconstruction activity. Using a familiar text that has been broken down into content words arranged in single sentences, students reconstruct the text by inserting appropriate links, selecting appropriate verb tenses, and grouping sentences into paragraphs.

Procedure

1. Select an excerpt from a text contained in the content-based readings that the students have already done and discussed in an earlier lesson focused on the meaning of the text and vocabulary (see Appendix A for a sample text). The excerpt should contain examples of the points of which you wish to make the students aware.
2. Prepare the text reconstruction activity by writing a new text in which you include the original content words, except for the target items, which may be absent or given in an uninflected form. (In Appendix B, for example, students have to provide a grammatically and contextually appropriate verb tense, insert linking words such as relative pronouns, and group sentences into paragraphs.) Indicate with single slashes where the students need to reconstruct the text, and present each sentence on a new line with double slashes at the end.
3. Explain the activity to the students. If this is the first time you have used such an activity, demonstrate a short text reconstruction on the blackboard.
4. Group the students into pairs or triads.
5. Give each pair or triad a handout of the text reconstruction activity.
6. Have the students work collaboratively on the task for approximately 20 minutes.

7. When the students have finished, give them a copy of the original text. Then have them compare their reconstruction with the original and note any differences.
8. Using an overhead transparency of the original text, elicit the students' alternative versions. Discuss whether they are grammatically correct and, where more than one version is possible, the effect an alternative choice of tense, modal, linking device, or paragraphing has on meaning.

Caveats and Options

1. The example in the Appendixes is from an advanced ESL content-based course on various aspects of contemporary Australian society. The text, from a segment dealing with legal aspects of Australia as a multicultural society, elicited an interesting discussion about how tense and modal choice reflects the writer's attitude toward the material cited.
2. Vary the activity according to the students' language proficiency level. Focus on other grammatical areas where choices are possible (e.g., passive/active voice) and or use different text types or sections of texts (e.g., abstracts, introductions, conclusions).

References and Further Reading

Rutherford, W. (1987). *Second language grammar: Learning and teaching*. London: Longman.
Wajnryb, R. (1990). *Grammar dictation*. Oxford: Oxford University Press.

Appendix A: Original Text

In a 1982 report, the Australian law reform commission argued that judges should take tribal law into account when sentencing but should not accept its dictates as grounds for exoneration. Significantly, the commission also ruled out the possibility that Western law could be used to enforce tribal law.

Chief Justice Martin's decision was made in response to a submission from Walker's barrister, John Tippett, that his client, or a member of his client's family, would receive tribal punishment for killing a man. Tippett argued that though payback was technically unlawful, it was "behaviour designed to settle a dispute between families and would take place regardless of what the court thought of it." Martin made legal history when he ruled that prison officers should record what occurred and report back to the court.

His decision has provoked enormous interest around Australia, particularly from lawyers keen to work out what kind of a precedent has been set. Paul Hennessy, a director of the NSW law reform commission, has criticised the report-back component of the sentence, arguing that it may actually force a spearing to occur that might otherwise not have been performed. Hennessy does, however, accept that aboriginal tribal law should have a special place in the judicial system, unlike the cultures and laws of other minority groups. Migrants, he argues, consent to the Australian legal system when they apply to come to this country. Aborigines, as prior occupants, have made no such choice.[1]

Appendix B: Text Reconstruction Handout

In a 1982 report, the Australian law reform commission argue / judges should take tribal law into account when sentence / but / not accept its dictates as grounds for exoneration //

Significantly, the commission also rule out / the possibility of western law / use to enforce tribal law//

Chief Justice Martin's decision / make in response to a submission by Walker's barrister, John Tippett, that his client, or a member of his client's family / receive tribal punishment for kill / a man //

Tippett argue / though payback / technically unlawful, it / "behaviour designed to settle a dispute between families and would take place regardless of what the court thought of it" //

Martin / make legal history / he rule / prison officers / record what occur / and report back to the court //

---

[1]From "White Law, Black Law," by W. Jamrozik, May 1994, *The Independent Monthly*, pp. 37–38. Reprinted with permission.

His decision / provoke enormous interest around Australia / lawyers keen to work out what kind of a precedent / set //

Paul Hennessy, a director of the NSW law reform commission / criticise the report-back component of the sentence, argue / it / actually force a spearing / occur / might otherwise not / perform //

Hennessy / accept, however / aboriginal tribal law / have a special place in the judicial system, unlike the cultures / laws of other minority groups //

migrants, he argue / consent to the Australian legal system / they apply to come to this country //

aborigines / prior occupants / make / no such choice //

Contributors

Joanna Tapper is a Lecturer in Communication Skills, and Neomy Storch is a Lecturer in ESL, both at the University of Melbourne's Centre for Communication Skills and ESL, in Australia.

Index to Activities

AUTHOR	TITLE	PART[1]	FOCUS	TOPIC	SKILLS[2]		LEVEL
Allen, M.	Support It!	II	recognizing generalizations	any academic topic	R W L S	V	intermediate +
Andrade, M.	Picture This!	V	activating vocabulary with visuals	any	L S	V	intermediate +
Andrade, M.	Vocabulary Classification	I	classifying field-specific terms	any academic topic	S	V	intermediate +
Bame, J.	Listening for Information Emphasis Cues in Academic Lectures	IV	taking lecture notes & recognizing emphasis cues	any academic lecture	L S		advanced
Bernier, A., & Snow, M. A.	Expanding Academic Vocabulary	I	identifying content-specific vocabulary	any academic topic	R	V	intermediate +
Bress, P.	From Debate to Essay	II	organizing an argument; debating a topic	any academic topic	W S		intermediate
Bricault, D.	Navigating a Syllabus	IV	scanning for information	any academic course syllabus	R S		intermediate +
Brinton, D. M.	A Day in the Life	V	writing from pictures	any societal problem	R W L S	V	intermediate +
Brinton, D. M., & Snow, M. A.	Advocate Your Position	II	teacher training, negotiation, & role play	implementing adjunct instruction	R S		ESL/EFL teachers
Brinton, D. M., & Snow, M. A.	Divide and Classify	I	classifying information from a content reading	any academic topic lending itself to classification	R S		intermediate +
Chandra-segaran, A.	What Does the Lecturer-Reader Want?	V	analyzing content course writing requirements	any academic writing topic	R W S		intermediate +
Connell, E. L.	Advertising and the Audience	I	classifying advertisements	any radio or television advertisement	L S		intermediate +
Connell, E. L.	Music Video Is the Story	V	building vocabulary	any popular cultural theme	W L S	V	intermediate

[1]I: information management; II: critical thinking; III: hands-on activities; IV: data gathering; V: text analysis and construction.
[2]R: reading; W: writing; L: listening; S: speaking; G: grammar; V: vocabulary.

AUTHOR	TITLE	PART[1]	FOCUS	TOPIC	SKILLS[2]					LEVEL
Connell, E. L., & Bradbury, L.	Environmental Facts Around the World	I	sorting & classifying environmental facts	any environmental problem	R		S			any
Connell, E. L., & Werner, D. F.	"How Do You Feel About . . .?"	II	values clarification	any controversial issue		W	S			intermediate +
Creese, A.	Journal Treasure Hunt	IV	learning bibliographic form	any academic research topic	R	W	S			intermediate +
Creese, A.	Methoding the Research	IV	examining the conventions of literature reviews	any academic topic	R	W	S			intermediate +
Esposito, M., Marshall, K., & Stoller, F. L.	Poster Sessions by Experts	III	presenting poster sessions	any theme-based unit	R	W L	S			any
Flowerdew, L.	Discussing Data	IV	determining relevant data for a report	any academic topic	R	W	S			high intermediate
Freeman, R.	Cross-Cultural Mathematical Consciousness-Raising	III	solving mathematical word problems	mathematics	R	W L	S			intermediate +
Freeman, R.	Observation or Interpretation, That Is the Question	I	classifying statements into observations & interpretations	any topic in science or social science	R	W L	S			intermediate +
Freeman, R.	Read All About It! Witch Hunts: The American Curse	IV	linking historical notions to the present	U.S. history	R	W L	S			intermediate +
Gajdusek, L.	Building a Life	V	combining sentences	life of a famous person	R	W	S	G		high intermediate
Goodwin, J.	Getting Into the Content	III	taking turns in a discussion	any	R	L	S			intermediate +
Harada, T.	Reinforcing Content Through Visuals	V	describing pictures related to content	any	R	W L	S		V	intermediate +
Heacock, C.	A Fact-Finding Mission	IV	locating key information	any	R		S		V	any
Heitman, C.	What Problem?	III	understanding environmental problems	any environmental issue		W L	S			any
Holten, C.A., & Brinton, D. M	Town Meeting	II	synthesizing information from sources using a simulation	any social, economic, or moral issue	R	W L	S			intermediate +

[1]I: information management; II: critical thinking; III: hands-on activities; IV: data gathering; V: text analysis and construction.
[2]R: reading; W: writing; L: listening; S: speaking; G: grammar; V: vocabulary.

AUTHOR	TITLE	PART[1]	FOCUS	TOPIC	SKILLS[2]			LEVEL
Huppauf, B.	Flowers in the States	III	linking state flowers to states	states of the U.S.	R W L S			any
Jensen, L.	Synthesizing From the Start	IV	identifying key information from an academic lecture & course syllabus	any academic course	R L S			intermediate +
Johns, A.	Taking Students Beyond Content	V	recognizing & producing genres	any genre	R W S			intermediate +
Kamhi-Stein, L. D., Koch, N., & Snow, M. A.	Making the Most of Office Hours	V	preparing for office hours	any academic course	L S			intermediate +
Kamhi-Stein, L. D., Krilowicz, B., Stein, A., & Snow, M. A.	A Scaffolding Approach to Library Research	IV	conducting library research	any research topic	R W L			intermediate +
Kamhi-Stein, L. D., & Snow, M. A.	Interpreting Tables and Figures	III	interpreting graphs	any academic topic	L S			intermediate +
Kaufman, D., & McConnell, K.	The Cereal Connection	II	analyzing & evaluating nutritional components	packaged breakfast cereal	R W L S			intermediate +; young learners
Kaufman, D., & McConnell, K.	Fruits for Thought	II	solving a problem collaboratively	food items	R L S			advanced; young learners
Kaufman, D., & Nelson, W.	Pumpkins: Resource for Inquiry	III	measuring & describing objects	food items	W S			intermediate; young learners
Kaufman, D., & Nelson, W.	What's a Button?	III	identifying characteristics & property words	buttons	W S V			intermediate; young learners
Kaufman, D., & Nelson, W.	Popping Corn	III	observing an experiment	food items	W S			intermediate; young learners
Koch, N., Krilowicz, B., Srole, C., Galanti, G., Kamhi-Stein, L. D., & Snow, M. A.	The Multistep Writing Assignment	V	writing a research paper	any academic topic	R W			intermediate +

[1] I: information management; II: critical thinking; III: hands-on activities; IV: data gathering; V: text analysis and construction.
[2] R: reading; W: writing; L: listening; S: speaking; G: grammar; V: vocabulary.

AUTHOR	TITLE	PART[1]	FOCUS	TOPIC	SKILLS[2]			LEVEL
Lange, E.	Serial Question Exchange for Review	IV	formulating content questions for test preparation	any academic reading	R	L	S	advanced
Mach, T., & Stoller, F. L.	Synthesizing Content on a Continuum	II	evaluating opinions	any academic topic	R		S	any
Mach, T., Stoller, F. L., & Tardy, C.	A Gambit-Driven Debate	II	presenting a debate	any controversial issue	R W		S	intermediate +
Magrath, D.	Thanks for the Visuals	II	sheltering content area presentations	any school subject	R W		S	low intermediate: young learners
Menconi, M.	Cities Alive!	IV	gathering information from sources	cities in the target culture	R		S V	high beginning +
Moore, T.	Finding a Critical Voice I	V	analyzing discourse structure	any review article	R		S	advanced
Moore, T.	Finding a Critical Voice II	V	analyzing summaries & author's use of citation devices	any review article	R		S	advanced
Moore, T.	Finding a Critical Voice III	V	analyzing the evaluation section of a report	any review article	R W		S	advanced
Morgan, E.	Test Cram Session	II	preparing for a content test	any academic course	R W		S	intermediate +
Murphey, T.	Learning What Learners Learn: Action Logging	III	examining the learning process via journals	any classroom experience		W		any; teachers & researchers
O'Shea, L.	Speaking Out About the Issue	II	understanding content through role play	any controversial issue	R	L	S	intermediate +
Park, J.	The Power of Persuasion	V	examining persuasive devices	any academic text		L	S	advanced
Partch, P.	Quiz Your Way to the Top With *Jeopardy!*	II	reviewing content using a game format	any theme-based unit		W L	S	any
Perentesis, S., & Tickle, A.	Feels, Tastes, Smells, Looks, Sounds Like . . . : Emotions in English	I	classifying vocabulary of emotions	any text dealing with emotions	R		S V	intermediate
Perez, A., & Romey, E.	Mystery, Mayhem, and Essay Planning	V	analyzing the structure of an academic essay	mystery	R W		S	advanced

[1]I: information management; II: critical thinking; III: hands-on activities; IV: data gathering; V: text analysis and construction.
[2]R: reading; W: writing; L: listening; S: speaking; G: grammar; V: vocabulary.

AUTHOR	TITLE	PART[1]	FOCUS	TOPIC	SKILLS[2]				LEVEL
Ribeiro, M. A. C.	Social and Economic Awareness	II	thinking critically about problematic issues	any social or economic issue	R W	S			intermediate; EFL learners in high school
Sagliano, J.	Graffiti Session	III	generating opinions about a topic	any theme-based unit	R W	S			intermediate +
Sagliano, J.	Now You See It— Now You Don't	V	writing effective paraphrases	any academic text	R W				intermediate +
Sagliano, M.	Feeling Empathy	II	understanding a controversial issue through role play	any controversial issue	R	S			intermediate +
Sagliano, M,	The Five-Minute Professor	V	recreating a lecture based on lecture notes	any academic lecture	R W	S			intermediate +
Sagliano, M.	Terms in Motion	III	matching terms & definitions	any academic topic	R W L	S		V	intermediate +
Sagliano, M.	Today's Contestants Are . . .	III	reviewing content using a game format	any academic topic	R W	S			intermediate +
Sasser, L.	Animal Classification	I	classifying animals	animals	W	S			beginning +; young learners
Silverman, M.	Identifying and Comparing Ancient Artifacts	I	classifying & comparing artifacts	archeology & cultural anthropology	R W	S	G	V	intermediate +
Strong, G.	Diagram the Discussion	V	using graphic organizers	any reading related to a problem or event	R L	S			intermediate +
Strong, G.	The 5W-1H Scan	II	forming wh- questions for prereading	any nonfiction text	R	S			beginning +
Strong, G.	Once Upon a Time	V	analyzing short stories	any short story	R W	S		V	intermediate +
Tanaka, K.	Discuss and Draw	III	creating graphic organizers to synthesize content	any academic topic	R W	S			intermediate +
Tapper, J., & Storch, N.	Paragraphing and Linking: A Reconstruction Activity	V	using linking devices	any academic text	R W		G	V	intermediate +
Upton, T.	Content Pursuit	III	reviewing content for test preparation	any academic unit	R L	S			intermediate +

[1] I: information management; II: critical thinking; III: hands-on activities; IV: data gathering; V: text analysis and construction.
[2] R: reading; W: writing; L: listening; S: speaking; G: grammar; V: vocabulary.

AUTHOR	TITLE	PART[1]	FOCUS	TOPIC	SKILLS[2]	LEVEL
Weed, K.	The Language of Art, the Art of Language	III	describing works of art	any example of graphic art	L S V	beginning–intermediate
Wilhelm, K. H.	"Wh" the Issue—Where Is It? What Is It?	II	identifying the main points of an argument	any academic topic	R	any
Wilhelm, K. H.	Whom Should You Believe?	II	identifying opinions & expertise	any controversial issue	R L S	intermediate +
Wilson-Allam, D.	Earth Summit: Think Globally, Act Locally	II	using simulation & debate to understand issues	social studies & environmental education	R W L S	high intermediate +
Winer, L.	Pictures to Paragraphs	IV	determining topics & subtopics in the prewriting phase	any academic topic	W S	high intermediate +
Wu, C.	Know Thyself!	II	developing language learning strategies	language learning	R W L S	intermediate +
Wu, C.	Write Your Congressman!	II	determining viewpoints	current political issues	R W L S	high intermediate

[1] I: information management; II: critical thinking; III: hands-on activities; IV: data gathering; V: text analysis and construction.
[2] R: reading; W: writing; L: listening; S: speaking; G: grammar; V: vocabulary.